The Government of the Qin and Han Empires

221 BCE–220 CE

The Government of the Qin and Han Empires

221 BCE–220 CE

Michael Loewe

Hackett Publishing Company, Inc.
Indianapolis/Cambridge

For further information, please address
  Hackett Publishing Company, Inc.
  P.O. Box 44937
  Indianapolis, IN 46244-0937
  www.hackettpublishing.com

Cover design by Abigail Coyle
Interior design by Elizabeth Wilson
Composition by SNP Best-set Typesetter Ltd., Hong Kong
Printed at Edwards Brothers, Inc.

Library of Congress Cataloging-in-Publication Data

Loewe, Michael.
    The government of the Qin and Han Empires : 221 BCE–220 CE /
Michael Loewe.
        p.   cm.
    Includes bibliographical references and index.
    ISBN-13: 978-0-87220-818-6 (pbk.)
    ISBN-10: 0-87220-818-4 (pbk.)
    ISBN-13: 978-0-87220-819-3 (cloth)
    ISBN-10: 0-87220-819-2 (cloth)
    1. China–Politics and government—221 B.C.-220 A.D.   2. China—
History—Qin dynasty, 221–207 B.C.   3. China—History—Han dynasty,
202 B.C.–220 A.D.   I. Title.
    JQ1510.L64 2006
    320.93109'014—dc22
                                                                    2006007916

The paper used in this publication meets the minimum requirements of
American National Standard for Information Sciences—Permanence of
Paper for Printed Library Materials, ANSI Z39.48–1984.

Contents

Preface

The following conventions are used in this book.

1. The terms 'Western Han' and 'Eastern Han' appear here in preference to 'Former Han' and 'Later Han'; use of the latter pair can sometimes become clumsy, for example, in denoting suggested periods for archaeological sites or artifacts as 'Late Former Han' or 'Middle Later Han'.

2. Years are identified below according to those of the solar calendar of the West, but these have no exact correspondence with those of the luni-solar calendars of Qin and Han. Thus the years which would have run in Western enumeration from 14 November 207 BCE to 2 November 206 BCE, and from 15 January 9 CE to 4 January 10 CE, appear below as 206 BCE and 9 CE. Different years are sometimes given in various writings for the foundation of Western Han, either as 206 BCE when Liu Bang 劉邦 became king of a part of China named Han 漢, or as 202 BCE when he assumed the title of emperor (*huangdi* 皇帝).

3. Some events and personalities feature on several occasions below as is appropriate for the different contexts in which they take their place. No apology is offered for a small measure of duplication.

4. Figures that follow personal names in parenthesis distinguish between persons who bore the same family name and given name; for example, at least six men in Western Han and two in Eastern Han are known to have borne the name of Liu Shun 劉順; Zhao Chongguo 趙充國 (1), who died in 100 BCE, is known only as the successor to a nobility; Zhao Chongguo (2), who died in 51 BCE, was a military leader of considerable renown. Accounts of the lives and careers of those who are mentioned here are available in Loewe, *A Biographical Dictionary of the Qin, Former Han and Xin Periods (221 BC–AD 24)* and de Crespigny, *A Biographical Dictionary of Later Han to the Three Kingdoms 23–220 AD*. Fuller references to primary and secondary sources are cited there than in the notes that follow each of the chapters below.

5.   Titles of official posts are rendered as in the first of the books listed immediately above and in the *Cambridge History of China Volume I,* where the versions adopted were chosen in an attempt to compromise systematically and consistently between various conflicting requirements (see *A Biographical Dictionary of the Qin, Former Han and Xin Periods,* pp. 757–78). In particular, care has been taken to avoid terms with misleading associations with officials of the later Chinese dynasties, such as 'censor-in-chief', or with dignitaries of the states of twenty-first-century Europe, such as 'ombudsman'.

6.   The terms 'bureaucrat' and 'bureaucracy' which appear in other writings may bear an implicit criticism of the ways in which officials of Qin and Han China exploited their authority. As such a criticism should not be applied universally to all the many officials on whose labours the operation of imperial government rested, they are not used here.

7.   'Standard Histories', which is the usual expression chosen to denote *Zheng shi* 正史, refers here to the *Shiji* 史記, *Han shu* 漢書, *Hou Han shu* 後漢書 and *San guo zhi* 三國志. Although the term is sometimes translated as 'Dynastic Histories', the works in question are not necessarily confined to a period in which a single dynastic authority claimed to rule over all of China.

8.   'Province' and 'provincial' are used in a general way to refer to parts of the empires that lay outside the metropolitan area, and which were governed as kingdoms or commanderies, as is explained in Chapter 3 below. 'Province' itself does not denote a particular type of administrative unit.

9.   'Laws' and 'legal' likewise refer in general terms to the remnants that we possess of the statutes (*lü* 律) and ordinances (*ling* 令) whereby the empires were governed; the terms do not imply the existence of a co-ordinated system of legislation or judicial procedure that was based on defined principles, such as Roman Law or Canon Law.

The author expresses his deep thanks to Deborah Wilkes and Elizabeth Wilson of Hackett Publishing Company for shepherding this book through the press and to Katherine Lawn for correcting errors that were of his own making.

Introduction

Addressed to non-specialist readers, this book attempts to present the main features of the means whereby China's first emperors governed their realms, and to do so without requiring previous reading. It is not intended to be a narrative account of the Qin and Han dynasties, which is available elsewhere, nor need it set out the minute details of imperial institutions that others have described in full. Historical facts, incidents and examples take their appropriate place so as to illuminate the ways in which men and women affected the operation of those institutions and to clarify how institutions could affect a person's way of life.

Our knowledge and understanding of these matters are necessarily limited by the extent and nature of the sources of information on which we can draw. These tend to give us a theoretical and idealised account of some, but not necessarily all, of those institutions; they remain tantalisingly silent about their implications in human lives and the practical means whereby they were operated. In this way it is possible to present the framework within which imperial officials worked and the inhabitants of the empire were controlled. Fuller research must precede an attempt to show how precisely the decisions and actions of imperial government depended on the established organs of administration, and how such conditions changed over the four centuries that are under consideration.

Our information derives from the hands of historians who set out to describe the Han dynasty and whose statements are now being steadily confirmed, amplified or corrected. Such verification is possible thanks to the discoveries of manuscript documents found mainly in tombs of the period and including a growing corpus of archival material written by officials and clerks of central and provincial government. The greater part of this new material dates from Western Han (206 BCE–9 CE), and some from the time of the dynasty's inception, but it cannot be necessarily assumed that the earliest evidence applies with equal force to the whole of the period.

A further and perhaps more general misapprehension has some-times arisen thanks to the way in which China's early historians and their successors in the West have focused on the material that con-cerns the Han dynasty and the years in which its emperors reigned to the neglect of some of China's other dynasties. They did so partly because they saw the Han empire as a time of ideal government and success, markedly different from its predecessors and successors. In so doing they gave rise to the impression that dynastic change neces-sarily affects the methods of imperial government and that the result-ing conditions of life changed radically as one throne tottered and yielded place to its successor. Such an impression cannot be taken for granted.

Such misapprehensions were due in part to the prevailing cir-cumstances in which much of imperial China's history has been written. Loyalty to the dynasty under whose aegis he was serving could oblige an historian to discredit the activities of its predecessor and to obscure the debt that it owed to the heritage it had received. For this reason due allowance is needed for the influence of prece-dents of pre-imperial times. To some extent, perhaps larger than has been realised, the organs of government of Qin and Han drew on those of the preceding kingdoms, and these may well have deter-mined the way of life of men and women in perhaps the same way before as after the foundation of those dynasties. Likewise, dynastic change after Han may well have altered the seat where the fount of authority was seen to reside. But for several centuries that followed the abdication of the last of the Han emperors in 220 CE, the admin-istrative theory and practice of Han times prevailed, standing as an exemplar to which emperors and officials of the third to the sixth centuries looked to solve their problems and which they could in no way ignore. We have to wait for the Sui (581–617) and Tang (618–907) dynasties to see major changes and initiatives set in.

Four Standard Histories, the *Shiji* 史記 (mainly by Sima Qian 司馬遷, ca. 145–ca. 86 BCE, and his father, Sima Tan 司馬談, d. 110 BCE), *Han shu* 漢書 (mainly by Ban Gu 班固, 32–92 CE), *Hou Han shu* (by Fan Ye 范曄, 398–446, and including chapters by Sima Biao 司馬彪, 240–306) and *San guo zhi* 三國志 (by Chen Shou 陳壽 233–297), provide basic information on the foundation and fall of the Qin, Western Han, Xin and Eastern Han dynasties. These works include terse records of major events, as in a diary; there are somewhat fuller narrative accounts of incidents, and essays on topics of major concern in public life and government. Two of these histories include chapters of tables which set out the succession of the kings and nobles of the empire. Much of the information is given directly, as an ordered description of the offices of the central government or a list of major administrative units of the empire. Narrative chapters, some in the form of biographies, carry reports that officials submitted by way of advice to the throne. Records of an emperor's actions include summaries of the decrees that he issued. Some chapters describe measures such as the punishments set down for disobedience of imperial orders or the type and rate of taxation that was to be levied. One of the tables, which gives the succession of holders of the principal offices of Western Han, follows a list of imperial offices and their complements of staff.

In no way do these histories provide an evenly spread coverage for the four centuries that are under consideration, and in the absence of chapters of tables for Eastern Han there is more statistical information available for the two earlier than the two later centuries. Fortunately these basic works may be supplemented by administrative records first discovered circa 1900 and supplemented subsequently by increasingly richer finds from sites that are spread throughout parts of Qin and Han China. The first of these finds consisted of documents compiled by military and civil officials who were serving in somewhat abnormal conditions. Their duties lay in maintaining the lines of communications and defensive forts at Dunhuang 敦煌, in the extreme north-west of the empire. Similar and more abundant finds, likewise dating from circa 100 BCE to circa 100 CE, followed shortly from Juyan 居延, somewhat to the east of Dunhuang but still on the perimeter. More recently sites have yielded documents written in the more normal conditions of governing the provinces of the centre rather than deriving from the military garrisons of the north-west. Of particular value have been two consignments of legal documents, dating from 217 BCE and 186 BCE, and a set of routine reports made at county level near the distant sea coast (found at Yinwan 尹灣, northern Jiangsu; 119 degrees east longitude and 34 degrees north latitude) circa 15 BCE. Numerous small pieces of inscribed bone and wood found at the site of a major imperial office, at Chang'an, testify to intensive clerical activity by officials and their assistants.

To our regret, so far no comparable documents have been found that refer to official practice in Eastern Han times. However our received literature includes fragments of short essays or treatises written mainly in Eastern Han times with the deliberate intention of describing the correct procedures for activities at the imperial court and the duties of officials. Such documents bring out the important place that the idea of hierarchy occupied in public life and the attention paid to ritual in the daily routines of the court and in relations between officials and their sovereign. Chapters of the histories include the views that officials expressed over choices of policy and problems of administration. One document that survives in toto sets out in dialogue form and retrospectively a debate between opposing parties on major issues of the day, in 81 BCE. Among the questions discussed were the imposition of controls on the population, the application of the laws, exploitation of the mineral resources of the empire and the value of an import-export trade.

Overall our writers and their documents were concerned with the lives and actions of those who exerted power in China's cities and counties rather than with those of the greater part of the population who received orders to pay the taxes that were due or to obey the imperial will. The histories are likewise more anxious to write of the successes of imperial government than to expose the weaknesses of its institutions. As a result much is left that is unknown; the implicit assumptions of our sources may well remain concealed from our eyes today.

Emperors and officials governed the Qin, Han and Xin empires, and material remains bear witness to their overriding presence. Archaeologists have identified perhaps thirty thousand tombs of the Han period, many of them of kings, nobles and officials, and some of convicts. They have also excavated parts of the capital cities of Xianyang 咸陽, Chang'an 長安 and Luoyang 洛陽, and occasionally the surviving traces of an imperial palace or the outskirts of an imperial tomb. They have investigated a number of major tombs identified as those of the kings, who ranked immediately below the emperors. Some tombs had been decorated with paintings or figures of officials proudly wearing their robes and hats, or riding in carriages to perform their duties. Officials of varied positions affixed their seals to their reports or orders, thereby expressing their authority to do so, and many of these have survived in tombs over the years to declare the titles and occasionally the names that the tomb occupants bore. Inscriptions on artifacts sometimes tell of the hand that an official took in ordering the manufacture of an article or inspecting the handiwork of the artisans who made it.

Han has been acclaimed as China's most successful empire, and a number of regimes which emerged subsequently adopted its name as their dynastic title, as in 221, 304, 338 and 551. The actions and lives of Western and Eastern Han emperors and officials as related in the Standard Histories have continually fascinated China's historians of later times and attracted the attention of scholars of the Song (960–1279), Ming (1368–1644) and Qing (1644–1911) dynasties. Building largely on the results of their labours and treating them with the disciplines and methods of European historians, Western and Japanese critics have imparted a critical sense to the subject. Overall, however, the four centuries in question have not received an equal degree of attention. In traditional Chinese scholarship, the two Standard Histories for Western Han, the *Shiji* and *Han shu,* have always been seen to possess greater literary merit than the *Hou Han shu;* the achievements of Western Han have earned a measure of praise while there has been a tendency to concentrate on some of the less reputable events that took place within the courts and palaces of the Eastern Han emperors and empresses at Luoyang.

In the profusion of secondary studies in European languages and Japanese, Western readers now have at their disposal translations of parts of the primary sources as well as monographs on many aspects of Qin and Han history. Such books concern dynastic and political events, the development of institutions, and contacts with Qin and Han's neighbours. Studies of economic practice and social distinctions accompany others on intellectual growth and religious practice, and those on a few outstanding poets and prose writers.

The institutions and ways of imperial government emerged and developed as conditions demanded; they cannot be judged as deriving from carefully thought-out theories of how best to control or promote the welfare of mankind. With more attention to mythological history than to established fact, writers of Han times called to mind the days of a glorious remote past, followed by the beneficent and successful rule of some of the kings of Western Zhou (1045–771 BCE). Some writers saw the rule of Zhou as based on the highest moral principles, which were reiterated subsequently in the precepts of masters such as Kong Qiu 孔丘 (Zhongni 仲尼; 551–479 BCE), known as Confucius. With the passage of the centuries there grew up a number of co-existent kingdoms, each exercising its authority over a limited area. In such circumstances we hear the voice of at least one writer (Xun Qing 荀卿, known as Xunzi 荀子; between 335 and 238 BCE) explaining the need to establish the rule of mankind by leaders who would introduce co-operative and corporate action in place of strife. Along with the moralistic values ascribed to some early regimes and their teachers, there were some strong persons who set up ways of governing a kingdom for material ends, so as to exercise unchallenged power over the population and to extend their own domains. By way of reaction others questioned the value of imposing authority on human beings and doubted how far the accepted guidance of the moralists could be trusted. Such were some of the varied traditions and expressions of thought that formed the intellectual background to the growth, consolidation and management of the Qin and Han empires.

China's own traditional writings and those of the Westerners who first interested themselves in these times leave the impression of a period of strength and stability that lasted for four hundred years with little change in political forms and practice, or in intellectual, cultural and religious developments. This view, of a pervasive stagnancy, will not stand scrutiny; gradual change and adaptation rather than sudden or radical innovation marked the continuities in public life. Certainly throughout those years imperial government took the form of an autocracy backed by ruthlessness, sometimes inadequately characterised as 'bureaucratic'. Certainly throughout Han times the organs of government were of the same form and the division of officials' responsibilities remained constant. But the degree to which those organs were able to exercise their power varied considerably, if only as generals and officials exerted their authority in newly acquired remote territories, or as the ability to recruit a sufficiency of civil servants grew. A rigorous or a liberal approach of senior officials or the degree of corruption in which they engaged could mark the efficiency of their administration.

In general it may be judged that government could well have gained in intensity between 221 BCE and 220 CE, but application of its orders can hardly have been uniform. At times the purposes of the offices of state may have been sharpened, at times blunted; officials might bear a title that had been formed decades before their own time and remained unchanged; the duties that they undertook may have been extended here, curtailed there or transferred elsewhere. Retention of the same titles for offices and officials for four centuries, and under other dynasties later, may well cloak different approaches to the problems of administration.

Paradoxically enough, it was the two emperors who have been subject to the most severe hatred for two thousand years whose regimes left a lasting heritage which their successors were happy to accept and to apply to their own problems. It was in the reign of the first of the Qin emperors (Qin Shi Huangdi 秦始皇帝; 221–210 BCE) that imperial institutions took shape; the succeeding emperors of Western Han adopted them as a means of governing their realm, and parts of that heritage such as the division of the land into counties may still survive today. Wang Mang 王莽 set himself up as emperor of a dynasty known as Xin 新 (New) from 9 to 23 CE. He gave out that he was following in the footsteps of the kings of Zhou 周, and that he was adhering to their traditions, and he re-named some of the existing institutions of government to accord with what he believed to have been their practice. Despite rejecting such nominal changes, the emperors of Eastern Han who followed could hardly jettison the moral support implicit in Wang Mang's claims and pretensions.

In whatever ways the methods of imperial government adapted to circumstance or were open to manipulation by unscrupulous leaders, they retained the same form in both Western and Eastern Han, different as those two periods were in many respects. Such differences are seen in the adoption of different objects of worship in the state cults, a different approach to hopes of immortality, the arrival of Buddhist influences and the growth of communities that are sometimes labelled 'Daoist'. The basis and purpose of imperial government was seen first as in the ambitions of Qin, and then in the ideals of Zhou, and the changed situation of the capital city reflected that difference. The training of officials and education of scholars reached stages in Eastern Han that could not have been achieved previously. Such advances perhaps owed something to two factors: the classification of literature by Liu Xiang 劉向 (79–8 BCE) and Liu Xin 劉歆 (46 BCE–23 CE) and their collection of texts to form a library in the palace; and the growth of the Imperial Academy, where increasingly large numbers of students took their places for training as the decades of Eastern Han passed by. Other changes that were no less significant took place. Different genres of poetry and prose were becoming dominant; Eastern Han saw the growth of new styles of burial and their attendant forms of art. Officials of Western Han might well have found difficulty in accepting the religious, intellectual and cultural terms with which their colleagues of some two or three centuries later were content.

Notes for Further Reading

Translations of narrative and biographical chapters of the Standard Histories appear in the works of Chavannes, Dubs, Watson and Nienhauser. Translations of chapters which have particular reference to economic conditions and legal matters can be found in Swann, *Food and Money in Ancient China,* and Hulsewé, *Remnants of Han Law.* For fragments of archival manuscripts, see Chavannes, *Les documents chinois,* Hulsewé, *Remnants of Ch'in Law* and Loewe, *Records of Han Administration.* Essays in Beasley and Pulleyblank discuss questions of historiography; narrative histories of the period are included in Bodde, *China's First Unifier,* the *Cambridge History of China Volume I* and de Crespigny's volumes. Bielenstein, *Bureaucracy,* provides a detailed study of the offices of the empire. See Hsu Cho-yun for agriculture; Wilbur and Ch'ü T'ung-tsu for social distinctions; Bodde, *Festivals,* for official religious practices; and Diény, Hawkes, Hervouet and Knechtges for literature. For the extensive evidence of art and archaeology, see Pirazzoli-t'Serstevens.

Major Dynastic Events and Institutional Changes

The entries below are limited to the principal events that affected the government and administration of the empires.

221 BCE	Foundation of the Qin empire; Li Si influential at court
210	Collapse of the Qin empire
206	Liu Bang nominated king of Han
202	Foundation of Western Han, with Liu Bang as emperor (Gaozu); organisation of government by Xiao He; capital established at Chang'an; review of existing laws by Xiao He and of court procedures by Shusun Tong
164	Reduction of the kingdoms
157–141	Consolidation of imperial government in Jingdi's reign
154	Revolt of seven kings suppressed; further reduction of the kingdoms
141–87	Reign of Wudi; establishment of training programmes for candidate officials at the academy; review of legal provisions (ca. 120, 110); adjustment to the calendar (104); establishment of regional inspectors (106); imposition of economic controls (from ca. 119); successful campaigns against the Xiongnu (127, 119); foundation of new commanderies in the north-west (104), Korean peninsula (111), south and south-west (111); growth of Han influence in Central Asia and of an export-import trade (ca. 100); policy of retrenchment in place of expansion (91)
81	Major debate on the purposes of government, economic, defensive and other policies

1

Emperors and Their Authority

Archaeology provides abundant evidence for the way of life that was practised in various areas of China at differing periods of pre-historic times. But with no written records to testify, there is no means of knowing in what ways those isolated communities chose their leaders or were forced to accept the will of their rulers. Much later China's own traditional historians tell of rule by the kings of Xia 夏. While a number of scholars are now prepared to accept that such a house or unit existed, there is no means of identifying settlements, artifacts or the evidence of communal living with such a ruling authority in historical terms. For a long time the dates of 2205 to 1766 BCE were suggested or even accepted as the dates of the Xia dynasty, but a definite relationship between "Xia" and the material evidence of archaeology has yet to be proved.

It is only from circa 1600 BCE that it is possible to validate the existence of monarchs who possessed spiritual and material powers that were sufficient to impose their will on the inhabitants of the land or over the walled enclosures that may perhaps be termed towns or cities. These were the kings of a line known as Shang 商 or Yin 殷, whose religious practices are known from surviving contemporary writings and whose powers of leadership and command stand revealed in the rich style of burial that their position demanded and received. The Shang line lasted until 1045 BCE.

The area over which the kings of Shang operated or perhaps ruled was limited, as was that of the kings of Western Zhou 周 (1045–771 BCE) who followed them; Shang and Western Zhou did not cover entirely the same territories. With the growing use of iron (after ca. 500 BCE), the more widespread use of writing and the growing sophistication of social distinctions and administrative methods there arose small communities, each owing obedience to its own lord, conqueror or ruler; insofar as the powers of these leaders were probably limited to small areas of land which included one walled settlement, they may perhaps be described as the leaders of 'city-states'. From a multiplicity of such independent and mutually antagonistic communities, in a period known as that of the 'Springs and Autumns' (Chunqiu 春秋; 770–481 BCE), there emerged only seven states, each with its own acknowledged royal house that could exert authority over major areas and the several cities situated therein. These kings were rivals, contending for the possession and control of ever wider territories at the expense of their neighbours; the period (480–221 BCE) is known as that of the Warring States (Zhanguo 戰國).

From such long drawn-out stages there arose China's first empires, which may be defined as regimes or authorities that claimed to govern all known territories and their inhabitants, other than those of a primitive, so-called sub-human, way of life whose conditions of human relationship were deemed to fall below the standard of civilised human beings. Such an empire was first established in 221 BCE by Ying Zheng 嬴政, king of one of the seven major kingdoms, who had succeeded in conquering or eliminating his rivals. Retaining the name of that kingdom, Qin 秦, for his new greatly expanded regime, Ying Zheng adopted a new title, *huangdi* 皇帝 'emperor', to replace *wang* 王 'king', under which his predecessor rulers had reigned; the new term was intended to emphasise the superiority of his own authority over theirs. Such a change was of both practical and symbolic importance, and whereas the Qin empire itself had come to an end within fifteen years, the title *huangdi* survived until 1910.

Later, one further feature was to illustrate this change. From quite soon after Qin, a Chinese empire could include subordinated kingdoms, independent to some extent, but owing prime allegiance to the emperor.

Only two emperors reigned over Qin, the second for scarcely three years, and by the time of his death (207 BCE) the authority of the dynasty had become tenuous. In the ensuing fighting that broke out, one protagonist for power named Xiang Yu 項羽 sought to set up a hegemony of nineteen separate small kingdoms over which he intended to preside. In doing so he named Liu Bang 劉邦 to be king of Han (206 BCE), but as events developed it was Liu Bang who succeeded in winning over or eliminating not only Xiang Yu but all other aspirants for power. By 202 BCE he had re-asserted Qin's principle of a single empire and proceeded to set up the Han 漢 dynasty, largely on the basis of Qin's experience and institutions and with his capital (Chang'an 長安, modern Xi'an 西安) situated to the west. Ten duly enthroned emperors of this dynasty, to be known as Western, or Former, Han, succeeded, reigning until 9 CE.

By that time, the fabric of empire had been weakened as the last of the Western Han emperors had been losing their power of attracting loyal support. It fell to Wang Mang 王莽, a relative of one of a former emperor's empresses, to attempt the task of building up a re-invigorated empire. Hoping to acquire support that would outface that of the eclipsed Western Han emperors, in 9 CE he established his own dynasty named Xin 新 (New). Unlike the first of the Qin emperors and Liu Bang (imperial title Gaozu 高祖), he had not earned a reputation as a forceful leader who was ready to suffer hardship with his comrades in battle. A victim of opposition, he met his death in 23 CE. Within two years the Han empire had been restored by Liu Xiu 劉秀 (2), who traced his descent to a great-grandson of Liu Bang and claimed continuity with the regime that the latter had set up but which Wang Mang had broken. Historians were to claim that such continuity had been no more than temporarily interrupted by Wang Mang's act of 'usurpation'. Liu Xiu (imperial title Guangwudi 光武帝) set up his capital city at Luoyang 洛陽, to the east and his dynasty is known as Eastern, or Later, Han. Twelve successors, including some who were very short-lived, followed him as emperor. The formal end of the Han dynasty was marked by the abdication of the last emperor in 220 CE, though it had lost its effective power of government from as early as 184 CE.

China must need wait until 581 for the re-establishment of a strong imperial dynasty. On several occasions before then, and then from the tenth century onwards, government of the land lay between two or more co-existent regimes. However in each case these regimes saw themselves as empires in the making, denied their full, rightful power; they did not see themselves as units attached to no more than a part of the land and co-existing with others in the same way as kingdoms had done in pre-imperial times and in the system that Xiang Yu had tried to introduce. Thanks to Qin, Han and Xin the imperial system had become accepted as the norm.

Ying Zheng of Qin, Liu Bang of Western Han, Wang Mang of Xin and Liu Xiu of Eastern Han had thus taken their places as leaders of the world. Each one took the opportunity to inaugurate a system of imperial government; both they and their successors either proclaimed their position as supreme governors or graciously and modestly acceded to the invitation of their supporters to adopt such a title. In much of these formal proceedings, sometimes reminiscent of a charade, they received advice and warnings from their counsellors: They should look to earlier examples of paragons of wisdom and philanthropy whose behaviour they should emulate; there were likewise evil tyrants who had exercised the highest powers but whose dire deeds must on no account act as precedents for them.

Drawing from both mythology and historical fact, these warnings served the purposes of those seeking power for themselves as well as those who wished to restrain the behaviour of their rulers. In the initial stages of human communities, it was told, Huangdi 黄帝, the 'Yellow Emperor', had brought benefit to mankind by teaching the arts that led to a civilised way of life and reduced suffering. Others, known as culture heroes, were responsible for teaching skills with which to raise crops from the soil, fashion objects of metal or treat the sick. At a later stage the basic forms of government took shape under the aegis and leadership of the blessed Yao 堯, Shun 舜 and Yu 禹, and the ways of life of those three heroes were seen as exemplary. Other monarchs who were likewise ascribed to these early, uncharted days of pre-history included the cursed Jie 桀 and Zhou 紂, who exploited their supreme positions to satisfy their personal fancies to the detriment of mankind.

These were by no means the only monarchs whose names and activities recur in the writings of the early empires. Officials would call on some of the kings of Western Zhou to praise and encourage an attention to ethical values and the modes of correct behaviour whereby a civilised society could be recognised (*li* 禮). Alternatively they could bring to mind kings or leaders of later days who indulged their personal whims to the danger of their kingdoms. Criticism of the past could become a sharp tool in the hands of propagandists, and its use could serve to support a prejudice. Writers of the Han dynasty did not credit the First Qin Emperor with the success of building the fabric of empire in which they themselves lived; they pointed to the severity of the rule whereby he achieved his ends.

The tales of monarchs of the past and the traditions that grew up around their names could easily bear on some of the problems that faced the emperors of Qin and Han, starting with that of the correct means of accession to the throne. Yao and Shun had each chosen their successors on the grounds of their merits and the trust that they inspired. Yu the Great, however, who had been chosen in this way to follow Shun, initiated a system of hereditary succession, and it was from his line that the Xia dynasty was said to have come. In the historical times of Shang-Yin, succession at one time passed from brother to brother, but such a practice did not constitute a precedent for later ages, when hereditary patrilinear succession was the regular norm.

That system was by no means free from irregularities or abnormalities. It could be supported by the practice of a regency or manipulated to serve personal ambitions, and there were occasions when, in principle, the merit of a candidate for the throne might take precedence over direct succession to a father. In the early days of Western Zhou, patrilinear succession had fallen to a person who, it was alleged or supposed, had yet to attain his majority; in time he was to be known as Cheng Wang 成王 (r. 1042 or 1035–1006). Tradition had it that it was thanks to the selfless behaviour of Cheng Wang's uncle, Zhou Gong 周公, that the kingdom survived intact; for, altruistically, Zhou Gong had been content to act as regent for the boy rather than seize the throne for himself. On several occasions in both Western and Eastern Han infants took their place as emperors, possibly filling the role of puppets, while other persons held fast to the reins of government. It could be claimed that by guiding a youngster to his august position and advising him thereafter such men were in fact following the example of Zhou Gong. Seven such 'regents' are known for Eastern Han, between 89 and 189 CE; they included Dou Xian 竇憲 in the reign of Hedi (r. 88–106 CE) and Liang Ji 梁冀 during that of Shundi (r. 125–144 CE).

In addition to the woman who was duly established as empress, a number of secondary consorts graced the imperial palaces. Such a system would perhaps ensure that a male child would be born who would in time take his father's place, but the price for such an assurance was paid in terms of the rivalry, dispute and violence that could arise all too easily. Frequently enough, both the established empress and the secondary consorts had been introduced into the palace thanks to presentation by one of the senior officials of government. By achieving such a result, perhaps for a daughter, those officials would seek to reinforce their own position with support from within the palace should the need arise. Contenders for power in government could easily involve their close relatives in the struggles for supremacy that might ensue, as occurred with considerable bloodshed in 91 and 6 BCE, and 79 and 124 CE.

Such dangers might come to the fore when it was necessary to nominate an heir apparent, whose choice lay primarily with the emperor. In principle the eldest son of the established empress would have the first claim, but there were occasions when a younger one was chosen, as in 60, 79 and twice in 106 CE. There were also ways in which an initial choice could be thwarted or changed. Possibly the sudden death of an emperor might leave this question unresolved, and in such circumstances the choice fell to the empress dowager; she in her turn might be subject to pressure from a senior member of the imperial family, such as the widow of a previous emperor. Alternatively, she might wish to seize the opportunity to strengthen the position of her own family. An empress dowager chose the heir to the throne in 89, 106, 125, 145 and 168 CE; in each case he was below the age of majority. On at least three occasions a highly placed woman did not hesitate to commit murder to eliminate a potential heir to the throne or to secure her position by eliminating the mother of one. Huo Xian 霍顯, wife of the prominent official Huo Guang 霍光, had Xuandi's empress Xu 許 murdered while pregnant (71 BCE) and had her own daughter substituted as empress in her place. In 12 BCE Chengdi's consort Zhao Zhaoyi 趙昭儀, and possibly her sister Zhao Feiyan 趙飛燕, had two sons borne to him by other women murdered. In 115 CE Andi's childless empress Yan 閻 had a secondary consort named Li, who had just given birth to a son, put to death.

Wang Zhengjun 王政君, empress of Yuandi (r. 48–33 BCE), exercised a dominating influence in public life in the next reigns, dying in 13 CE after her nephew Wang Mang had been established as emperor. The Empress Dowagers Ma 馬, Dou 竇, Deng 鄧, Yan 閻 and Liang 梁 were equally powerful, during the reigns of Mingdi (r. 57–75), Zhangdi (r. 75–88), Hedi (r. 88–106), Andi (r. 106–125), Shundi (r. 125–144) and Huandi (r. 146–168), respectively. The strength of an empress dowager may be seen in the ways in which she succeeded in some of her aims or wishes, whatever those of the emperor may have been. Dou Taihou 竇太后, empress of Wendi (r. 180–157 BCE), survived throughout the reign of his immediate successor, to die early in the reign of her grandson Wudi (r. 141–87 BCE). She had been a devotee of a certain type of thought that may be generally termed mystical and was at variance with some of the political ideas of the day, and she insisted that members of her family, including two future emperors, received instruction therein. But a change was noticeable after her death in 135 BCE, when other influences, of a more realistic frame of mind, allowed a number of significant changes to be introduced into imperial policies. It was the family of Yuandi's empress Wang 王 that prevented him from substituting another son to take the place of his nominated heir apparent, her own son. Somewhat later, in the face of the pressure of the Empress Dowager Fu (2) 傅, Aidi (r. 7–1 BCE) was obliged to dismiss some of his ministers (5 BCE). Wang Zhengjun played an important part in the rise to power of her nephew Wang Mang.

An empress who failed to give birth to a son could find herself deposed in favour of one of the minor consorts, who would be elevated to her position on a boy's birth. Should an empress fall out of favour with the emperor she could likewise be disestablished, and possibly the nomination of her son as heir could be revoked in favour of that of her successor, as occurred in 43 CE. Such a result might also follow from the will or pressure of one of the minor consorts or, more probably, from one of her relatives who held high office. A son of the newly declared empress would duly take the place of the one who had been dispossessed. An extreme example of these rivalries occurred three years after the death of Fu Taihou 傅太后, at first one of Yuandi's minor consorts. To ensure that she and her family would be seen to be utterly degraded, the Wang family, of whom Yuandi's established empress was a member, had her tomb desecrated and her body re-buried in a much less honourable style.

A system of hereditary succession was not strong enough to preclude disputes or acts of violence that followed an emperor's death, nor could it ensure that a man with a strong character, a sense of duty and noble virtues would become emperor. There are however some hints that such qualities demanded attention and could override a claim of close kinship. At a critical moment in 74 BCE, when succession to the throne lay in doubt, one senior official cited authority of a traditional canon to suggest that if a choice lay open between two candidates of equal standing, the one with greater merit would have a better claim. Two emperors of Western Han, Xuandi (r. 74–48 BCE) and Yuandi seriously considered displacing their named heirs, in one case owing to basic disagreement over the aims and methods of imperial government, and in the other owing to disillusionment with the character of the man whom he had originally named.

In addition to these possible irregularities and dangers, the security of the throne might be subject to dispute by an emperor's relative who claimed a closer degree of kinship with the founder of the line or with one of his successors than the current incumbent could boast. A fear that such a person could be persuaded to launch a plot to seize what he saw as his rightful position might lead a government to take precautionary action that could be ruthless. On several occasions in Eastern Han it was the empress dowager who saw to it that an infant sat on the imperial throne. Strong-minded officials manipulated the succession in two somewhat exceptional cases. After eliminating the duly nominated heir to the First Qin Emperor, they substituted a weak man of their own choice to succeed him (210 BCE). In 74 BCE they deposed Liu He 劉賀 (4), a young man who had taken no more than twenty-seven days to demonstrate his unfitness to rule.

There was no accepted right whereby a woman could take her place on the throne. Having secured powers of control, Gaozu's widow the Empress Lü 呂 (dominant 188–180 BCE), had two infants nominated emperor in succession. She herself, as we are told, did not hesitate to contemplate or perhaps commit violent or criminal acts by which to eliminate threats from would-be rivals and to maintain her position of dominance over the court and government. It is perhaps due to such occurrences that fears or warnings of such a possibility recur in the pages of the Han histories.

From the outset, it was accepted that the emperor held supreme powers of government, assisted as he might be by the supporters who had led him to the throne and then by the officials who served him. It was from him that all authority to govern the population and administer the land devolved. Unchallenged by others, in theory he determined the appointment of men to high offices of state, choosing those whose ability and loyalty he could trust. Consulting them as he would, in the early days he was in no way bound to comply with their wishes; time had to pass before officials would find themselves able to voice criticism of an emperor's decision. It was from the emperor's hand that orders were forthcoming, in the form of decrees that were to be of universal force; regulations that concerned human conduct and activities and which were to be of legal validity required his sanction and approval. When the trial of a criminal case raised doubts or a decision for punishment or pardon lay outside the scope of an official's authority, the case could pass to the emperor as the final arbiter.

As a religious functionary, the emperor was of the sole rank that entitled and perhaps obliged him to perform certain rites that were denied to others. Ideally he did so at regular intervals, at first at sites that lay outside the capital city but later at altars to its south. These services were addressed to the highest of various divine powers who were believed to affect human welfare; the emperor's attention to these rites could affect the lives of all of his subjects. He took part regularly in some of the sacrifices, invocations and prayers that were intended to relate the people of Earth directly to the care of Heaven, for the emperor was seen as the essential intermediary to bring this happy state of affairs to pass. Preparation for his worship of Heaven, introduced circa 30 BCE, would require a hundred days of vigil. At crucial times and seasons he presided over acts of divination that would give guidance for the future and its tasks.

The emperor stood at the top of the social scale. He took precedence over members of his own family; should his father still be alive when he ascended the throne, as was the case of the founder of Han, he granted him a suitable dignity and title that would preserve the correct order and degree of kinship. Likewise he granted the title of king to his sons or close relatives and could determine the degree of precedence to be accorded to a visitor from outside the empire, such as the leader (*Shanyu* 單于) of the Xiongnu 匈奴, a people of Central Asia, in 51 BCE. On a more general level, he conferred titles or orders of rank (*jue* 爵) to many members of the population, which involved legal privileges and obligations as may be seen below (p. 136). Such conferments were described as acts of imperial bounty, which could take other forms, such as the distribution of food to those whom a natural disaster had left suffering or destitute. A general amnesty for criminals might accompany some of these acts.

The founding emperors may have risen to their positions of eminence thanks to their military powers and leadership, but it was very rarely that their successors stood at the head of their forces when engaged in battle. Wudi, 'the Martial' was the posthumous title of one of the Han emperors whose reign was marked by courageous military activity and territorial expansion, but it was the emperor's generals who undertook the long marches and fought the campaigns. Prestige did not attach to heroism; only exceptionally was or could a Chinese emperor be credited with the same manner of success as an Alexander or a Julius Caesar.

Although the emperor was the final source of authority for actions taken to govern the land and administer its people, it was not necessarily from him that direct orders, for example, for a method of taxation, the conduct of criminal trials or the promotion of agriculture, derived. Such proposals may have resulted from consultation by senior officials who had been ordered to concern themselves with a particular problem of government. Or they may have resulted from the initiative of an official who, finding himself facing a problem, proposed a means of solution and requested imperial approval. Imperial decrees might consist in no more than a curt word of permission to follow such a proposal. They might otherwise enunciate a general principle of government, such as the need for criminal sentences to be seen to be fair; they might refer to the importance of moral sanctions in governing the empire rather than a reliance on severe penal sanctions; they might demand advice over some matter of detail; or they might order an inspection of certain conditions such as those of suffering, whether incurred by natural causes of flood or brought about as a result of human activities.

Suggestions for the way to govern the empire came from below, sometimes passing from one level of official to another until they reached the stage for submission to the emperor. Orders to implement those suggestions were delivered in the opposite direction, until they reached those who would be responsible for the work that was necessary and that might draw hatred upon them. In all this, the existence, purpose and function of the emperor was essential, as without him there would be no authority to act and no means of guaranteeing obedience to the orders that an official, junior or senior, might transmit.

The emperor's powers may perhaps be regarded as nominal, being seen in his approval of the proposals that reached him; they may appear to be restricted, allowing little scope for independent initiative; or they may appear to be no more than those of an agent dutifully and necessarily responding to the influence brought to bear upon him. Such pressures could derive from a senior imperial consort, as in the reigns of Huidi (r. 195–188 BCE), or the non-adult Eastern Han emperors Hedi (r. 88–106 CE), Andi (r. 106–125), Shundi (r. 125–144), Huandi (r. 146–168), Lingdi (r. 168–189) or Xiandi (r. 189–220); or from senior officials, as in the reigns of Zhaodi (r. 87–74 BCE) or Xuandi (r. 74–48 BCE); or from a combination of both such parties. Perhaps it is only exceptionally that we know of a strong emperor who moulded the course of dynastic history (Gaozu, Wang Mang, Liu Xiu). But whether strong or weak, old or young, an emperor was necessary in constitutional terms, as without him there could be no authority to govern.

There were also ways in which an emperor formed an essential element in intellectual and religious terms. Reacting against the concept of an empire whose existence depended solely on force, Han thinkers explained it as an integral part of the whole cosmic system, whereby the realms of Heaven, Earth and Man were interlocked with one another and interdependent; the person of the emperor came to be seen as the instrument whereby this link was maintained. His description as *tian zi* 天子 'son of heaven' which was drawn from pre-imperial practice, served to demonstrate this function.

An emperor might well regard himself as supreme, with unquestioned authority over all beneath the skies. Officials would recognise the force of this ideal in the conduct of their relations with him, and in their formal behaviour they would be careful to display the respect due to his position. But they might also harbour other ideas. Some of the thinkers who had lived in the pre-imperial age had proclaimed the value of *wu wei* 無為, the unconscious exertion of influence on affairs without taking any positive action to do so. This ideal could have had an immediate attraction for ambitious officials of Han times who could cite it as the most noble way in which an emperor could fulfil his task; for it would imply that it left full scope for themselves to govern in a positive manner as a situation demanded while the emperor sat by with his arms folded and his robes flowing. Such a situation was perhaps idealised in a conventional expression which refers to the kings as saintly and his ministers as intelligent and loyal (*sheng wang xian chen* 聖王賢臣).

In the early days of Western Han, the system of imperial government was still on trial; initiated by Qin who practised it, as was alleged, with unnecessary severity, it had come into question after Qin's collapse and was restored in a slightly different form under Han. To the emperors and officials of Eastern Han, however, empire had been practised successfully for over two centuries and could be regarded as the norm. To those who upheld the dynastic order, an emperor was the *huangdi* 'lord of all', or the *tian zi* 'son of heaven'; to historians and perhaps some officials, he was *shang* 上 'the higher authority'. On earth he must be seen to be all majestic, living in a style that lay far beyond the reach of most mortals. He must be secluded from the cares and tribulations of the world by living within a mighty palace, or in one of several such palaces; absence from his palace must be for approved reasons only, such as visits to the sites where the cults of state were performed, or escape from the city during the heat of summer. In Western Han his palaces lay in different parts of the city of Chang'an; of the two palaces for Eastern Han at Luoyang one lay at a dominating situation to the north of the city. In Western Han imperial consorts were housed in separate palaces.

Ritual prescriptions set an emperor apart from other mortals. They governed many of his daily activities and are seen particularly in the attentions paid to him when dead. Only for his line could there be as many as seven shrines dedicated to the memory of ancestors. At his death the gates of the palace and the city were closed and troops received orders to stand by on alert. Lamentations at prescribed intervals punctuated the long series of the steps preparatory to burial. The corpse was encased in a suit of jade within the innermost of up to seven coffins. A solemn intonation of texts reminded those present of the precepts and ideals of the past. Before the closure of the coffin the heir stepped forward to pay his last respects prior to taking his place as his father's successor. Carpenters planed down the dowelling, then the coffin was placed on its hearse for the journey to the place of burial, which could be as far as seventeen kilometres' distance from the city of Luoyang. Parties of strong men hauled at the ropes; a choir of sixty voices with eight bells accompanied the cortege.

Work started on the construction of the tomb soon after an emperor's accession. This would be in a large walled park which enclosed several ritual halls such as the shrine in which his memorial tablet would be preserved. Surmounted by a tumulus, which was visible in at least one case from Chang'an city, the tomb may have been built as a complex set of corridors and rooms; possibly it simulated arrangements in the palace, with an audience chamber standing immediately to the front of living quarters. The furnishings of the tomb and the burial equipment would have been of a higher grade than that of any others, and excavation of tombs of the kings, immediately below emperors in social terms, gives an idea of the opulence and the expenses that were likely. The ritual halls received daily, monthly or seasonal offerings. Once a month a procession set out from one of them to convey the deceased emperor's headdress and robes to the shrine where the memorial tablet was installed, to receive reverence from his descendants.

The First Qin Emperor, Han Wudi and Guangwudi visited their domains quite frequently, mainly for religious purposes. The occasions also provided an opportunity to uphold dynastic prestige by displaying imperial majesty both in person and in fact. Such journeyings were not an unmixed blessing for the areas through which the progress moved, as the expenses that the localities bore might well be high. On some occasions these were offset by the grant of an imperial bounty such as exemption from tax for a particular region.

Bounties showed an emperor's philanthropy. In some of his decrees he might express acknowledgement of his own shortcomings, thereby indicating that he was devoted to maintaining traditional moral values and standards of behaviour. Disingenuous as the tone and message of these decrees may perhaps appear to be, they may also have served the persons of some of his officials by diverting blame for an unsuccessful decision or the onset of a calamity away from themselves and on to his own person. As the final judge of certain criminal cases the emperor would best be shown to practise clemency and to find it difficult or impossible to tolerate the imposition of a severe punishment such as death. He should refrain from indulging in personal pleasures, be they of wine, women or song. He should give an example of thrift rather than extravagance, for those of lower status would soon be emulating his standards, thereby ignoring social distinctions and incurring expenditure that reduced their households to poverty. Emperors should uphold the principles and practice of that acknowledged code of behaviour (*li*) which strengthens the relations within a family and on which the organisation of individuals and families into cohesive communities might depend. Thanks to the force of their personality, emperors should be able to attract the adherence of potential rivals and of leaders of non-Han peoples who were willing to be received in the empire. They should encourage scholarship and promote the production of literature as outward and visible signs of a civilised way of life.

As the decades passed and emperors succeeded one another ideas of the proper function of an emperor developed and changed in many respects. The edicts and memorials of the day bring out a contrast between the view that his position depended on material strength, in realistic terms, as in Qin, and the expectation that he stood possessed of saintly qualities, as were ascribed to the kings of Zhou. These views are seen in the writings of essayists, including Lu Jia 陸賈 (ca. 228–ca. 140 BCE), Jia Yi 賈誼 (201–169 BCE) and Dong Zhongshu 董仲舒 (ca. 179–ca.104 BCE). Ban Biao 班彪 (3–54 CE) made an early attempt to describe the place of sovereignty, and thoughts on the subject are latent in the memorials that officials submitted to the throne by way of either encouragement or reproach. Other factors which affected the practice of imperial sovereignty arose from the growing activities of the civil servants and the conduct of the administration. Officials had evolved correct procedures for their business and found ways of bringing their advice to bear on decisions of public policy.

With the passage of time, officials were voicing their criticism of their masters more readily. In the early days of Jingdi (r. 157–141), Yuan Gu 轅固 had raised the question of the means, legitimate or not, by which the Han empire had been founded, and the emperor had abruptly closed the discussion, in some embarrassment. Early in Chengdi's reign, Du Qin 杜欽 had tried in vain to warn the emperor of the likely results of his personal excesses. A few years later Gu Yong 谷永 had reminded him that sovereigns must reign in the interests of their people and had called him to task for allowing disorderly behaviour at court.

Some officials may have found a way of upbraiding Mingdi, said to be a narrow-minded man, for revealing confidential matters and exposing his officials to calumny. It was early in his reign that Zhongli Yi 鍾離意 personally criticised him for putting the pleasures of the hunt before attention to business and for expending public effort and resources to build a palace at a time of drought (60 CE). Shortly before 76 CE, Zong Jun 宗均 disputed his emperor's decisions in a steadfast manner, and towards the end of his reign Andi (r. 106–125 CE) merited a rebuke from Chen Zhong 陳忠 for tolerating the scandalous way in which a woman whom he favoured (not a consort) was demanding and receiving undue respect from officials. In a personal and direct way, circa 160, Chen Fan 陳蕃 berated Huandi for failing to recognise the gravity of his charge and for squandering his inheritance in a life of idleness. Wang Fu 王符 (90–165 CE), who lived through a time when the standard of government was low, expressed his distrust of the hereditary system of succession. He called for an emperor who would put public before private interests and take a personal part in upholding the fabric of the empire. In a lighter tone we read of an incident in which Guangwudi's sister teased him for his lack of power; as a commoner he had been able to take all sorts of action, legal or not, but as emperor he could hardly get his orders obeyed.

Restrictions on an emperor's freedom could perhaps be irksome, as when Yang Bing 楊秉 rebuked the newly acceded Huandi, at the age of about 15, for paying a visit to an official's home. As seen above, his duties started at his father's funeral, to be followed by the formal call that he paid at the shrine dedicated to the founder, there to pay his respects and announce his inheritance of the charge to govern mankind on earth. Formality and traditional procedures guided his steps; carriages, of different designs and with different designations, served him for travelling for different purposes. Regulations determined the type of decree or rescript in which he expressed his will, authorised by one of six different seals of jade and ornamented with carving. Controlled movements of standing and sitting and of announcing formulae showed the correct way for granting an audience. In the same way, when the empress was attending to her task of encouraging the growth of silkworms, she followed the prescribed steps rather than letting her interest fasten on the natural processes at work.

We read of irresponsible or frivolous behaviour by some emperors; of Yuandi, who fell ill and rather than attend to the business of state concentrated on music or played the game of aiming copper pellets to fall on a drum; and of Chengdi, who liked to escape from the palace and wander around the town incognito with his associates. Aidi shocked some of his ministers by offering to abdicate in favour of his close companion. In 181 CE Lingdi, who also enjoyed moving around in public places incognito, took to playing at shops in one of the women's palaces, putting on tradesmen's clothes and making merry. How far such accounts tell of the regular behaviour of those emperors and how far they are exaggerated by a spiteful historian may well be in question. It can perhaps be imagined that they indulged in such frolics by way of relaxation, disabused of any thought that they were playing a part of some importance in public life. Or they may have been seeking a deliberate and conscious escape from an atmosphere in the palace that was inhibiting, frustrating and tense.

Notes for Further Reading

For the kingdoms of the pre-imperial age, see chapters in *CHOAC*, and, for further information, Keightley, Shaughnessy, and Lewis; for the dynastic history of Qin and Han, see *CHOC*; Bodde, *China's First Unifier: Li Ssü*; and Bielenstein, *The Restoration of the Han Dynasty*. Balazs, pp. 187–225, writes of some of the protests expressed in Eastern Han; these are also seen in Pearson. Fragments of various texts collected in *Han guan liu zhong* describe the procedures for an emperor's actions; for the burial arrangements for Han emperors, see Loewe, 'The Imperial Way of Death in Han China' and 'State Funerals of the Han Empire'. References to select subjects will be found in primary sources as follows: a debate on legitimacy (*SJ* 121, p. 3122); Guangwudi and his sister (*HHS* 77, pp. 2489–90); Lingdi's habits (*HHS* 8, p. 346, and 54, p. 1777); precedence of merit over kinship (*HS* 68, p. 2947); views expressed by Chen Fan (*HHS* 66, p. 2164); Chen Zhong (*HHS* 46, p. 1558); Yang Bing (*HHS* 54, pp. 1769–70); Zhongli Yi (*HHS* 41, p. 1408); and Zong Jun (*HHS* 41, p. 1411).

2

The Structure of the Central Government

Comparison of the ways in which the early Chinese empires operated with those of other pre-modern regimes can be no more than a matter of speculation, but it may nonetheless stimulate valuable enquiry. Although no attempt at such a comparison will be undertaken here, it may be asked whether the governments of Qin and Han were organised in a more systematic and intensive manner than that of the Roman Empire and perhaps of any other regime prior to that of Byzantium. Such a question would involve consideration of a number of features some of which had emerged even from the outset of imperial China, shortly after 221 BCE, and had developed in a marked way by the close of Eastern Han (220 CE).

Qin and Han practice drew on the experience and precedents set in the earlier kingdoms, and many of Qin's and Han's institutions survived to form characteristic features of government in later times. An established complement of civil servants staffed the organs of administration each one with its defined responsibilities; a senior official who was appointed to such a department and supported by an assistant supervised the work of his subordinates and their clerks. Steps to achieve the purposes of government depended on organising and controlling the population in units of five persons of less. A division of responsibilities could serve to check the growth of a monopoly of power; civil servants advanced in their careers according to a structure that marked their seniority and determined their salary; social privileges and economic advantages separated officials both from the lower orders of humanity who were subject to their instructions and from those whose high status rested on circumstances of birth.

In ideal terms that were by no means always realised, government lay in the hands of men of proven ability, intellect and loyalty who strove to maintain impartiality and to preclude favouritism. There was no concept of basic distinctions between the consultative, administrative and judicial functions of an official, whose duties might embrace the performance of religious rites and the collection of tax, the promotion of education and the conduct of military campaigns. A conscious sense of seniority and hierarchy pervaded the manner of government and the authority reposed in officials, who must needs comply with set procedures in transacting their business and in their relations with their colleagues, senior and junior alike.

The Standard Histories include detailed descriptions of the offices of the central government for both Western and Eastern Han, setting out the titles of officials with short notes of when their office was founded, their rank, salary and responsibilities, and changes that occurred at various junctures. The entries list their subordinates along with their duties, and their complement with changes of title from time to time. In some instances we are not given a precise figure for the number of incumbents, but a statement such as 'no fixed quota', as may be seen in the cases of the counsellors (*dafu*大夫) who could be counted by the ten and the gentlemen (*lang* 郎) who could rise to a thousand. In addition to this basic, theoretical information, we possess for Western Han a list in chronological order of those men who were appointed to the highest, altogether fifteen, posts of state. The list shows that these offices were in general filled continuously; subordinate offices were not always filled on a regular basis, and it can only be expected that that practice was far from uniform throughout Han times.

Calling doubtless on the earlier practice and schemes of some of the kingdoms, Qin set up a series of offices in its capital city of Xianyang 咸陽 with which to govern the whole empire. It imposed this system on the kingdoms that it had conquered, and the founders of Western Han were ready, and one may perhaps think relieved, to be able to take over an existing system without major change, except for the organisation of provincial units. With some modification, these organs of government remained largely unaltered until the close of Eastern Han, and many of their characteristics and features survived thereafter. As greater numbers of trained men became available, it became possible to expand the scope of the administration to meet demands and problems. At times a sharper edge could be given to government, perhaps by re-ordering the subordination or responsibilities of some of the lesser departments. Rivalries and contests between individuals and groups could bring to light the growth of favouritism or a need to control excessive ambition. A division of the highest responsibilities between two officials of equal status may be seen as an attempt to do so, in the case of the most senior post of all (chancellor) or for the management of finances. The same precaution is seen in the appointment of military commanders and the posting of garrison troops in the capital city.

On a few occasions the titles of some of the major offices of state underwent change, as occurred in 144 BCE, in Wudi's reign and under Wang Mang 王莽, but there is no means of judging whether such changes recognised an altered function of an office or signalled that a major change was being envisaged. Thus the most senior official to be concerned with the conduct of criminal cases was first termed *tingwei* 廷尉; in 144 BCE this was changed to *dali* 大理, but it reverted to *tingwei* in 137 BCE. Whether such changes were intended to correct current abuses and weaknesses, to emphasise a particular purpose of an institution or to make a more intensive way of government possible may not be known. Wang Mang's changes of officials' titles may well have sprung from ideological motives, insofar as they deliberately evoked an affiliation with practices ascribed to the kings of Zhou of much earlier times (1045–771 BCE). For a growing change of attitude that had been set afoot some six or seven decades previously came to fruition under Wang Mang. Han had been founded as the heir to Qin's ideals, systems and ways of government; Wang Mang and his supporters looked to Zhou models, supposedly backed by the ethical ideals of a more liberal and humane dispensation.

Records that are far from complete give hints of some of the ways in which the principal offices of state emerged to govern communities of the Shang and Western Zhou periods, and then those of the many minor units that arose and finally those of the seven major kingdoms, none of which controlled more than a part of China and of which Qin formed one. In no case have we a full statement of a system or organisation, and we depend for our knowledge of such ideas on the titles of officials; these varied from kingdom to kingdom, some to be adopted in the early empires.

The term *San gong* 三公, which is usually rendered 'Three Excellencies', denoted the three (or at times two) officials who stood at the most senior level of the civil service and imperial administration.

In Western Han times these were the chancellor (*chengxiang* 丞相), imperial counsellor (*yushi dafu* 御史大夫) and supreme commander (*taiwei* 太尉). That last post was not filled on a regular basis, and the chancellor was superior to the imperial counsellor. A major change in 8 BCE led forward to a somewhat different situation that prevailed in Eastern Han and involved the use of different titles. The office of *da sikong* 大司空 (usually translated as grand minister of works) replaced that of imperial counsellor, and that of *da situ* 大司徒 (grand minister over the masses) replaced the chancellor. The third member of this most senior consultative group was the supreme commander, and the three officials existed on terms of equality. A further difference in Eastern Han as compared with Western Han is seen in the subordination of three of the nine specialist departments (to be described below) to each of the *San gong;* such a marked assignment of responsibilities had not been seen in Western Han.

At the extreme head of imperial government, second only to the emperor, stood the chancellor (*chengxiang*). In especially meritorious cases, this official was accorded the more dignified title of chancellor of state (*xiangguo* 相國); occasionally the office was split between two chancellors, one of the Left and one of the Right, and as seen it was later replaced by an officer entitled *da situ* or *situ*. He is described as being responsible for assisting the emperor and managing all the multifarious matters of government. For Eastern Han it is said that his duties and activities included the promotion of ideals of social and ethical behaviour, such as respect within a family and integrity; assessment of merit and advice on the consequent bestowal of rewards or sentences to punishment; and the supervision of state sacrifices and funerals. He could proffer direct advice to the throne, as was done by Wei Xiang 魏相 (67–59 BCE) who once urged adherence to traditional ideals and policies and attention to maintaining supplies of food as needed by the population in times of emergency. Li Si 李斯, earliest of the chancellors, in Qin (221–207 BCE), claimed to have upheld the emperor's right to exercise authority and to have introduced a number of practical measures, such as the use of a unified, formalised script and the construction of roads. Xiao He 蕭何, chancellor from 206 to 193 BCE, has ever been cited as one of the 'founding fathers' of Western Han, being credited with the basic work of organising imperial government, thanks to his possession of the state documents and records of Qin. We also hear of weak or ineffective chancellors such as Shi Qing 石慶 (112–103 BCE), who took no part in the energetic and active policies of the day.

In Western Han the imperial counsellor was the deputy or immediate assistant of the chancellor, with the general duties of seeing that the institutes of state were properly maintained in their due form and co-ordinating the work of all officials. One of his assistants was responsible for the safekeeping of maps, registers of the population and certain secret documents. In the conduct of their duties they could at times affect major issues of state, as when Zhou Chang (1) 周昌, who held the post from 203 to 197 BCE, prevented the replacement of a duly nominated heir apparent which was intended to serve particularist interests in the palace. Chao Cuo 鼂錯, who held the post from 155 to 154 BCE, took deliberate action so as to bring about a revolt by seven kings; he foresaw that it could be suppressed in conditions that favoured the central government. Zhang Tang 張湯 (121–115 BCE) put forward suggestions that concerned the coinage and the iron and salt industries. Gong Yu 貢禹 (2) took steps to reduce the extravagant expenditure of the palace (44 BCE). Some of the imperial counsellors are known for the personal parts that they played in questioning the hold that certain favourites had on the reins of power. Zhang Tan 張譚 (33–30 BCE) presented an indictment in one of the early cases where a eunuch had risen to eminence; in 5 BCE Zhao Xuan 趙玄 suggested the degradation of a man who had angered the empress dowager.

Not surprisingly relations between the chancellor and his immediate colleagues varied. In 89 or 88 BCE the chancellor co-operated with the imperial counsellor and one other colleague in suggesting the establishment of colonies in Central Asia. Yu Dingguo 于定國, for the somewhat long period of eight years during which he held the post of chancellor (51–43 BCE), enjoyed the trust of Chen Wannian 陳萬年 (imperial counsellor from 51 to 44) regularly concurring with his views; however, there was no such measure of agreement with Chen Wannian's successor Gong Yu (2). As *situ,* in 121 CE, Yang Zhen 楊震 could submit memorials deploring the unduly high privileges extended to the daughter of the emperor's foster-mother, but these protests were to little avail. He could also refuse to nominate certain persons for office simply because they were protégés of those who held comparably high positions; he did so only to find that his colleague the *sikong* was willing to nominate them and to speed them on the way to early promotion.

As distinct from the posts of chancellor and imperial counsellor, that of supreme commander was filled only rarely, and never on a regular basis. It features at the outset of the Han empire, being held by a few men known to be capable of decisive military achievement, such as Zhou Bo 周勃 (1) (196–195 and 189–179 BCE) and his son Zhou Yafu 周亞夫 (154–150 BCE). Zhou Bo had taken an active part in the fighting that attended the foundation of the dynasty and in securing it from rebels; Zhou Yafu saved the empire and the central government from disruption in 154 BCE. After 140 BCE the post was not filled until 51 CE, being held initially by men of military ability but subsequently by civil officials. One of the latter (Yang Zhen) delivered a stern rebuke to his emperor for tolerating the excesses of favouritism (123 CE).

Confusion may sometimes arise with the title of marshal of state (*da sima* 大司馬), which was first conferred in 119 BCE to enhance the dignity and raise the status of two outstandingly successful generals (Wei Qing 衛青 and Huo Qubing 霍去病) for their leadership on the field of battle. But the gift of this title did not constitute appointment to a paid position as an official. Subsequently on no less that twenty occasions between 87 and 1 BCE the title was granted to salaried officials who held leading posts in the government, to the point that some of them could exercise complete control, but whose strength and reputation did not necessarily rest on their military skills or triumphs. When Huo Guang 霍光 received the title in 87 BCE, the dynasty had recently passed through a severe crisis and the imperial succession lay in doubt; at the same time he was appointed to the salaried position of general-in-chief (*da jiangjun* 大將軍). In effect he was acting as regent, guiding the hands of two emperors who were under age (Zhaodi and Xuandi) while a duly appointed chancellor was complaisant enough to tolerate his exercise of power. As the fifth member of his family (that of the empress dowager of Yuandi) to hold the title, Wang Mang, who received the appointment in 8 BCE, was in a strong position to maintain the leading role that that family was already playing in public life and to prepare the way for his own advancement. There were also times when the title was conferred on a person who held a post as a general in the armed forces (see Chapter 4) but who did not act as regent.

A further development came later. On a number of occasions in Eastern Han nomination of the emperor had fallen to an empress dowager who had deliberately chosen to name a child or youngster who was under age to hold that august position. In such circumstances the empress would entrust the government of the empire to one of her own close relatives, upon whom there would be conferred the title of general-in-chief. As such they possessed controlling powers and are usually described as 'regent'. Dou Xian 竇憲 was the first of these (89–92 CE), and Ho Jin 何進 was the last (184–189 CE). Regents affected the conduct of public affairs sometimes for a few months or perhaps for a few years, and altogether over thirty-seven years. The longest period of tenure was that of Liang Shang 梁商 (135–141 CE) and his son Liang Ji 梁冀 (141–159 CE).

Immediately after the three most senior posts previously mentioned the list of offices for Western Han enters briefly those of the senior tutor (*tai fu* 太傅), grand tutor (*tai shi* 太師) and grand protector (*tai bao* 太保). Described as 'ancient offices', they do not appear for Qin times. In theory the senior tutor provided instruction and guidance for the emperor, but only four men held the title in Western Han, in 187, 180 and 1 BCE and 1 CE. All the emperors of Eastern Han except one appointed a senior tutor at their accession, but the post was never filled more than temporarily. It was usually given to an elderly man with a high reputation whose willingness to serve the dynasty could be taken to convey moral support. Kong Guang 孔光, a descendant of Confucius in the fourteenth generation, held the titles of senior tutor and grand tutor in 1 CE.

Along with the senior tutor, the grand tutor and grand protector were said to have existed under the traditional system of the kings of Zhou. It was Wang Mang who introduced the last two in imperial times, perhaps partly with the intention of displaying his affinity with those praiseworthy rulers of old whom he wished to see as his predecessors.

These three titles were in fact of honorary rather than practical concern. As distinct from the three most senior officials and the nine ministers of state to be described below, those who held these titles did not carry administrative responsibilities. Immediately after listing them, the treatise of the *Han shu* enters a brief note on the titles of four generals, which will be considered below (Chapter 4).

Placed below the three most senior functionaries, the three dignitaries and the generals were the nine ministers of state (*jiu qing* 九卿), who each headed a named department of government that was responsible for ceremonial, executive or military matters. Their duties comprised care of ritual observances and charge of the academicians; security of the palace and the provision of counsellors to the throne; control of the guards; arrangements for transport; conduct of trials and judicial affairs; relations with non-Han peoples; precedence within the imperial clan; agriculture and taxation; non-agricultural production; and technical activities. There were however no set distinctions between these types of duties such that any one type would be the exclusive responsibility of one the nine ministers. Thus, officials whose duties lay in providing advice to the throne came under the jurisdiction of the superintendent of the palace; the two superintendents of state visits and of agriculture, rather than the superintendent of ceremonial, saw to the performance of certain rituals. The treatise gives the nine offices in the descending order of seniority that is followed here.

The superintendent of ceremonial (*fengchang* 奉常 until 144 BCE; thereafter *taichang* 太常) is said to have been responsible for 'the rituals carried out at the imperial shrines', but in fact his duties were more widespread. Of his most senior subordinates, who included directors for music, prayer, sacrificial meats, astrology, divination and medical practice, it is the director of astrology (*tai shi ling* 太史令) that is best known as it was the post held by the historians Sima Tan 司馬談 and his son Sima Qian 司馬遷. The director of astrology maintained the records of events, drew up the calendar and advised on the choice or avoidance of auspicious and inauspicious days for holding state sacrifices, weddings and funerals; he also supervised some of the tests for entry into the civil service.

A large staff served the needs of the superintendent of ceremonial. In addition to his own assistant he could call on the services of two specialist assistants who attended to the Devotional Hall (*Ming tang* 明堂) used for ceremonial and religious purposes and the observatory. Other subordinate officials looked after the shrines, chambers of rest and parks of the imperial mausolea and, in Western Han, of the five sites where the religious cults of state were performed. The settlements that were established in towns at the imperial tombs were under his jurisdiction until they were transferred to the senior administrators of the metropolitan area (43 BCE). Under the director of astrology there were thirty-seven men awaiting appointment as officials, including specialists in the calendar and various methods of divination; two were responsible for sacrifices to expel evil influences and two for making prayers for rain.

The director of prayer (*tai zhu ling* 太祝令) read those incantations, presumably aloud, and performed the rites of welcoming the spirits and escorting them back to their place of habitation. In addition to his staff of twenty-five, the director of music (*tai yue ling* 太樂令) controlled 380 musicians and the court's company of dancers. One notable change occurred in 159 CE when the post of inspector of the imperial library was created, to be under the superintendent of ceremonial, to take charge of documents and books. Previously such duties had rested within the office of the imperial counsellor, and later with that of the superintendent of the lesser treasury.

The academicians, who came under the jurisdiction of the superintendent of ceremonial, were scholars who were familiar with past precedent and current practice. Numbered by the ten, from 136 BCE they included specialists in interpreting the five texts selected for special or even scriptural attention. The academy admitted fifty students for a year's study, and before final enrolment they needed the approval of the superintendent of ceremonial. In the course of time this institution grew to the extent of including up to a thousand students, and its complement was modified as occasion demanded.

Shusun Tong 叔孫通, who was the earliest superintendent to be named (200–197 and again from 195 BCE), had persuaded the first of the Han emperors that he must take account of the importance of formal procedures in government and behaviour at court. Some of those who held the post were brought up on a charge and dismissed on technical grounds, for example, in 117, 107 and perhaps 100 BCE, for failure to keep sufficient sacrificial animals as duly prescribed for the needs of the state's cults at Yong 雍.

When in 81 BCE a storm dislodged tiles of the shrine dedicated to Wendi, the superintendent of ceremonial was dismissed. In 66 BCE Su Chang 蘇昌 was dismissed on the grounds of disclosure of secret information, to be re-appointed in 62 BCE.

The superintendent of the palace (*langzhong ling* 郎中令 until 104; thereafter *guangluxun* 光禄勳) was charged with control of the 'gates and doors of the palaces and their halls'. To fulfil these duties, which included securing the buildings and their grounds from criminals and intruders and policing admission to different parts of the palaces, he could call on the company of the gentlemen, or gentlemen-at-arms (*lang* 郎). The performance of such duties included a search for arms held by visitors summoned to the palace, and at least one man (Xiao Wangzhi 蕭望之) who was later to become a leading official refused to suffer this indignity, at the cost of forfeiting nomination for a post. The superintendent of the palace was also responsible for the safety of the emperor when travelling, and two regiments of cavalry (*Qimen* 期門 and *Yulin* 羽林) who were under his supervision accompanied the emperor on his journeys. In addition his staff included a large number of officials who provided advice to the throne and a number of messengers who served to carry out missions as was required.

There was no fixed complement for the gentlemen of the palace and gentlemen in attendance, and their number could rise to as many as a thousand. Some of them were men who had already been selected as being capable of service as officials and who were on probation awaiting appointment. To carry out their duties effectively they were armed.

Founded in 128 BCE and renamed *Huben* 虎賁 in 1 CE, the *Qimen* regiment of up to a thousand cavalrymen stood to arms to escort the emperor. The *Yulin* regiment was founded in 104 BCE, the men being chosen as the sons or grandsons of those who had died on active service, with some preference for those of families of good repute from the north-west. Ranking below the *Qimen* these armed cavalrymen likewise provided an escort. They included famous soldiers such as Zhao Chongguo 趙充國 (2), of Longxi, who was responsible for successful military and colonial initiatives in the north-west (from 61 BCE), and Gan Yanshou 甘延壽 who, without the necessary authority, took the field against a leader of the Xiongnu in 36 BCE. The two regiments featured in the coup led by a eunuch in which the regent Dou Wu 竇武 was forced to suicide in 168 CE.

Also on the staff of the superintendent of ceremonial were the gentlemen consultants (*yi lang* 議朗) and various types of counsellor (*dafu*) who were expected to answer questions that were posed, perhaps in the name of the emperor, to provide him with information or to reprimand him for errors of government. There was no fixed number of counsellors, whose degree of seniority ranged widely, reaching almost to the top of the scale of grades and salaries. Unlike the nine ministers of state, the counsellors did not usually initiate proposals or take the first steps in tendering advice; they usually acted in response to orders.

Examples of their activities follow. In 28 BCE Gu Yong 谷永, as counsellor of the Palace, and Du Qin 杜欽, as gentleman consultant, together expressed the view that it would be unwise to accept the surrender of one of the leaders of the Xiongnu 匈奴. As leader of the gentlemen of the palace, in 43 CE Zhang Chun 張純 gave advice on the proper arrangements for services to the memory of the imperial ancestors. Zuo Xiong 左雄, who was appointed gentleman consultant in 126 CE, was to be known later for his outspoken criticism of contemporary abuses and scandals.

There were seventy imperial messengers in Western Han, but the number was reduced to thirty-five in Eastern Han.

With the assistance of a number of military officers subordinated to him, the superintendent of the guards (*weiwei* 衛尉) commanded the guards' units stationed at the principal imperial palace. In Eastern, and presumably Western, Han they checked officials and others who came to deliver written documents or presents to the throne and those who were presenting themselves for audience. In some cases production of a tally was needed to secure entry. At one time the post was combined with that of a general, but this was not a regular arrangement, and from time to time officials with the same duties as that of the superintendent of the guards were set up to protect the other palaces in Chang'an and Luoyang. Li Guang 李廣 and Han Anguo 韓安國 (1), who served in successful campaigns against the Xiongnu in 134 and 129 BCE, had both held this post, as did Lu Bode 路博德, who fought both in the north and the south (112 BCE) and played a part in the construction of the defence lines of Juyan in the north-west. So also did Zhang Qian 張騫, after returning from his pioneer journeys in Central Asia.

The superintendent of transport (*taipu* 太僕) was responsible for supplying carriages and horses for the imperial use and for the army, and for stockbreeding for those purposes. His subordinates controlled at least thirteen sets of stables in Chang'an and perhaps as many as thirty-six pasture grounds that were situated mainly in the north-west, raising altogether some 300,000 head of horse. Du Yannian 杜延年 (1), known for his liberal rather than oppressive administration, and the part that he played in having Liu Bingyi 劉病已 (reign title Xuandi) placed on the throne, had been superintendent of transport in 80 BCE.

The superintendent of trials (*tingwei* 廷尉; at times termed *dali* 大理) who was responsible for punishments that included the death penalty did not take part in all trials. As the senior authority for the conduct of legal matters and for giving judgement in criminal cases, he received reports from the provinces of cases that were in doubt and gave a decision when necessary. He also gave his opinion in disputes that involved legal issues. Of the superintendents of trials of Western Han, Zhang Shizhi 張釋之 (probably from 160 or 158 BCE) intervened at the highest levels to ensure that sentences to punishment were not more severe than those authorised by the laws. As a boy Zhang Tang 張湯 (*tingwei* from 126 BCE) had once staged a mock trial of some rats that had damaged his household's stores; later, as an expert in legal matters, he enforced the laws severely. Yu Dingguo 于定國 held the post from 69 BCE for seventeen years before promotion to imperial counsellor and then chancellor.

Leaders of non-Han communities who accepted Han suzerainty came under the control of the superintendent of state visits (*da honglu* 大鴻臚; previously entitled *dian ke* 典客 and then *da xingling* 大行令). His subordinates included those who served in an office of interpreters, as required for negotiation with peoples of both the north and the south, and he had charge of the residences kept for senior provincial officials who were called to Chang'an. He also received officials who came to the capital to present the annual accounts of the kingdoms and the commanderies.

The superintendent of state visits also saw that the due procedures and rites attended the visits paid by Han kings (see Chapter 3) and non-Han kings on their arrival at the capital city. He ensured that the succession passed correctly to the heirs of the Han kings and non-Han leaders, and possibly also of the nobles, at their decease. One of his subordinates was responsible for the ritual act of renewing the fires at the winter solstice for senior offices and at the summer palace.

As early as 202 BCE a man named Xue Ou 薛歐 held the title of superintendent of state visits, though the call to undertake all of the activities just described can hardly have been made already. His successors included Wang Hui (1) 王恢, in 136 BCE, who was well familiar with the non-Chinese peoples of the north and led a military expedition to assist a friendly king of Nan Yue in the south. It was in this capacity that Xiao Wangzhi (61–59 BCE) successfully argued against renewal of matrimonial relations with the leaders of Wusun in the north-west.

The superintendent of the imperial clan (*zongzheng* 宗正; *zongbo* 宗伯 for a short time from 4 CE) was responsible for regulating and maintaining the correct status and degree of kinship between members of the imperial family. His subordinate staff included directors and guardian officers of the houses of the imperial princesses. He received annual registers of the members of the imperial family which were submitted from the provinces. Should any such member be charged with a crime that was punishable by hard labour or a more severe sentence, as a first move the case was brought to the attention of the superintendent of the imperial clan; one, Liu Shou 劉受 (1), may have been involved in just such an affair in 122 BCE. The list of those who held this office is not complete; all those who are named were members of the imperial family themselves. Liu Yingke 劉郢客 (1), the earliest to be named (186 BCE), became king of Chu in 179 BCE. The most famous man to hold the post was the litterateur Liu Gengsheng 劉更生 (2), for two years from 48 BCE; he is known more usually under his later and more usual name, Liu Xiang 劉向 (1).

Of all the nine ministers, it was the superintendent of agriculture (*da sinong* 大司農; first known as *zhi su neishi* 治粟內史 and as *da nongling* 大農令 between 143 and 104 BCE) whose work affected the greater part of the population most comprehensively and intensively. This is because it was his officials who were concerned with the working occupations of the great majority of the people and with the collection and use of taxation, whose burdens none, except the highly privileged, could avoid. Whereas the work of the superintendent of agriculture bore on those many men and women who worked the land, the offices of the superintendent of the lesser treasury (*shaofu* 少府) affected those who worked as artisans, craftsmen and perhaps tradesmen, living in the towns.

The superintendent of agriculture is said tersely to have been responsible for crops and money, and to this we may add valuable and precious commodities. His subordinates included five directors. The one for the Great Granary received the grain delivered as tax from the units of the provinces, and he was custodian of a standard set of weights and measures. The two directors for price adjustment and stabilisation (*junshu ling* 均輸令) and equalisation and standards (*pingzhun ling* 平準令) collected tax that was delivered in other types of kind and saw to the distribution of those items; they also contrived to stabilise prices of staple commodities, as between periods or areas of famine and glut. Another director (*dunei ling* 都內令) had charge of storing money and valuables, and one (*jitian ling* 籍田令) maintained the lands reserved for the annual ceremony in which the emperor handled the plough, by way of invoking a blessing for an agricultural work of the empire. There were also two other offices, at a slightly lower level, which were concerned with some aspects of the administration of the state monopolies (salt, iron and liquor). Some of the offices which were subordinate to this superintendent received seasonal reports from the provincial units with registers of grain and money in hand, and separate entries for those items whose records were incomplete.

The senior officials of sixty-five offices were posted to the provincial units as supervisors of granaries, agricultural work and water supplies. They may have been responsible for implementing the detailed regulations of the Statutes on Agriculture, whose text was completely unknown until recent discoveries of copies of parts, dated 217 and 186 BCE. Other subordinates of the superintendent of agriculture who were attached to select places in the provinces included one who supplied sacrificial victims, one who regulated transactions in the markets of Luoyang and one who had charge of the famous Ao 敖 Granary at Xingyang 榮陽.

The terse descriptions of the functions of the superintendent of the lesser treasury (*Shao fu* 少府), as bearing responsibility for taxation on lakes and pools, or for the clothing in the palace and equipment used by the emperor, are far from adequate to describe the wide-ranging work of the office. They do not mention the all-important fact that at times the exercise of power moved from the chancellor to one of the subordinates of this official. The entry for the office for Western Han lists sixteen departments, each with its own director, and twelve more subordinate offices. Other departments are named for Eastern Han, when the office had been substantially re-organised, with the transfer of some of its minor divisions to the charge of some of the other nine ministers. Whereas the term *shaofu* was retained throughout Han times, the titles of some of the subordinate officials were changed in 104 BCE. Overall, it may be said that the office was responsible for looking after the needs of the emperor and the palaces as well as for a number of items of imperial administration; it was also in charge of a number of eunuchs who were employed in various capacities.

Subordinate officials of the superintendent of the lesser treasury provided supplies of clothing and palace furnishings, medical attention and medicaments and the writing materials that the emperor needed. They conducted the services and sacrifices that were needed within the palace compound, and they employed three thousand slaves for the preparation of food and drink. They looked after the paintings of paragon leaders of old and praiseworthy officials of the empire that were displayed in some of the palace's halls, and they were responsible for the parks, orchards and detached palaces. Skilled craftsmen and artisans were employed in the workshops of the superintendent to manufacture precious artifacts for daily use and some of the equipment used in imperial funerals.

Subordinate to the superintendent of the lesser treasury was the Secretariat (*shangshu* 尚書), often under the leadership of a director (*shangshu ling* 尚書令), and it was this department that came to control many aspects of government. Its power depended partly on its access to the documents that passed to and from the throne. The leader of the Secretariat would open one of the two duplicate copies of proposals and reports and was in a position to suppress any that were not to his liking. The office was already strong by circa 40 BCE; some seventy years later its powers could essentially rise to be higher and more effective than those of the three officials who stood at the head of the administration. In addition the superintendent of the lesser treasury had charge of the 'Orchid Terrace' (*Lan tai* 蘭臺), which was a repository for state documents. An example of the power of the *Shangshu ling* is seen in 160 CE, when the man who held the office took the lead in praising a man of distinction whose integrity had been brought into question.

During Western Han the *Shao fu* was responsible for collecting certain dues from non-agricultural work and products and controlled expenditure of these so as to meet the needs of the palace; in Eastern Han this latter task passed to the superintendent of agriculture. The *shaofu* controlled the issue of tallies and credentials whereby imperial messengers and officials appointed to a special commission could declare and make use of their authority. Some of these tallies conveyed permission to call out armed forces for a stated purpose. One of the departments, the Bureau of Music, provided orchestras and choirs for ritual ceremonies and by way of entertainment, controlling a large number of performers.

Eunuchs played a comparatively minor role in Western Han, their numbers, functions and activities growing during Eastern Han. Two had risen to prominence during Yuandi's reign (r. 48–33 BCE) but it was not until some century or more later that they began to form a defined and cohesive group that was capable of affecting dynastic destinies. However, from early in Han times eunuchs had served in a number of offices which were nearly all under the supervision of the superintendent of the lesser treasury. Until 29 BCE some of them had been appointed to be palace writers (*zhongshu* 中書), their duties matching those of their colleagues in the Secretariat and bringing them inside the palace for their work. Eunuchs served in posts and with titles as personal attendants of the emperor, carrying out missions as ordered. They managed the women's quarters of the palace and enquired after the health of princesses and consorts. They were responsible for the emperor's wardrobe and looked after the parks, gardens and lodges of the palace. In addition the director of the office that was responsible for the manufacture of choice items of equipment (*Shangfang* 尚方) was a eunuch. Possibly eunuchs were appointed to this post and put in charge of the emperor's wardrobe because the staff there included young girls who were engaged in embroidery and similar work.

From time to time the assignment of specialist offices and tasks was transferred from the charge of one of the nine ministers to another. The physician-in-chief (*tai yi*) was at first subordinate to the superintendent of ceremonial, but in Eastern Han the office was moved to the superintendent of the lesser treasury; the latter official, however, at one time lost control of the selection of grain (*dao guan* 道官) and of one of the workshops responsible for manufactures

(*Kaogong* 考工), which came under the superintendents of agriculture and transport, respectively.

Of the same rank as the nine ministers, and sometimes classed with them, the superintendent of the capital (*zhijinwu* 執金吾; before 104 BCE *zhongwei* 中尉) could rely on resources with which to patrol the capital city, maintaining law and order outside the palaces and handling emergencies such as those due to fire or floods. Conscript servicemen were available to him for these purposes, and his subordinates included some with military titles such as major (*sima* 司馬) or captain (*hou* 候). The arsenal of Chang'an was in his charge. His subordinate staff was reduced considerably in Eastern Han.

Other senior officials with specialist functions acted independently of the nine ministers and were of lower grade, usually being supported by assistants and subordinate offices. There were the senior and junior tutors to the heir apparent, providing him with guidance and instruction. The court architect (*jiangzuo da jiang* 將作大匠; until 144 *jiangzuo shaofu* 將作少府) had charge of the palace buildings and ancestral shrines, arranging for any work that was needed in their parks; he also ordered trees for planting on the sides of the highways. Supplies of stone and timber, kept carefully under the supervision of his subordinates, were at his disposal for these purposes. Supervisors of the households of the empress and the heir apparent (*zhanshi* 詹事; after 18 BCE combined with the office of *da changqiu* 大長秋) were responsible for domestic arrangements in their residences and the religious ceremonies conducted there; their subordinates included eunuchs.

From 115 BCE the superintendent of waterways and parks (*shuiheng duwei* 水衡都尉) took charge of the major hunting park that was reserved for imperial use. Subordinates took care of the stables, horses and dogs needed for the hunt, and of the upkeep of buildings in the park and the collection of fruit or vegetables produced there. As the collector of certain taxes and controller of the mint, the superintendent of waterways and parks also shared some of the financial responsibilities of empire with the superintendents of agriculture and the lesser treasury. The post of colonel, internal security (*sili xiaowei* 司隸校尉) was founded in 89 BCE. The incumbent could call on a force of up to 1,200 convicts with which to perform his duties of arresting criminals and detecting crime. In 106 BCE regional inspectors (*cishi* 刺史) had been appointed to look for cases of corruption and dereliction of duty by officials in the provinces, and in the same way the colonel, internal security, carried out such duties in the seven major administrative units of the metropolitan area and adjoining commanderies. Such duties were retained in Eastern Han. At one time the holder of the post had been concerned only with supervising convicts engaged in public works.

Attention will be paid below to senior officials listed alongside those named above, such as the director of dependent states, the metropolitan superintendent and the commandant, orders of honour (see Chapter 3), as well as colonels of the city gates and central ramparts. There were also the posts of commandant, attendant cavalry and commandant, imperial carriages.

Appointments to these senior posts are recorded as deriving from the emperor. In some instances the choice may have rested on his own judgement; in others it may have been due to persuasion or pressure brought to bear by those who were in close proximity to the throne, whether imperial consorts and their relatives, senior officials themselves or eunuchs. When Xiao He, chancellor of state, lay dying in 193 CE the emperor asked him whether Cao Shen 曹參 would be a suitable successor. That five members of the Wang family who were relatives of the Empress Dowager Wang held the title of Marshal of State between 32 and 7 BCE tells its own story.

A number of officials who were assigned to the major offices of government that have been described above were posted to work in the provinces, supervising establishments such as the salt and iron agencies, until in Eastern Han these were transferred to local control; or, as we may perhaps surmise, they were appointed to work in the arsenals situated outside the capital city, the pasture grounds of the north, two clothing agencies, ten agencies for the manufacture of equipment and two for the production of fruit. Such offices were termed *Xian guan* 縣官, or *Du guan* 都官, and the number of those officials may perhaps be included in the thirty thousand estimated to have been in the complements of offices in Chang'an city in 5 BCE. There is no means of determining how those thirty thousand were distributed among the major organs of government whose scope and activities varied widely, as has been seen. Nor are we given figures for the clerks of the lowest levels upon whose labours the orders of government eventually depended. However, some idea may perhaps be gained from what is known of some of the smaller organs.

The subordinate staff of the superintendent of agriculture in Western Han included his two assistants; the directors and assistants of five specialist divisions; the heads and assistants of two other divisions; all inspectors of granaries and agriculture in the commanderies and kingdoms; and the heads and assistants of sixty-five other offices. For Eastern Han, the superintendent of the imperial clan had one assistant, one controller of the household and an assistant for each of the princesses (whose numbers varied), together with other officials of no fixed complement. In addition he controlled a personal staff of twenty-two men, including six who were on horseback and two who were legal experts, eighteen apprentices and one physician.

Such were the offices of the central government. The chapters which follow will describe those of provincial government, the sources from which officials were drawn or trained and the organisation of the armed forces. It was largely from the structure and practice of the central government of the Han empire that there evolved the ideal of a civil service that was to form so marked an element in China's social, political and intellectual tradition. Whereas as yet it would be hard to discern a formal or theoretical distinction between differing aspects of government, such as legislative, administrative and judicial, the system embodied the means of assigning specialist responsibilities to specified offices. Some of the main organs of government were directed to the personal needs of the emperor, some to evolving and implementing the means of governing an empire.

In the early stages the emperor called on loyal supporters whose merits he had seen proven, often on a field of battle; experiments followed in entrusting powers of command to his close relatives. With the passing of the decades it became possible to call on men of experience and ability to shoulder major burdens of state, and there would develop an association between possession of such gifts and the benefits of a scholarly training. Long before the titular end of the Han dynasty in 220 CE a civil service had come into being with hierarchies and grades, methods of recruitment, chances of promotion and dangers of dismissal. Admission into this profession was to spell a recognition of a man's talent and become a source of pride to the members of his family.

Notes for Further Reading

For a full account of the complement of all officials for Qin and Han times, see Bielenstein, *Bureaucracy*, which includes information from the specialist chapters of the *Han shu* and *Hou Han shu* (*HS* 19A and *HHS* treatises 24 and 25) and details seen in other primary sources. For the *San gong*, see Bielenstein, *Bureaucracy*, pp. 7–12; for regents, pp. 151–52, and the same author in *CHOC*, p. 282; for imperial counsellors, see *Men Who Governed*, pp. 155–75, and p. 70 for the estimate of thirty thousand officials in the central government.

For the powers of the Secretariat, see *HS* 74, p. 3135, and *HHS* 54, p. 1771; Chen Zhong's criticism of it voiced shortly before 124 CE, and before becoming its leader, is seen in *HHS* 46, p. 1565; for criticism by Zhongchang Tong (ca. 200 CE), who traced the problems to the time of Guangwudi, see *HHSJJ* 46.15a note, and Balazs, pp. 213–25. Figures are given for the number of *lang* in Eastern Han in *HHS* 54, p. 1772, and 66, p. 2161. Swann, pp. 64–65, discusses measures to equalise or stabilise prices; and Bodde, *Festivals*, pp. 294–302, writes about the renewal of the fires. Hulsewé, *RCL*, pp. 21–27, gives an English translation of the Qin Statutes on Agriculture of 217 BCE; for remnants of reports drawn up for the receipt and disbursal of grain and money, as submitted from commanderies in the north-west, see the documents described in *RHA*, vol. 1, pp. 20–23. Primary sources refer to persons who are mentioned above as follows: Gu Yong and Du Qin (*HS* 94B, p. 3808); Yang Zhen (*HHS* 54, pp. 1761, 1764); Zhang Chun (*HHS* treatise 9, p. 3193); Zhou Chang (*SJ* 96, p. 2677); and Zuo Xiong (*HHS* 61, p. 2015). For Li Si, see Bodde, *China's First Unifier*.

3

Provincial and Local Government

As is hardly surprising, the newly founded Han government was content to accept the heritage of a working empire bequeathed by Qin and to make use of such of its administrative records as survived after its demise. Although the importance of the emperor and the part that he played in government changed vitally as between those emperors who were forceful and those who were complaisant, little structural change was introduced until the occasions in Eastern Han when control of the government came into the hands of the regents.

Such continuity was not the case with provincial government, in which the founders of Han combined elements of different traditions. The Qin empire had been formed by taking over territories from its neighbouring kingdoms and amalgamating them with lands that were firmly under its existing rule. Such newly acquired lands were administered as units that were termed commanderies (*jun* 郡) or counties (*xian* 縣), and there was no difficulty in establishing new such units as occasion demanded. From such beginnings and accretions, the whole of the Qin empire was governed as thirty-six, or perhaps as many as forty-six, commanderies under the control of governors (*shou* 守), who were appointed by the centre. Some of these commanderies were established in areas that had been taken over in the south-west (Shujun and Bajun; modern Sichuan) at the end of the fourth century BCE, or in those that had been penetrated in the south (Nanhai; modern Guangdong); Liaodong in the north-east and Jiuyuan in the north-west marked the extremities of the defence lines known as the Great Wall.

However, government of China as a single unit was an innovation and a short-lived one at that; there could be no certainty that it would be seen again after the virtual collapse of Qin in 210 BCE. Emerging as apparently the leading protagonist from the ensuing civil warfare, Xiang Yu 項羽 sought to set up a system of a pre-imperial type; it was to consist of nineteen separate kingdoms over which he would claim to act as overlord. Some of these kingdoms were led by survivors of the royal houses that Qin had destroyed, such an arrangement signifying a rejection of the imperial system. One of the kingdoms, named Han 漢, was placed under the rule of Liu Bang 劉邦, whom Xiang Yu had relegated to a subordinate position but who had attained a dominant position after some years of warfare. It can only be surmised that, living as he had under pre-imperial, imperial and post-imperial dispensations, and fired by a personal ambition, Liu Bang deliberately chose to re-instate an imperial system under his own control as his chosen way of asserting his authority and governing China. He did so with one major change: the institution of kingdoms as an element in provincial government.

Like the Qin dynasty, the Han dynasty was established in the west, with its capital at Chang'an 長安 in place of its predecessor's choice of Xianyang 咸陽. The relatively secure position where it was situated was organised and governed as the metropolitan area, which came to be divided into three parts as time went by. Stretching in all directions, the adjoining lands were governed as fifteen commanderies, but in a new venture the regions east of a north-south line that ran roughly between 110 and 115 degrees were incorporated as kingdoms of the empire. In time the number of commanderies rose to reach 83 in 1–2 CE and 80 in 140 CE, whereas the extent of the lands made over as kingdoms was severely reduced by founding commanderies in parts of them. The number of kingdoms varied from time to time, with 20 and 19 existing respectively at the dates just given.

The situation, size and names of some of the original Han commanderies may well have been identical or closely identical with those of Qin; some may even have derived from arrangements made in some of the other pre-imperial kingdoms. The establishment of new commanderies in Han, particularly in the south and the north-west, could in no way spell immediate and total occupation of new territories and the enforcement of intensive government by officials. At its lowest level it could signify no more than the penetration of new lands by tradesmen or explorers, followed by the despatch of an official with orders to set up his headquarters as governor and administer the land and its peoples as best he could. In such circumstances a governor and his staff might find themselves isolated in remote spots such as the Korean peninsula or Hainan Island, among inhabitants who were not accustomed to the ways of life of the newcomers or could not understand the language that they spoke. Han officials might suffer from the absence of suitable company and the material comforts that they were used to enjoying in their home surroundings.

The further afield a commandery lay from the metropolitan area, the larger the territory that its governor would have to try to control. The smallest of the commanderies in area were those that followed the course of the Yellow River to the sea and lay along its northern and southern banks, in the modern provinces of Hebei, Henan, Jiangsu and Shandong; the largest were those of the south-west and north-west, whose external boundaries were not necessarily certain. Many of the smaller commanderies had come into being when territory was removed from the charge of the kings, as was achieved by government policies in 164, 154 and 121 BCE. The larger commanderies were founded following the expansionist moves towards Central Asia, the lands south of the Yangzi River and the south-west between 115 and 110 BCE. Figures that we have for the years 1–2 and 140 CE show the degree of variation (see pp. 48–9 and 197–201 below).

The boundaries, extent and internal organisation of the commanderies were anything but fixed for all time. The governors (*shou* 守 until 148 BCE; thereafter *taishou* 太守) were appointed by orders of the central government which could likewise exercise powers of promotion or dismissal. The governors enjoyed a high salary and status from which they could advance to become one of the nine ministers, such as the superintendent of agriculture, state visits or the lesser treasury. A number of governors rose immediately to be one of the three metropolitan superintendents (see p. 52 below). Of four members of the imperial Liu Family who had been governors, three rose to be superintendents of the imperial clan. A governor could also be demoted for failure in his administration, or dismissed after indictment as a criminal.

It may be estimated that by the end of Western Han perhaps 100,000 officials were engaged in administering the provinces of the empire. The governors of a highly populated commandery might be responsible for a registered population of two and a half million registered individuals, those of the remote commanderies at the perimeter for less than fifty thousand; they could also be held accountable to some extent for the activities of those persons who had not been registered, living by means of criminal activities or evading apprehension as deserters or vagabonds. The governors were responsible for security, for the maintenance of law and order and, if at the perimeter, for defence. They held judicial powers with which to implement the laws, judge lawsuits and disputes and suppress crime; at times they took command of armed forces. They were enjoined to promote agriculture and education. If posted in regions such as the south (modern Guangdong and Guangxi), they could earn merit by teaching refined habits such as those of wearing clothes or regulated marriages to folk who were as yet unassimilated. They collected revenue which was payable to the centre, and they controlled the registration of the population and the call-up of those members who were due for statutory service as labourers or soldiers.

A number of annual duties fell to the governor. He would tour the constituent units of the commandery, providing relief for those who had suffered by reason of natural disaster. He reviewed the condition of criminals under detention in prison to ensure that their sentences were fair; he submitted accounts of tax collected and other matters, as will be seen below (Chapters 9 and 10). The governor reported on the achievements or failures of officials working under his authority. He forwarded the names of men recommended as being suitable for office, sometimes by a quota of one to every 100,000 inhabitants of the commandery.

Much of this work fell to the officials of the constituent divisions of the commanderies, which are to be described below. The governor's own staff was relatively small, including one assistant, with some specialist officials to be responsible for military weapons and, in commanderies at the border, for horses. Little is known of the subordinates who served in various bureaus such as those of merit, banditry or consultation, but a recently found diary kept by an official of the Bureau of Merit has records of the journeys that he made from one county to another in the course of his duties in 11 BCE. From other documents we learn that there was a total of twenty-five junior officials or clerks attached to the governor of the exceptionally large commandery of Donghai (modern Shandong and Jiangsu) at that time.

Matched with the governor and of the same rank, the commandants of the commanderies (*Wei* 尉 until 148 BCE; thereafter *Duwei* 都尉) were responsible for defence, military duties and the use of conscript servicemen, and for precautions against acts of violence and crime. He too was supported by an assistant, and in circa 10 BCE the commandant of Donghai could call on a staff of ten clerks. Except for commanderies at the borders the office was discontinued from 30 CE, its duties passing to the governor. Reference follows below (Chapter 4) to the organisation and staff of the commandants in the commanderies of the north-west. The offices of both governor and commandant had been instituted in Qin times, and it is perhaps possible to see here an attempt to ensure that complete control of the commanderies did not fall into the hands of a single senior official.

If he was lucky, a governor who had shown himself to be an efficient administrator might earn praise and merit promotion. After serving as regional inspector (see p. 53 below) for Yangzhou (modern Zhejiang and further south), circa 65 BCE Huang Ba 黃霸 became governor of Yingchuan (modern Henan), where he saw that the contents of imperial orders were made clear to all. He dispensed relief to those who were in distress, suppressed crime, promoted agriculture and increased the numbers of the registered population. In 55 BCE he rose to become chancellor, with the honor of a nobility (see pp. 49, 146 below). As governor of Kuaiji (modern Zhejiang), circa 53 CE Diwu Lun 第五倫 eliminated cattle sacrifice with its attendant impoverishment; transferred to be governor of Shu (modern Sichuan), he stamped out corruption. As imperial counsellor (ca. 76) he was strong enough to submit memorials criticising unduly harsh government and the recommendation of unsuitable persons for office.

In some cases a governor so endeared himself to his flock that they staged a demonstration if he was called elsewhere, even to the point of instituting religious services. As governor of Shu in Wendi's reign, Wen Weng 文翁 strove to improve the cultured way of life of the commandery by sending select persons for a scholarly education in Chang'an and by setting up schools in Chengdu. In recognition of his achievements a shrine was erected in that city, and annual services were performed in his memory. Diwu Lun was once summoned to face a legal charge (62 CE), but such was his popularity that the local inhabitants tried to prevent him from proceeding by land to answer the call and he could do so only by a secret withdrawal by boat. Bao Yu 鮑昱 was appointed governor of Runan (modern Henan) at a time between 62 and 74 CE, when the commandery was suffering heavy losses owing to the collapse of some of the dykes. He proposed the construction of water gates made from stone, which resulted in a major increase in supplies of water for irrigation and a growth of the population.

Governors or commandants who had freed a commandery from crime might acquire a reputation for harsh application of the laws or even for oppression, but such conduct would not necessarily ban appointment to a higher level. When Commandant of Guangping (modern Hebei), Wang Wenshu 王溫舒 stopped at no measures, however ruthless, with which to suppress crime, and other senior provincial officials came to imitate his methods. In due course he became superintendent of trials (115 BCE), and then of the lesser treasury (109), to be appointed metropolitan superintendent of the right (see p. 52 below) in 107. As governor of Bohai (modern Hebei) circa 80 CE, Zhou Yu 周紆 deliberately left general orders for a pardon or amnesty unopened and disregarded until decisions had been made and sentences pronounced for all outstanding criminal cases in the counties of the commandery.

Arising from humble beginnings with the help of a few supporters, Liu Bang passed several years of hard fighting before emerging as the victor of all his rivals. His campaigns led to the occupation of large areas of land, which were left for others to control while he himself moved to win his next objective. It was in such circumstances that some of those men who had shown their abilities as military leaders when fighting with him became the effective masters of the lands that they had helped him to conquer. To ensure that he retained their loyalty and that they would not be tempted to set themselves up as independent or rival leaders, Liu Bang agreed to their assumption of the title of king, the very title that he himself held at the time as king of Han. In some cases, such as that of Han Xin 韓信, he had had little choice in the matter in view of the powers that lay in their hands and the part that they had played to win the lands that they now occupied. Some of these men were surviving members of the royal families of kingdoms that Qin had conquered and incorporated into its empire.

Liu Bang's acceptance that some of his closest friends and associates would carry the title of king, to rule over broad tracts of territory, may be interpreted as a means of rewarding them for their support, deterring dissidence and establishing an administrative control. But the situation changed in 202 BCE with his assumption of the title and position of emperor (*huangdi* 皇帝), thereby signifying his superiority over all other leaders and his requirement of their fealty. In those circumstances, doubts could soon arise as to whether all these kings were prepared to accept such a position, or whether, situated at a long distance away from the palace and the capital city, one of them might choose to abjure his loyalty to Han and make common cause with the potentially hostile non-Han leaders of the north. By a series of moves between 202 and 195 BCE, all except one of these kings were eliminated, to be replaced by Liu Bang's own kinsmen (two brothers, one cousin and six sons). The one remaining king (Wu Rui 吳芮), who was not a member of the Liu Family, ruled over Changsha (modern Hunan), which lay far away in the south and was out of contact with a would-be challenger to Han authority.

In this way there came about a major change in the form of the empire, as compared with that of Qin. The Han empire now included both commanderies governed by officials who were appointed on merit and were subject to dismissal, and kingdoms to be ruled by the emperor's kinsmen, succeeding one another on an hereditary basis. The two principles might well have come into conflict, the one of direct control imposed from the centre and the other of reliance on family ties designed to ensure loyalties to the centre. As the decades and the generations passed those ties slackened; the family relationship of some of the kings to the emperor grew more and more remote, and fears arose in the centre that some of them might challenge the emperor's right to his supreme position.

Some of the kingdoms within Liu Bang's empire bore the same names and were situated in parts of the same territories as their predecessors of pre-imperial times or in the dispensation of Xiang Yu. But they were not necessarily set up precisely in the same area, and their size and importance varied widely, as may be seen in the case of Chu. This had been one of the mightiest of the kingdoms of pre-imperial times; as one of those set up by Xiang Yu it had occupied large areas of the centre and the south. However, in the Han empire it existed as no more than an enclave to the south of the Shandong peninsula.

In 195 BCE the ten kingdoms formed a large unbroken block on the east side of the fifteen commanderies. The nineteen kingdoms of 108 BCE lay dispersed mainly as small pockets surrounded by the commanderies, and by 2 CE all except Changsha, now committed to a member of the Liu Family, had been reduced even more drastically. Some of these survived into Eastern Han and some new kingdoms were created then, but by that time the distinction between kingdoms and commanderies had almost vanished. The story of the kingdoms is mainly one of Western Han.

Investiture of the kings could sometimes require a special rescript from the emperor which specified the scope of their territory or authority. On one occasion in 117 BCE, when the nomination of three kings was a matter of controversy, the rescripts included a note of warning to the three men not to exceed the bounds of their powers. As a symbol of their temporal power they received a parcel of soil bound within a coping of thatch; they also received a seal fashioned in gold, of which no examples have been identified so far. Back in their kingdoms, they set up shrines dedicated to the gods of the soil and the crops.

In social terms the kings took precedence over all other persons except for the emperor and empress; exceptionally, in one revealing incident of 51 BCE, it was determined that in a state visit to Chang'an the leader of the Xiongnu 匈奴 should rank above the kings. No remains have been identified of the palaces in which they lived in their own domains, but a number of imposing tombs, adorned and furnished with rich articles, tell of the wealth that they could command and the importance attached to a display of their status by building an imposing mausoleum. Some of these tombs, such as the one at Beizhuang 北莊 (modern Hebei) that is dated circa 90 CE, were made for kings who reigned after the time when they had been stripped of their main powers of government.

At regular intervals the kings were required to attend at court to render homage, and special lodges were built to house them for this purpose at Chang'an and Luoyang. Apart from these statutory visits they were kept away from the capital as much as was possible. A protest was voiced at the particular favours that Zhangdi (r. 75–88

CE) granted allowing some of them to prolong their visits to the capital.

When first established the kingdoms were administered by a set of offices that replicated those of the central government. The kings could call on the help and advice of a chancellor, a royal counsellor and superintendents of trials, the lesser treasury, the royal clan and transport. Academicians and counsellors, messengers and gentlemen-at-arms served in their courts. But by a major reduction of their powers in 145 BCE most of these senior posts were abolished, and the central government assumed responsibility for choosing men to fill such official posts as survived. These included the kings' chancellors, now to be known by a less dignified title. Following further changes, by 8 BCE the remaining senior officials of the kingdoms became barely distinguishable from the governors and commandants of the commanderies.

In the early decades of the Han dynasty some of the kings could acquire financial support from resources such as the copper mines in their lands. Until 145 they could raise revenue by means of taxation, but they lost this power when it came under control of the central government. They may have been able to call on conscript labour, and authority to call out troops, presumably conscripts, depended on the receipt of orders from the central government. Messengers conveyed such orders, bearing a copper or bronze tally that was fashioned in the shape of a tiger, and before mobilising his forces a king was obliged to produce his half of the tally to be matched with the one brought from the centre. Clearly, when seven kings raised a revolt in 154 BCE they dispensed with such formalities. One of the charges brought against the king of Hengshan in 122 BCE was that of manufacturing arms in his kingdom, together with seals cut for the officials whom he would appoint once he had become emperor.

Some of the kings did indeed rise to become emperors, notably Liu Heng 劉恒, king of Dai from 196 BCE until his elevation in 180 BCE, who came to be known as Wendi. Appointed king of Jiaodong in 153 BCE, at the age of four, Liu Che 劉徹 was named imperial heir apparent in 150 BCE and became emperor in 141 BCE (Wudi). Summoned to Chang'an in 74 BCE at a time when the dynastic succession was not settled, Liu He 劉賀 (4), king of Changyi (modern Shandong), rode at speed to take up his position, to last no more than twenty-seven days before being deposed. The historians pillory some of the kings, such as Liu Jian 劉建 (3), king of Jiangdu (modern Zhejiang) from 127 to 121 BCE, and Liu Qu 劉去, king of Guangchuan (modern Hebei) from 91 to 70 BCE, for their gross behaviour, cruelties and excessive use of their powers. Appointment of an official to take a post in one of the kingdoms could in effect mean removal of an independently minded man from public life and an opportunity to raise a protest; in this way Dong Zhongshu 董仲舒 was sent circa 140 BCE to be chancellor of Jiangdu when Liu Fei 劉非 was king. In 124 BCE he was sent in the same capacity to Jiaoxi (modern Shandong); Jiaoxi's king Liu Duan 劉端 (1) had already shown that he saw no reason to refrain from inflicting harm on his ministers when he wished to do so.

Ranking below the nine ministers, the director of the dependent states (*dian shuguo* 典屬國) was responsible for relations with those non-Han leaders and their peoples who had given way to Han pressure. These had expressed their allegiance to the emperor by accepting the establishment of 'dependent states' in which they lived, subject to the orders of imperial officials. These states, of which the first was set up for the king of Kunye 昆邪 in 121 BCE, were under the charge of a commandant and his assistant and a director of interpreters. In 28 BCE the office of *dian shuguo* was amalgamated with that of the superintendent of state visits (see p. 28 above). Of the six dependent states that existed in 140 CE, five were in the west (Guanghan, Shu, Jianwei, Zhangye and Zhangye Juyan) and one (Liaodong) was in the north-east.

In Han times the kingdoms, commanderies and dependent states were organised as major units comprising the minor constituent units of four types, that is, counties, sometimes called prefectures (*xian* 縣); nobilities, sometimes called marquisates (*hou* 侯); estates (*yi* 邑); and marches (*dao* 道). By 2 CE 1,577 of these units had been established; there were 1,179 in 140 CE, and it is likely that some of the territorial and administrative divisions made in this way have survived until now. Counties were graded in two or perhaps three degrees, depending on the size of the population. The magistrates of those with ten thousand or more registered households bore the title of *ling* 令; those with ten thousand or less that of *zhang* 長. All magistrates were supported by an assistant and minor staff, the rank and salary of the magistrate and the number of men on his staff varying according to the size of the population.

The counties consisted of an identifiable area of land which included at least one town, probably walled. In theoretical terms, within a county ten hamlets (*li* 里) formed a group or village known as a *ting* 亭, with its own head; ten *ting* formed a district (*xiang* 鄉). It was on the shoulders of the junior officials of the counties and the districts that there fell the main burden of administering the greater part of the population. They were responsible for maintaining the standards of a cultural way of life and setting up schools. They gave a hearing to parties who were in dispute and could pass judgement and determine sentences if the laws of the empire had been disobeyed. They collected the poll tax and the land tax, rendering accounts to the commandery; they patrolled and policed the land to suppress banditry and robbery. They dispensed relief at times of suffering; they maintained communications by land and water.

The magistrates were appointed by the central government, and their administration was divided among a number of bureaus (*cao* 曹), such as those for merit, markets and litigation, each with its own head. Recently found manuscripts provide records of officials who were in post in the commandery of Donghai and its thirty-eight constituent units, of which eighteen were counties, eighteen nobilities and two estates, for a year close to 10 BCE. In one document the total number of officials is given as 2,203, in another as 2,202. The records give this information for seven large counties that were under a *ling,* at the grade of 1,000 or 600 *shi,* and for two categories, of nine and four counties, that were under a *zhang,* graded at 400 and 300 *shi.* (For the grades of officials, see p. 78 below.) Whereas we are told of the main distinction between the *ling* and the *zhang,* as above, we do not know on what criterion the two categories that were under a *zhang* were divided. It may perhaps be suggested that this depended on the size of the population, such as above or below five thousand households. The nobilities were likewise divided into two groups, whose administrators (*xiang* 相) were of the grades of 400 and 300 *shi.* The numbers of officials were as given below (Table 2).

Attention will be paid below (Chapter 9) to the orders of honour (*jue* 爵) whereby members of the population could merit or be

Table 1.   Registered inhabitants and sub-units of select commanderies and other units.

WESTERN HAN (1–2 CE)						
	(1)	(2)	(3)	(4)	(5)	(6)
Commanderies						
Runan	461,587	2,596,148	5.62	37	12,475	70,167
Peijun	409,079	2,303,480	4.96	37	11,056	54,877
Chenliu	296,284	1,509,050	5.09	17	17,428	88,767
Nanhai	19,613	94,253	4.80	6	3,268	15,708
Dunhuang	11,200	38,335	3.42	6	1,866	6,389
Kingdoms						
Zhongshan	160,823	668,080	4.15	14	11,487	47,720
Changsha	43,470	235,825	4.42	13	3,343	18,140
Sishui	25,025	119,114	4.75	3	8,341	39,704
Total, empire wide	12,366,470	57,671,400	4.66	1,577	7,841	36,570

EASTERN HAN (140 CE)						
	(1)	(2)	(3)	(4)	(5)	(6)
Commanderies						
Runan	404,448	2,100,788	5.19	37	10,931	56,778
Shujun	300,452	1,350,476	4.49	11	27,313	122,770
Chenliu	177,529	869,433	4.89	17	10,442	51,143
Hejian	93,454	634,421	6.78	11	8,495	57,674
Jiuzhen	46,513	209,894	4.51	5	9,302	41,978
Yizhou	29,036	110,802	3.81	17	1,708	6,517
Kingdoms						
Chen	112,653	1,547,572	13.7	9	12,517	171,952
Rencheng	36,442	194,156	5.32	3	12,147	64,718
Zhao	32,719	188,381	5.75	5	36,543	376,676
Dependent states						
Guanghan	37,110	205,652	5.54			
Zhangye	4,656	16,952	3.64			
Total, empire wide	9,698,630	49,150,220	5.1	1,179	8,226	41,688

Figures are given for registered households (1) and registered individuals (2) of select commanderies and kingdoms and for their ratio (3); for the number of counties in the commanderies (4); and for the average of such items for the counties (5) and (6).

Table 2.   County officials in Donghai commandery circa 15 BCE.

	(a)	(b)	(c)	(d)	(e)
Total Number of officials in the county	603	511	141	227	574
Variation between units	60–107	27–86	22–66	50–65	21–56
Village heads (ting)	271	224	54	49	82

(a) Counties under a ling; *(b) counties under a* zhang *of 400* shi; *(c) counties under a* zhang *of 300* shi; *(d) nobilities under an administrator (*xiang*) of 400* shi; *(e) nobilities under an administrator of 300* shi.

assigned places on a social scale with corresponding legal and economic privileges. The highest of these orders as granted in Han times was that of the noble (*chehou* 徹侯, *liehou* 列侯 or *tonghou* 通侯), which was bestowed by imperial decree on the sons of the kings, or as a reward for meritorious services or as a mark of favour. In addition, the grant of these titles could serve several purposes of government. The nobilities could act as instruments for local administration, they could satisfy the ambitions of the younger sons of kings and they could be established so as to reduce the powers of the kings.

Nobilities were held on an hereditary basis, being exceptionally granted to seven women. Extensive records in the histories, which probably derive from documents kept in the government's offices, list in tabular form a total of 788 nobilities that were granted between 201 BCE and 5 CE. The tables give the names of the beneficiaries and their successors, and dates of the original ennoblement and of closure of the line owing to death without a successor or to crime. A citation notes the circumstances of or reasons for the nobility being granted, such as military service, loyalty at a time of revolt or plot or fulfilment of a commission such as care for religious buildings.

The tables also include one highly important detail, as to the extent of the authority that the nobility commanded. This consisted of the right to collect taxation from a specified number of households within a named locality, whose name formed the title of the man thus honoured. Nobles were by this means encouraged to maintain law and order in that locality and to exercise control over the inhabitants. They were required to render the tax that they collected to the central government while retaining for their own use 200 cash for each registered household in the nobility.

To carry out these obligations, the nobles were assisted by an administrator and other members of his staff, whose number varied in accordance with the number of households and could reach as many as sixty-five. The households over which the nobles possessed these rights could number no more than a few hundred; exceptionally they could be as many as nearly twenty thousand, if continued and protracted service had earned an official cumulative increases in the size of the estate. From the reign of Xuandi (r. 74–48 BCE) onwards, a number of nobilities were evidently formed in areas that had hitherto been organised as districts of the commanderies.

Both the creation and the closure of a nobility could be brought about with comparative ease, and a Han government could make use of the system to considerable advantage. In the initial stages of the dynasty when there were not too many trained officials on whom it could call, the gift of a nobility would reward one of Gaozu's henchmen, remove him from the capital city where he might possibly cause trouble and set him to administer an area that needed controlling. If in later years an expansionist policy led to the penetration of remote territories, the creation of nobilities could act as a first step to imposing an administration. If leaders of non-Han peoples declared their loyal allegiance to Han, they could be rewarded with a nobility and its responsibilities.

But as more and more officials were forthcoming for service it became less necessary to make these arrangements, and in certain circumstances it was deemed wise to bring some of the existing nobilities to an end. This could be managed with relative ease, by raising a legal charge against the incumbent. In one incident of 112 BCE the government suppressed over one hundred nobilities at a blow; they had been created nearly a century previously by Gaozu. The emperor could not have the same hold over their loyalties as when they were founded, and by 112 BCE there were more officials available for posting as magistrates than there had been at the start of the dynasty. On closure of a nobility, the control of the households settled there would pass to the magistrate of an adjoining county or to the governor of the commandery.

Unfortunately we have no records of the nobilities of Eastern Han that are comparable with those of the earlier period. For Western Han they were set out in the official lists in the three categories of those given to the sons of kings, those given for merit and those bestowed by reason of close relationship to the imperial family or for favouritism. The numbers of the nobilities created during Western Han for these three reasons reached 406, 280, and 102, making a grand total of 788. Many of these did not survive the death of the original holder or his immediate successor; exceptionally one that was granted to Xiao He 蕭何 in 201 BCE lasted for nine generations until the defeat of Wang Mang in 23 CE, but this was brought about by re-creation of the line after a break on several occasions. By far the greatest number of nobilities given to the sons of kings, totalling 178, were dated in Wudi's reign between the years 128 and 124 BCE. The largest number of those given for merit was 137, during Gaozu's reign, and the number of those existing at different periods of the dynasty varied from 140 (in 180 BCE) to 26 (10 BCE), at one time falling to 21. A few of the nobilities created in Western Han survived into the reign of Wang Mang and even into Eastern Han.

Of the two other types of constituent unit of the commanderies, the estates (*yi*) were lands which were made over to provide an income for female members of the imperial family, such as an empress dowager, empress or princess (emperor's daughter). The marches (*dao*) were small areas whose inhabitants included non-Han persons. In the Statutes of 186 BCE the marches are frequently mentioned in direct conjunction with the counties as seats of authority. This may be seen in a legal provision which ordered that officials of both types of unit who destroyed or altered official buildings and residences without authority to do so were to be fined and made to pay for the damage they had inflicted.

Removed from the direction of the central government, in Eastern Han the agencies for the production of salt and iron were transferred to the care of local authorities. Thirty-four agencies for salt and forty-eight for iron are named in the lists of the *Han shu* for 2 CE, but recently found documents now show that these numbers must have varied, as others than those mentioned in the history existed in Donghai commandery circa 10 BCE. The agencies were under the control of a head official or his assistant; staff at the three salt agencies that are named varied between twenty-six and thirty, and that at the two agencies for iron between five and twenty.

Special arrangements existed for the control and administration of the area in which the capital cities of Xianyang (for Qin) and Chang'an (for Han) were situated, and which extended as widely as some three commanderies or more. In Qin times and initially in Han this large area was in the charge of an official who was entitled metropolitan superintendent (*neishi* 內史) and ranked immediately below the nine ministers. In 155 BCE the area for which this official was responsible was split into two, to be controlled by the two metropolitan superintendents of the left (*zuo neishi* 左內史) and the right (*you neishi* 右內史). In 113 BCE an area was detached from that of the metropolitan superintendent of the right to form the commandery of Hongnong.

In 104 BCE the title *jingzhao yin* 京兆尹 'governor of the capital' replaced that of metropolitan superintendent of the right, and the term *zuo* 左 *neishi* was replaced by *zuo pingyi* 左馮翊; in the same year, areas formerly under the *you* 右 *neishi* were detached to be placed under the control of an official entitled *you fufeng* 右扶風. This title replaced that of commandant, orders of honour (*zhu jue zhongwei* 主爵都尉), an official whose responsibilities had included some matters with which the nobles were concerned. Collectively these three officials, rendered as governor of the capital and metropolitan superintendents of the left and the right, became known as the 'Three supporters' (*San fu* 三輔). Like their colleagues of similar rank who attended to specialist duties, these three senior officials were supported by assistants and directors of offices concerned with matters such as the food, animals and supplies needed for sacrificial purposes. There was also a director of Chang'an's four markets.

After the transfer of the capital to Luoyang (25 CE) these three officials still remained on the establishment of government, with responsibility for provincial administration in their areas, in the same way as if they had been governors of commanderies. In 39 CE a new dignity was added to the commandery of Henan, wherein lay Luoyang, by naming its governor *Henan yin* 河南尹. Like his predecessors of Western Han he controlled a staff who looked after specialist tasks, such as Luoyang's markets and the supplies for the sacrifices. In addition the governor of Luoyang was responsible for the all-important Ao 敖 Granary at Xingyang 榮陽 (in modern Henan), which had earlier featured as a strategic prize to be won by those fighting in civil warfare.

Both Chang'an and Luoyang were under the control of a magistrate (*ling*). The five cities of Luoyang, Linzi 臨淄 (in Qi commandery; modern Shandong), Handan 邯鄲 (Zhao kingdom; modern Hebei), Wan 宛 (Nanyang; modern Henan) and Chengdu 成都 (Shu commandery; modern Sichuan) are sometimes named as Han's five capitals or emporia by virtue of their importance as commercial centres. Figures that are given for ten exceptionally large cities of 2 CE (see Table 3 below) may suggest that in general terms the number of members of a household in the cities was less than that of one in the countryside.

Inspection of the performance and behaviour of officials in the provinces dates to Qin times but it was not maintained regularly in Han until 106 BCE, when thirteen regional inspectors (*cishi* 刺史) were appointed to receive edicts and submit detailed accounts of work done in specified provincial regions, each of which included

Table 3.   Registered inhabitants of ten cities at 2 CE.

	(a)	(b)	(c)	(d)
Luoyang	52,839			Henan (Henan)
Yangdi	41,650	109,000	2.6	Yingchuan (Henan)
Yanling	49,101	261,418	5.3	Yingchuan (Henan)
Wan	47,547			Nanyang (Henan)
Chengdu	76,256			Shujun (Sichuan)
Lu	52,000			Luguo (Shangdong)
Pengcheng	40,196			Chu kingdom (Jiangsu)
Chang'an	80,800	246,200	3.0	Jignzhao yin (Shaanxi)
Changling	50,057	179,469	3.5	Zuo Pingyi (Shaanxi)
Maoling	61,087	277,277	4.5	You Fufeng (Shaanxi)

(a) Number of households; (b) number of individuals where available; (c) average number of persons per household; (d) locality in Han times, with modern provinces in parentheses.

kingdoms and commanderies. It was evidently intended that these officials should look for instances of inefficiency, oppression, corruption and injustice and report such evidence directly to the centre. They made a tour of their regions once a year, inspecting the conditions of those who were incarcerated in prisons and of conscript servicemen who were under local charge; they also assessed how officials were performing their duties, possibly submitting a recommendation for promotion or dismissal. They looked for cases of oppression by the great families and for the failure of officials to implement decrees. They checked whether officials were putting private before public interests, to see if they were practising extortion, handling criminal cases in an arbitrary fashion or recommending candidates for office unfairly. In addition they kept a sharp lookout for evidence of bribery or corruption.

At the grade of 600 *shi* 石 the regional inspectors ranked below the governors, whose work they were examining, and they were clearly of lower status than the kings, whose kingdoms lay within their spheres of authority. Thirteen provincial regions (*zhou* 州), or twelve in Eastern Han times, covered the whole empire except for the metropolitan area. They did not constitute administrative units of which the commanderies and kingdoms formed constituent parts. The metropolitan area itself, together with some adjoining commanderies, formed a fourteenth or thirteenth region, where the colonel, internal security (*sili xiaowei* 司隷校尉) took on the duties of a regional inspector. At times the title of these officials was changed from *cishi,* with its implication of exerting pressure or threat, to that of *mu* 牧 'shepherd', thereby conveying the impression that these officials were appointed to look after the welfare and interests of the population; at the same time their rank was raised to the level of governors of the commanderies.

The regional inspectors stood possessed of considerable powers, as may be seen in an incident of about 160 CE, when one of them had the governor of Jiyin commandery brought up on a charge of profiteering. But it cannot necessarily be assumed that the regional inspectors were all paragons of fair-minded, benevolent administrators. A few years later Yang Bing 楊秉, the supreme commander (*taiwei* 太尉), raised a case against the regional inspector of Yizhou (modern Yunnan), an area in the south-west that had been subject to oppression. It was alleged that he had sequestered large sums of money, murdered eight members of a resident's family, seized that resident's house and behaved outrageously when drunk. As a result the regional inspector committed suicide.

Notes for Further Reading

For counts of the population, see Bielenstein, 'The Census of China', pp. 135–45; for royal tombs, and the site at Beizhuang, see Loewe, 'State Funerals of the Han Empire', p. 28; for the king of Kunye, Hulsewé, *CICA*, pp. 75, 213; for the activities of two regional inspectors, *HHS* 54, pp. 1771, 1773; for protests at the kings' sojourn in Luoyang, *HHS* 41, p. 1414; for the Statute on Damage to Official Buildings, *Zhangjia shan*, p. 188 (strip no. 410).

See *Men Who Governed* for: the Bureau of Merit (pp. 53–59); diary of an official (p. 60); investiture of Wudi's sons (Chapter 12); kingdoms (Chapter 11); nobilities of Western Han (Chapter 9); nobilities' staff (p. 69); powers of the kings (pp. 371–82); staff complements in the commanderies and counties (pp. 60–75, 84–85); types of counties (pp. 64–66, 80–81); women holders of titles (p. 292).

References in primary sources to individuals who are mentioned above include: Bao Yu (*HHS* 29, p. 1022); Diwu Lun (*HHS* 41, p. 1397); Huang Ba (*HS* 89, pp. 3627–32); Wang Wenshu (*HS* 90, p. 3662); Wen Weng (*HS* 89, p. 3627); and Zhou Yu (*HHS* 77, p. 2494).

4

The Armed Forces

The Qin, Han and Xin dynasties were founded, brought to a close and in the case of Han restored by leaders who attracted supporters and relied on armed forces to achieve their aims. Once established, the rulers of those dynasties could not but have been aware that they lay open to similar action, should their antagonists or rivals resort to the very methods that they had employed, in order to take their place. And before long those rulers needed to face other dangers. Leaders of non-Han peoples whose homes lay beyond the perimeter of their own domains, be they Xiongnu 匈奴, Qiang 羌, Wuhuan 烏桓 or Xianbei 鮮卑, could all too easily and suddenly disrupt the livelihood of the Han farmers and townspeople. Threats to dynastic continuity or outbreaks of civil fighting led to a call on armed forces on several occasions in Western Han, such as in 180, 154 and 91 BCE, and they featured in the moves to unseat Wang Mang and to restore the Han dynasty. Preventative measures designed to secure defence led to campaigns such as those of Wei Qing 衛青 in 129 and 119 BCE. Huo Qubing 霍去病 took Chinese forces deep into Central Asia in 121 BCE; Ma Yuan 馬援 suppressed dissident Qiang tribesmen in 35 CE and eliminated the two Tr'ung 徵 sisters who were challenging the Han presence in Jiaozhi commandery (modern Vietnam) (42 CE). In addition, the Han government itself would initiate military activity. Li Guangli 李廣利 led an expedition to promote Han interests in Central Asia from 104 to 102 and again from 101 BCE. Li Ling 李陵 fought courageously in those parts in 99 BCE, and Ban Chao 班超 set out to re-establish Chinese influence in Central Asia from 91 CE; in the meantime military operations had extended to the south. Further need for the support of armed forces lay in the regular, permanent measures for security against local riots, as was seen in a mutiny led by Su Ling 蘇令, a worker in an iron foundry, in 14 BCE, and in the disturbances raised by a poseur named Wei Fan 維氾 who claimed spiritual powers in 41 CE; government forces were unsuccessful in their efforts to bring the Yellow Turbans under control (184 CE).

By contrast with Rome, no tradition of military heroism developed in China's early empires. On rare occasions successive members of a family followed in one another's footsteps as leaders of armies, as may be seen in the case of Meng Tian 蒙恬. He is best known as the officer who unified Qin's defence system such that it constituted a 'Great Wall'; his father and grandfather had both acted as generals in the kingdoms of the Warring States. Roman soldiers were sometimes led by a foreigner such as Stilicho; Han troops were at times placed under the command of leaders who were not exclusively of Han stock, such as Gongsun Hunye 公孫渾邪 and Gongsun He 公孫賀.

Chinese histories for the Qin and Han period include few descriptions of battles as fought or of the basic preliminary preparations. We may perhaps not be in error in presuming the requirements of certain conditions that applied elsewhere, as in Rome. Effective military service and action would have depended on whether skilled generals and junior officers were available to provide leadership. Successful campaigns needed sources of well-organised servicemen who had received training and learnt to accept a discipline. The armed forces needed reliable supplies of food, clothing and equipment. Generals had to be able to communicate with the forces under their command and with their home government; they needed experience so as to know how to adopt the right strategy or tactics.

In the unsettled conditions of the Warring States men had arisen who had gathered around them a force prepared to fight with them, perhaps in reaction against oppression, perhaps to defy the authority and will of kings and their officials or to protect themselves from apprehension and dire punishments as criminals or deserters. Such leaders (*jiang* 將) operated independently; their objectives may have been limited; they might seize supplies as they found them, profiting from the shortages and weaknesses of their opponents; and they would probably have little idea of an overall strategy. Such independent leaders took their place in the dynastic story that attended the collapse of Qin (after 210 BCE) and again in movements such as those of the Red Eyebrows and Xinshi 新市, Pinglin 平林 and Xiajiang 下江 companies who rose up towards the end of Wang Mang's reign.

Successful dynasties were created by agreement of some of these leaders to take concerted action in support of one of their own members, to accept his overlordship and to continue with their support once he had ascended a throne and taken the title of emperor. Such had been the story with Gaozu and eventually with Guangwudi. Once acting in support of an acknowledged emperor, these leaders forfeited their independence in return for a confirmation of their powers and a recognition of their status. Accepting commissions or orders from a central government, they relied on that government for material help. They may be termed 'generals' (*jiang* or *jiangjun* 將軍), trusted to campaign on behalf of their emperor and capable of taking command of a force in such a way that it could be brought into action independently of other military ventures. They were trusted to retain that degree of loyalty when they were situated at a remote distance from the centre, where they might be open to temptation to make over to another party. They had become members of an established order of imperial government.

With some exceptions there was no marked or rigid distinction in early imperial times between civil and military responsibilities; rather, there was an expectation that, if called to service, men of quality would be ready and able to work in either capacity. In this way, when operating in the south with the title of *fubo jiangjun* 伏波將軍 (general who calms the waves), circa 40 CE, Ma Yuan advised on the division of one large, unwieldy county into two parts; he saw that walls were built round towns, initiated irrigation works and explained to the natives the differences between the statutes of Han and Yue 越.

Historical documents devote comparatively little attention to official posts that were specifically founded for military purposes, such as those of general or colonel, and only a few such posts existed on a permanent basis. Ranking above the nine ministers of state, the generals of the van and the rear, of the left and the right, were acknowledged as senior members of imperial government. But these posts were not always filled, and in time the titles did not necessarily imply an active command in the field or anything more than a civic appointment.

Generals who bore different titles and who were invested with temporary rather than permanent authority took the lead in the campaigns and large-scale fighting of the early decades of Han, and particularly those of the first half of Wudi's reign. Named as general of chariots and cavalry (*juji jiangjun* 車騎將軍) or of agile cavalry (*piaoqi jiangjun* 驃騎將軍), officers set out to complete the task that had been allotted to them, perhaps to lead an expeditionary force against the Xiongnu, or later the Qiang, Wuhuan or Xianbei. Some other titles bore a definite reference to the task that was in hand, such as 'general posted to serve beyond the Liao River' (*du Liao jiangjun* 度遼將軍; 'general commissioned to attack Ershi (Sutrishna)' (*Ershi jiangjun* 貳師將軍); or 'general of the towered warships' (*louchuan jiangjun* 樓船將軍). The bearers of such titles, having completed their task, might well proceed to hold other posts with civilian responsibilities or duties.

On a few occasions two generals were commissioned to lead separate but co-ordinated campaigns that were planned to coincide at the same time on different sides of an enemy stronghold. Such intentions depended on careful planning and timing, and on the willingness of the two commanders to co-operate. This worked satisfactorily enough in the attacks made by land on Nan Yue 南越 (modern Vietnam) in 112 BCE. But the necessary conditions could not always be met, as was seen in the land and sea expeditions sent to attack Chaoxian 朝鮮 (in modern Korea) in 109 BCE.

An incident of 127 CE illustrates attempts to co-ordinate operations by two forces and the difficulties that could occur. Ban Yong 班勇, who had successfully brought a number of the leaders in Central Asia to accept Han suzerainty, wished to attack Karashahr (close to Lake Bostang). The governor of Dunhuang led three thousand men from four commanderies; local communities produced an additional force of forty thousand. Ban Yong advanced along the southern route round the Takla Makan desert, the governor along the northern route, with an agreed time for a rendezvous. The governor, however, was anxious to redeem himself from punishment for a previous crime by a marked success in battle, and he struck at Karashahr by himself. By bringing about its surrender he evaded a death sentence. Arriving late for the rendezvous, Ban Yong was imprisoned and dismissed.

There are obvious reasons why a Han government would be reluctant to commit all the forces at its disposal to the control of a single commander-in-chief. As has been seen above (see Chapter 2), the post of supreme commander (*taiwei* 太尉) was filled only sporadically. The titles of general-in-chief (*da jiangjun* 大將軍) and marshal of state (*da sima* 大司馬) were at times given to successful commanders as a reward for merit, but they came to signify the exercise of full civil power, with no certainty that the holder had had experience as a military commander or would be acting in that role. In Eastern Han times the title of general-in-chief indicated and corresponded with that of regent (see p. 22 above).

Held at a lower level than that of general, the title of colonel (*xiaowei* 校尉) could designate officers who held independent responsibility for commanding small forces for a specific task and perhaps for a limited period of time. These included five officers who commanded the units of troops stationed permanently in the capital city, each with his own separate headquarters and encampment. These officers ranked highly, at 2,000 *shi* 石, as did three other colonels, one of whom was responsible for a force of archers who were still under training. The colonel of the city gates (*cheng men xiaowei* 城門校尉) had charge of security at those sensitive points and was authorised to close them at crucial moments that might cause unrest, such as at the death of an emperor. Appointed first in 48 BCE, the Wu and Ji colonel (*Wu Ji xiaowei* 戊己校尉) worked independently to set up agricultural colonies way over in Central Asia. Presumably he led Chinese servicemen to work in the territory of a non-Han leader. By 74 CE this post had been split into two.

As has been seen (p. 45 above), the kings of the empire required the authority conveyed by a tally before they could call out armed forces. The imperial decrees which appointed a general to his rank would likewise specify the task for which he was entitled to use the forces at his command. In one famous incident of 36 BCE two officers acted on their own initiative to stage an attack on a recalcitrant leader of the Xiongnu, forging the document that gave them the necessary authority to do so. On return to Chang'an they faced legal enquiries, finally to be exonerated.

Further down the scale, and ranking below the colonels, were the majors (*sima* 司馬) and captains (*hou* 候). These were posted to a variety of duties; a major and a captain served at the orders of the colonel of the city gates.

The garrison forces who manned the forts, walls and communication lines in the north-west left behind them remnants of documents, mainly in rubbish pits. These derived from sites such as Dunhuang 敦煌 and Juyan 居延 which were maintained, perhaps not continuously, between 100 BCE and 100 CE. Drawn up at the headquarters and orderly rooms of comparatively small units, these records show how the defence lines were organised. As they originated in special points in the empire which required a constant watch against the danger of marauders, they do not necessarily refer to arrangements and conditions that were a normal feature of provincial government throughout the empire.

The commandants (*duwei* 都尉) of the commanderies in these sensitive areas bore as titles the names of the sections of the borderland for which they were responsible, such as Juyan or Jianshui. They controlled perhaps four 'companies', which each consisted of a number of units that may be termed 'platoons'. Each platoon was under the command of a captain and consisted of a number of 'sections' of perhaps two to four, or even ten, men; each section was under the orders of the section head (*sui zhang* 燧長), who received pay by the month.

Conscripts, volunteers and convicts on reduced sentences filled the ranks of the forces under a general's command. In Western Han, except for those who enjoyed privileged social status, males aged between twenty-three (or at times twenty) and fifty-six were obliged to serve in the armed forces for two years, one of which was spent in training and one on duty as a guardsman or in the static defence lines of the north. These men formed the bulk of a commander's infantry. In addition to their statutory service, they were subject to recall in times of emergency.

Perhaps in return for certain privileges, members of families that were not stained with a criminal record could volunteer to join the forces, and others might respond to an appeal to do so. Han cavalry forces may have included these men as well as volunteers who were not of Han ethnic origin or cultural assimilation, being natives of the lands that lay to the west, outside the empire. Convicts were at times drafted to join the Han forces, and those convicts who had benefited from an act of bounty and were working out their time in less severe conditions than their comrades were also found in the garrisons of the north. Some of these convicts took part in an expedition that Ban Chao led in 80 CE to confirm the adherence of some of the non-Han peoples of Central Asia. In certain circumstances conscripts may have served in the armed forces for several years together with their families; records indicate that they might be sent to the north by way of a long march from a commandery or kingdom in central China.

In general, however, Han armies were staffed by men who were on short-term tours of duty, and this condition may have affected the length of time for which it was practical to plan or sustain an expedition. Figures given in the histories for the numbers of servicemen engaged in fighting, whether on the Han or the opposing side, are notoriously unreliable, as are those of the casualties inflicted or suffered, or of the booty taken, perhaps in the form of livestock. Greater trust may perhaps be placed in the figures that a seasoned officer might quote in his pleas for forces that he judged necessary for a task, or in the warnings given by some of the difficulties of maintaining a large force in the field. But here again serving officers may have been tempted to ask for more than they knew that they could expect, and those who were decrying a proposal may have exaggerated the scale of the difficulties.

Figures that we have for the size of Chinese forces that were in the field during various episodes between 133 and 90 BCE rise as high as 300,000. According to the histories, when Li Guangli set out on his unsuccessful long march to Central Asia in 104 BCE, he led six thousand cavalry and 'ill disciplined youths' by the ten thousand. In his second attempt (101 BCE) he led sixty thousand men from Dunhuang and a further 180,000 conscripts. Sixty years later an officer named Feng Fengshi 馮奉世 marched out to suppress a rebellion of some of the Qiang (proto-Tibetan) peoples. Denied the force of forty thousand that he had requested, he led twelve thousand cavalry, only to fail in his objective; he finally gained this when supplied with sixty thousand men.

Officials of the central government, ruling China from their offices in Chang'an or Luoyang, may well have failed to recognise the hazards and dangers of campaigning, particularly at long distances from the capital in terrains and climates to which conscripts from other parts of the empire were not accustomed. Ma Yuan returned from suppressing insurgency in the deep south (Guangxi and Vietnam) in 44 CE; 40 to 50 percent of his forces, as we are told, had succumbed to illness or had died. Disturbances that arose in the same area in 137 CE led to discussions at court, and it was left to a junior official, Li Gu 李固, to point out the difficulties of supplying a force of forty thousand men, as was proposed, over so long a distance, and to warn of the weak, unhealthy state in which the men would arrive to fight an enemy. He urged that only officers of proven ability should be sent on the expedition and that non-Han native leaders should be recruited to fight for the empire. His advice assured the expedition of its success.

Reference appears above (see pp. 26, 27, 33) to the various military dispositions at Chang'an. The superintendent of the palace (*guangluxun* 光祿勳) held command of two special regiments with which to ensure security within the palace. The superintendent of the guards (*weiwei* 衞尉) could call on forces to keep watch for security outside the palace and to check admission thereto. The superintendent of the capital (*zhijinwu* 執金吾) could call on conscripts to control any act of insurgence that broke out inside Chang'an city. The same principle of dividing the armed forces and their command is seen in the establishment of the Southern and Northern Armies, or barracks, there. Of these, the Southern Army was staffed by conscript servicemen who took their turn of duty for a year at a time. By contrast the Northern Army included a standing force that was on a permanent basis, and it continued to exist in Eastern Han. Command of the Southern Army was divided among five colonels, those of the Central Ramparts, the Garrison Cavalry, the Infantry, the Picked Cavalry and the Chang 長 River.

Perhaps some 3,250 servicemen were needed to man the defence lines which may have run for 1,000 kilometres from Dunhuang to Shuofang. There were in addition the conscripts who had been detailed for agricultural work and were settled on the farms sponsored by the state. These farms extended on a specially built line of fortifications that ran from south to north along water courses and lakes whose care and maintenance lay with the same body of men. Conscripts were also put to making bricks with which to build the watch-towers, and they undertook the work of maintaining these buildings in a good state of repair. They operated a regular system of signalling both to keep constant contact with the neighbouring units along the line and to raise the alarm at times of emergency. Such work followed careful time schedules and regulations for the types of signalling to be used, whether by day or night and whether for normal purposes or to give warning of impending danger. Units responded to receipt of a signal sent by flag, flare or woodpile with the correct acknowledgement by the same means. The men who were on the watch kept alert to spot any signs of intrusion or unaccounted movements of man or beast. They checked the passage of men, women and children, and animals and commodities through points of control; they set out to patrol the areas outside the immediate vicinity of the defence lines. Their officers drew up reports for all such activities. Some of the equipment that was needed for this work, such as pulleys or flags for the signal posts, or javelins, were issued to the troops on the spot.

The Qin and Han system of bestowing degrees of social status together with legal and other privileges (see Chapter 9 below) had started as a means of rewarding and thereby encouraging military valour. The degree of insistence on maintaining discipline in the armed forces varied widely, sometimes in accordance with the character or will of a commanding officer. One general (Cheng Bushi 程不識), who was fighting a defensive battle to protect Han territory circa 134 BCE, demanded strict conformity with the rules, to the point of causing his men hardship; he nonetheless commanded a force that was capable of fighting effectively. Li Guang 李廣, who fought on a number of occasions during Wudi's reign, won his men's affection by allowing them far greater freedom from restrictions, leading them into battle without forcing them to adopt drill formations, sharing his prize money with them and attending to their welfare. An incomplete document from the north-west which is dated 29 CE records a case of failure to observe the regulations for signalling, thereby, as was alleged, leading to the capture of an officer and his horse and provoking a legal investigation.

The rations of grain and salt that were provided for the servicemen presumably derived from the stores collected by way of taxation and retained in official granaries; the salt would have come either from privately owned salt mines or from the government's agencies. Fortunately there are a few sets of figures which give an idea of the quantities that were needed. Circa 61 BCE Zhao Chongguo 趙充國 (2), a highly experienced senior soldier who had served in the north-west, gave the figures of 27,363 *hu* 斛 of grain and 308 *hu* of salt as the requirement for a force of 10,281 men, amounting to a monthly ration per man of 2.6 *hu* (519 litres) of grain and 0.03 *hu* (0.6 litres) of salt. A somewhat more meagre estimate was given by

Zhuang You 莊尤, who was arguing in 9 CE against the despatch of a force of 300,000 men for a campaign that was inteneded to last for 300 days; he reckoned that the men would each require 18 *hu,* that is, 1.8 *hu* of grain per month. In addition the documents found in the rubbish pits of the north-west disclose a distribution of a ration of 3.2 *hu* (638 litres) of grain and 0.03 *hu* (0.6 litres) of salt for a month.

Other documents from those sites record the issue to conscript servicemen of tunics, trousers, socks and sandals; presumably these items came from the state's agencies for textiles and clothing. Zhuang You also referred to the needs of transporting food supplies by ox-drawn wagons, itself involving supplies of fodder for the animals. It was probably to ease the difficulty of sending supplies, whose condition could easily decline, over long distances, that the government set up a line of sponsored farms in the north-west, at sites where water was available.

The arms, armour and vehicles that an army required were presumably manufactured under government control in the agencies for iron or other official workshops. A major arsenal in which these items were stored had existed in Chang'an since the outset of Western Han, being placed under the control of the superintendent of the capital. Excavation of the site where it had been built shows that by perhaps 20 CE it consisted of seven separate buildings set in two groups. The largest measured 205 by 25 metres; weapons were probably stacked on separate racks or shelves according to type.

Of all items found at the site of the arsenal, arrowheads were the most numerous, but more is known about the types of military equipment and the numbers of items held in store from a document that dates from 13 BCE. This came from a site in eastern China (Yinwan; modern Jiangsu), and it is questionable whether it records the goods that were kept in a local arsenal or in the main one in Chang'an, as the very large number of items suggests. The two sections of the list bear entries for 58 and 182 different types of article respectively, with a grand total of 23,153,794 items; these included bows of various types and some twelve million arrows, 564 trolleys with combined crossbows, 1,741 flags, and numerous swords, sword-belts, coats of armour and drums.

With an exception that is mentioned above we do not know at what point in the preparation for a campaign or the call-up of servicemen these items were distributed to commanders or issued to troops. Records kept by the defence forces in the north-west show that different types of bow and crossbow were classified according to the pressure required for loading. Some of these were mounted in wooden frames that were attached to the walls of the forts; they afforded protection to the archer and enabled him to rotate his bow so as to bring it to bear where it was needed. Triggers carried a scaled device which enabled him to take aim according to the distance from his target. Officials inspected the defence posts of the north-west and reported on their state of readiness, deficiencies in the equipment and the state of consumable items, such as bows and bowstrings, helmets, axes, rope, flares, flags and woodpiles used in signalling, and dog kennels. Before these defence lines had been built, legal regulations of 186 BCE controlled the use and storage of poisonous arrows needed for action against robbers who were not of Han stock; there seems to be no reference to their use in other connections.

Towards the end of Western Han fifty-three texts on military matters stood on the shelves of the imperial library, classified under four types. Lost as most of them are, their titles suggest that they were concerned with tactics such as the proper use of weapons and fighting techniques, and many of them included illustrations. Some of these texts alluded to divine beings or heroes, perhaps with advice to seek their help or emulate their deeds. One text on silk that is not mentioned in the catalogue of the library but has been excavated recently shows illustrations of climatic conditions and the different shapes of comets together with explanations of how such signs can give guidance to a commander or warn him of his plan's risk of failure.

Officials repeatedly voiced a warning that warfare can be dangerous and should be avoided if possible. Possibly Han governments bore such advice in mind when they showed willingness or took steps to come to terms with an adversary, as could be achieved by several ways. It might be possible to set up a regular agreement of friendship that might imply Han's delivery of large consignments of valuable gods, such as silk, to the other party, who might be the Xiongnu. Or else an emperor could seal a compact by selecting a princess to be a bride to one of the non-Han leaders, such as the ruler of Wusun 烏孫. Diplomacy of this type would involve subjecting a young girl to living conditions that she could hardly find amenable, in the hope that she would give birth to an heir who would be friendly to her own family and dynasty. Requests from a non-Han leader for such a mark of Han good will, as from the ruler of the Yuezhi 月氏 people in 90 CE, were not always accepted.

One of the motives for prolonging the protected line of communications deep into Central Asia may have been the hope of separating the Xiongnu from the Qiang, who were each capable of threatening Chinese integrity; it was hoped that the line would prevent the two parties from joining forces. A further strategic motive may perhaps be discerned in the Han policy towards the groups of people and their leaders who were settled on the oases that skirted the Takla Makan desert. Controlling supplies of water as they did, they could ensure success or spell disaster for a Chinese trading caravan, and should they succumb to the blandishments of the Xiongnu or others, Han interests would suffer. Han policy aimed at preventing such influences from proving dominant.

A sense of strategy may be seen in two ways, first in the timing or phasing of Western Han's thrusts or ventures of exploration. Gongsun Hong 公孫弘, who became imperial counsellor in 126 BCE, had strongly advised suspending operations in the south-west, where the maintenance of communications was causing heavy casualties, in favour of concentrating Chinese strength on building effective defence lines in the north. It was in fact only after the campaigns fought in the north in 119 BCE that the threats of enemy activity were lifted in those areas and the north-west; attention could then move to the north-east, south-west, south-east and Central Asia.

Secondly, some twenty-five years later it had become apparent that China had overspent its strength. A far-sighted official named Sang Hongyang 桑弘羊, who was executed for conspiracy in 80 BCE, suggested that the best way of maintaining a Chinese presence among the communities of Central Asia lay in setting up state-sponsored colonies there on sites that were suitable for farming. A colonial policy of this type was taken a step further in 60 BCE with the creation of the post of protector general of the Western Regions, who would oversee Chinese activities and relations and co-ordinate these ventures.

At least one official of Western Han showed that he had a shrewd idea of tactics, despite apparently no experience on a field of battle to his name. This was Chao Cuo 鼂錯, who died at the hands of the executioner in 154 BCE after tendering wise advice but falling foul of his rivals. As a junior official early in Wendi's reign he saw fit to submit his views on military problems, at a time when the Xiongnu had been making repeated incursions into Chinese commanderies. He stressed the importance of three factors, terrain, training and discipline, and weapons, and he described the types of territory that would favour infantry, cavalry, halberdiers, short-spearmen and swordsmen. Arms, armour and bows had to be in excellent condition so that they could fulfil their purpose. In the lands of the north neither Chinese horses nor men could compete with the Xiongnu, whose skills were adapted to that type of terrain; they could shoot with their bows while on horseback and could face the hardships of climate and deprivations of hunger that the Chinese could not withstand. However the Xiongnu were liable to be worsted in flat territory, and they could not face small squads of five or ten mobile archers. Given the right ground Chinese light cavalry could throw a large body of the Xiongnu into confusion; Xiongnu armour could not withstand a mass volley of arrows, and if forced to fight when dismounted the Xiongnu were no match for the Chinese.

A few examples show how Han generals were able to exploit tactical advantages. In 37 CE Ma Yuan saw the wisdom of avoiding a battle if his aims could be achieved by other means. In 88 CE Ban Chao was able to trick his Qiang adversaries in the north-west into withdrawing from his own objective, which he was then able to take with an inferior force. Chao Cuo had already realised the advantages of using non-Han forces to fight against their neighbours who were also not of Han stock or cultural affiliation, and in 78 CE Ban Chao mustered ten thousand men from Kashgar (modern Shule 疏勒), Kangju 康居 (probably around Samarkand) and other non-Han areas to attack Gumo 姑墨 (near modern Aksu). In 94 CE Ban Chao is said to have had a force of seventy thousand men from Kucha and elsewhere with which to attack Yanqi (modern Karashahr 焉耆).

It is open to doubt how far the term 'professional' may be applied to Han concepts of military needs, the means of maintaining armed forces in sufficiency and the use of armies in the field. Records from the orderly rooms of the north-west show clearly that the units stationed there served under a strict command; they were subject to working orders in a manner of which civil officials could be proud. They kept records of letters and documents that they received and sent, together with the times of despatch and delivery; they submitted accounts for the expenditure of money and reports in which officers acknowledged receipt of their pay, either in cash or in textiles. The clerks wrote out scrupulous lists of stores of grain as received and as issued in accordance with the scales laid down according to age and sex. As in services in other cultures, so here some of the records were made out in duplicate.

Notes for Further Reading

For units at the capital see Bielenstein, *Bureaucracy*, pp. 114, 117. Hulsewé writes in *CICA* on the Wu and Ji colonel (p. 79, note 63); the gift of a bride to Wusun and her subsequent misery (pp. 147–50); and the protector general (pp. 30–33, 64). Yü Ying-shih discusses the place taken by material goods such as silks in relations with non-Han leaders (Chapters 2 and 3). See *RHA* for: inspectors' reports at Juyan (vol. 2, pp. 151–68); the issue of equipment (vol. 2, pp. 61–63); military dispositions in the north-west (vol. 1, pp. 76–77, and vol. 2, pp. 384–87); rations and clothing at Juyan (vol. 2, pp. 67–71, and 261–73); signalling (vol. 2, pp. 221–25). See Loewe, 'The Campaigns of Han Wu-ti', for Li Ling's campaign in 99 BCE (pp. 119–22); numbers of Han forces (p. 93); *Men Who Governed*, pp. 76–78, for the list of military equipment; and 'The Han View of Comets' for comets and military predictions. For a sketch map of places in Central Asia, see Hulsewé, *CICA*. An excavation report on the site of the arsenal at Chang'an appeared in *Kaogu* 1978:4, pp. 261–69.

See primary sources as follows: for Ban Chao (*HHS* 47, pp. 1571–86); Ban Chao's expedition in 80 CE (*HHS* 47, p. 1576); Ban Yong's campaign of 137 CE (*HHS* 47, p. 1590); Chao Cuo, (*HS* 49, pp. 2278–81); dissidence and its suppression in 41 CE (*HHS* 1B, pp. 68, 24, 838); Feng Fengshi (*HS* 79, pp. 3296–98); the fight against the Xiongnu leader in 36 BCE (*HS* 70, p. 3013); Gongsun Hong (*HS* 95, p. 3840); Li Gu (*HHS* 6, p. 258); Li Guangli (*HS* 61, pp. 2699–700); military texts in the imperial library (*HS* 30, pp. 1758–59, 1761–63); Ma Yuan (*HHS* 24, pp. 827–50); Ma Yuan's 'civil' work in the south (*HHS* 24, pp. 838–40); his use of non-Han forces in 78 and 94 CE (*HHS* 47, pp. 1575, 1581); the protector general (*HS* 70, p. 3006); the request of the Yuezhi for a princess (*HHS* 47,

p. 1580); Sang Hongyang (*HS* 96B, p. 3912); the Tr'ung sisters (*HHS* 24, p. 838); Zhao Chongguo (*HS* 69, pp. 2985–86); and Zhuang You (*HS* 94B, p. 3824).

Information about signalling will be found in the newly discovered documents from Juyan (EPF16 1–17 and EPT68 81–102). For poisonous arrows, see *Zhangjia shan* (Statutes), strip no. 19.

5

The Officials

Officials stood apart from other mortals in imperial China. They were members of what may be termed the only profession, admitted thereto thanks to hard-won qualifications, to sponsorship or to favouritism. They received salaries paid by the state. In social terms their distinction from others did not depend on circumstances of birth such as descent from an imperial or royal family, but their degree of dignity and the respect that they received for their authority could rise to be higher than those accorded to princes or nobles. A theoretical classification of the people of the empire according to their occupations placed officials within the *shi* 士, persons of education and ability with some powers of leadership; these ranked above the farmers, artisans and merchants of the three other types of occupation.

Whereas the society of the early empires did not include other definable groups of persons who could collectively be treated as 'professional', it did not lack specialists in intellectual proficiency and skills such as medicine, astronomy or mathematics; indeed the complement of officials provided for the inclusion of posts for a few persons with just those gifts. In addition there were men and women who studied the occult and advised how the messages from the supernatural world should best be interpreted and exploited, for the benefit of the emperor or the empire. There were those who sought means that may be described now as irrational with which to bring earthly bliss to individuals in particular or mankind in general. There were physicians who practised independently, treating patients in the highest reaches of society. None of these practitioners, however, attained the same measure of respect as did the specialists in learning and documents who became officials and received the support of the state.

Officials served the monarchs of the Shang-Yin kings and their successors of the house of Zhou. Long after the time when those kings had lost their effective power of rule the tradition associated with the offices of Zhou lived on to attract respect or call for emulation. There resulted treatises which set out to describe the systems and complement of those officials, written long after the time when their accuracy could be supported by verifiable records. There is however one difference between such accounts and those that we have of imperial times that requires attention. For pre-imperial times there is not the sharp distinction seen for Qin and Han between the dignitaries of the court and the functionaries who were appointed to implement a government's commands. The distinction became unavoidable with the foundation of the first empires.

Careers in the civil service, which in time would become highly competitive, could spell long years spent in junior offices before promotion to the most senior posts that carried empire-wide renown. Such eminence reached no more than a fortunate few, and a career could just as easily be cut short with disgrace, owing to a failure to fulfil one's duties or to involvement in political antagonisms. These results were possible because in their higher positions officials would in effect be leading members of a government from whom the emperor requested advice. Their proposals and actions in that capacity might win widespread popular praise; they might equally well excite enmity and hatred among rivals.

It was in Qin and Han times that the distinction of the official and the prestige attached to his position may be traced; such prestige would rise to considerable heights in the more sophisticated conditions of the Tang (618–907), Song (960–1127 and 1127–1279), Ming (1368–1644) and Qing (1644–1911) empires. During those mediaeval and late dynasties, families whose members had never seen a provincial capital, let alone the imperial capital city, and whose resources were far from great, would be ready to make considerable sacrifices to provide the means whereby a chosen member could be left free to concentrate on study for the examinations that he would face. Once successfully over such hurdles, a young man would return to his native place of domicile, bringing with him honour to his family and prestige to his village. Parents shared the renown attendant on their son, destined as he might be to reach the highest levels of the empire. It was in Qin and Han times that the moves that led to these social conditions started; it was also in Qin and Han times that there emerged the titles of many official posts that would survive until the close of the imperial age, vitally different as their duties may have become.

We have no means of assessing what proportion of the nearly sixty million registered inhabitants of 1–2 CE were literate. We can surmise that the 130,000 officials who were in post in 5 BCE necessarily had to master the three arts of reading, writing and arithmetic. Possibly such rudimentary skills were also needed by many men of a lower order, such as the constables or watchmen who carried out the basic work of administration as ordered by their superiors up and down the land.

Much of the administration of an empire depended on steady, routine and repetitive work, often in the form of preparing seasonal, monthly or daily reports, perhaps of accountancy or of the receipt and distribution of stores. If daily entries were needed such documents might take the form of a ledger in which the successive days of the calendar were clearly written to await the insertion of the relevant figures. Officials would receive instructions, such as orders to comply with a decree, to call out military forces or to adopt a newly authorised calendar; such instructions came from their superiors whether of the provinces or the central government, and on receipt an official would pass them down to his subordinates for the requisite action. Or officials might received documents from below, such as the legal dossier of a case that was sub judice; after taking action or recording the opinions and advice such as the limits of their own positions allowed, they would submit such documents to higher authorities for comparable action.

Much of the work of officials concerned taxation, security or criminal proceedings. They would report the action that they had taken to face an abnormal or disastrous situation such as one caused by floods; they might give reasons to explain what could appear to be a failure in their task, for such might be construed as dereliction of duty for which they could face prosecution and trial. With increased seniority an official would find himself governor of a commandery with responsibility for the welfare and control of a registered population of anything between a few hundred thousand and two and a half million (for sample counts, see p. 48 above). At an even higher level, in the central government, he would supervise a host of specialist offices and their directors and advise the emperor on weighty matters of policy. For such tasks he must be familiar with precedents, good or ill, and he must be aware of the prevailing conditions of the empire. Whether in the provincial or the central government, a senior official must be capable of exercising authority on a wide enough scale to preclude an outbreak of dissidence.

From the outset of empire it may well have been apparent that there was a need to recruit, train and attract persons to join the civil service. We learn that youths of seventeen years could be enrolled to receive instruction, so that they would be able to read documents written in different styles of script and acquire a familiarity with some approved texts of literature. Such arrangements were designed to prepare young men to serve as clerks of a fairly low grade, and after three years they faced a test of their abilities. At the same time other young men were being trained to become prayer reciters, or diviners who operated with the traditional media of turtles' shells; some of those who were at the early stages of training in the mystique of divination might face a test of a practical nature.

Rules for this type of training and testing existed from at least 186 BCE, and different methods of recruitment soon arose. From 165 BCE, or possibly earlier, decrees were ordering senior officials who were installed in the capital city or the provinces to recommend persons of intelligence and fine character, or those able to express themselves cogently, for direct appointment to the service. Sometimes a quota was fixed for the number of men to be recommended. Calls for men of distinction in this way became frequent during Wudi's reign (r. 141–87 BCE), with the introduction of a new criterion, identified as a sense of family responsibility and of known integrity (*xiao lian* 孝廉). These steps brought at least two hundred and perhaps as many as three hundred names forward for recommendation annually, and some of the recommended young men entered the service at a higher level than that of those trained according to the rules mentioned above. In Western terms the difference may be compared with that between an officer and gentleman and a non-commissioned officer.

At much the same time (ca. 124 BCE) a further and more advanced style of testing was introduced. A complement of fifty pupils aged eighteen and above were chosen by officials from the provinces for presentation at the Imperial Academy (*Taixue* 太學) in Chang'an; the lucky few who were chosen were also exempted from the state's obligations of tax and service. Following an assessment of their character and abilities they became pupils of the academicians, scholars who specialised in the interpretation and teaching of approved literary texts. After a year's training they were tested and either posted to a suitable office or dismissed; those officials who had recommended a failure were liable to punishment. The quota rose on several occasions, possibly reaching three thousand, as we are told, in the reign of Aidi (r. 7–1 BCE); if we may believe our figures it rose further to thirty thousand or more by the middle of the second century CE.

The conduct and content of some of these tests and methods of selection did not pass without criticism. As director, astronomy (*tai shi* 太史), Zhang Heng 張衡 presented a memorial in 133 CE in which he protested that the tests concentrated on details of textual competence and abandoned the search for the quality of family responsibility and integrity.

Other methods of finding talent and recruiting officials arose. An order of 106 BCE, which was perhaps not fully implemented until later, called on the regional inspectors and the governors of commanderies to submit the names of men of flourishing talent (*mao cai* 茂材) or special ability for appointment to office. In 62 and 35 BCE, and perhaps earlier, a roving commission set out on a tour of the empire to discover such persons. Or else, an imperial rescript would ask at large for responses to questions that could concern the moral or material state of the empire; the answers might be graded as alpha, beta or gamma with appointment to a suitable post to follow. There were also the so-called gentlemen (*lang* 郎); these were men who had been recommended in one way or another and were singled out for nomination as a *lang,* thereby being well set on the competitive career of the civil service. There was no limit to the number of these persons, which could perhaps reach a thousand. They provided the emperor with a personal escort and could act as his advisory attendants.

There were other means of reaching these privileged positions, either by purchase or perhaps more regularly by sponsorship. Officials of the most senior rank were entitled to sponsor a son or a brother as a *lang,* and particular cases of merit, such as specialisation in the *Changes of Zhou* or in music, could perhaps be sufficient to gain nomination. There were penalties for sponsoring those whose abilities proved to be inadequate; nonetheless there could be no certainty that those nominated were necessarily men of intellectual ability and integrity, as was desired.

With some exceptions appointment to office was in theory open to all, without restriction. It could fall to men who were not entirely of Han ethnic origin, such as Gongsun Hunye 公孫渾邪 or Jin Midi 金日磾, of Xiongnu stock. Gongsun Hunye held offices in the reigns of Wendi (r. 180–157 BCE) and Jingdi (r. 157–141 BCE), serving in the campaign to suppress rebel forces in 154 BCE. Jin Midi might well have become regent to a newly enthroned young emperor (Zhaodi; r. 87–74 BCE). A member of the imperial family of Liu regularly filled one of the senior posts of government, that of superintendent of the imperial clan (*zong zheng* 宗正), but otherwise members of that family held office only rarely. A ban on holding office could be imposed as part of a criminal's punishment both on the criminal himself or herself and on family members. Tradesmen, bond servants and officials guilty of financial misdemeanours or some other crimes were excluded from appointment. Officials in the provinces were sometimes able to nominate their own favourites and could arouse criticism for choosing unsuitable persons. In addition such patronage could not necessarily be effective permanently. When Liang Ji 梁冀 was removed from his all-powerful position of regent in 159 CE, some three hundred of his subordinates and clients were dismissed with him.

Eunuchs are first seen in powerful positions in the reigns of Xuandi (r. 74–48 BCE) and Yuandi (r. 48–33 BCE), but they were not appointed to senior offices, and it was only between circa 159 and 189 CE that they became a major force in dynastic history. Some offices of a lower level, such as those of the palace writers (*zhongshu* 中書), were regularly filled by eunuchs while they existed, and eunuchs served in subordinate ways in the Secretariat (*Shangshu* 尚書). As holders of supernumerary titles (see below, p. 79) they could be in a privileged position that was not available to all those appointed to office. Their part in public life is discussed below (see Chapter 12, p. 185).

The initial steps towards an official career could sometimes depend on luck, perhaps when a high dignitary was visiting a village in the country and chanced to spot a youth who showed a promise of talent. A first appointment could thus be that of an aide or subordinate to an official of the central government. More frequently it would be at an unspecified low level at a settlement in the countryside, under the orders of a sub-division of a county known as a district (*xiang* 鄉). From there, appointment could lead to a post in the office of a magistrate who controlled a county. Service could follow in one of the specialist departments of administration which were controlled by the central government in the capital; these offices were responsible for a diversity of matters such as religious rites, the distribution of grain, musical performances or the manufacture of choice, luxury items of bronze.

Alternatively, a man might perhaps be transferred to an office that was likewise under central control but which was situated in the provinces, such as a government mint or an arsenal. Successful completion of duties, avoidance of implication in crime or acknowledgement of merit in the annual reports framed by a man's superior could lead to a better posting, perhaps as assistant to the director of one of those specialist departments mentioned above, or perhaps as one of the many counsellors, whose duties might lie in commenting on suggestions laid before the government or in warning of the dangers inherent in a proposed course of action. Appointment as a magistrate of a county, which might include ten thousand registered households or fifty thousand individuals, could follow as the next stage, and thereafter a return to Chang'an or Luoyang might be possible. A posting there could well be at a higher grade than that held previously, or the promotion might be to assistant to one of the nine ministers of state (*jiu qing* 九卿) or to director of one the departments under his jurisdiction.

Meritorious service, patronage by a high-ranking official or a stroke of good fortune could then result in appointment as a governor of a commandery, the highest position to be held in provincial administration. Successful in such a post, a man might next be appointed to one of the most senior offices of the central government, such as tutor to the heir apparent, or court architect, or even to an office with supreme responsibility for matters such as finance or security. Finally the way might lead forward to the highest of all offices of the empire, imperial counsellor (*yu shi dafu* 御史大夫) or chancellor (*chengxiang* 丞相).

It may thus be observed that in the course of a successful career an official might move alternatively between the provinces and the centre, with the general principle that the senior posts in a commandery were not open to natives of that area. Promotion brought with it increased prestige and an advance up the scale of salaries. This scale was marked in a notation of measures of grain to which an official was entitled, but payment was probably made partly in kind and partly in cash. There were basically sixteen ranks on the scale, ranging from that of 10,000 to 100 measures. A further mark of distinction might be seen in the style and colour of the sashes and seals that officials were entitled to carry, ranging from seals in gold and silver at the top to those in copper. They were entitled to wear a special type of headdress with their robes; as their duties took them from place to place they travelled in luxury, riding in carriages.

These signs of the position held in the hierarchy may well have been on display in the formal calls of courtesy that junior officials paid to their superiors. Seals were often buried with an official, thus displaying the dignity of the position that he had held on earth. There were perhaps two crucial points of advance in an official career; one occurred on reaching the rank and salary of 1,000 measures of grain, the rank of magistrates of the most populous counties and of the assistants of the nine ministers of state. The second major step was marked by rising to a salary of 2,000 measures, as was the due of governors of commanderies and the most senior officials of the central government. In general the expression 'two-thousand-measures men' (*er qian shi* 二千石) became a term for referring to the most important men in the government.

Appointment to the senior posts could sometimes be for a temporary period only. If abnormal conditions obtained when a post fell vacant it could be filled by an official nominated to act in an acting rather than a substantive capacity. No general statement is possible for the length of tenure of a position; two to perhaps four years seems to have been the norm for the imperial counsellors before their promotion to chancellor; Ni Kuan 兒寬, who did not reach the latter position, lasted for eight years. Some of those who served in the highest places started their real careers at an advanced age, as may be seen in the cases of Gongsun Hong 公孫弘 and Yang Zhen 楊震. Of these two, Gongsun Hong had been dismissed from a minor post in his early years and came to the fore in public life at the age of sixty, to hold appointment as chancellor from 124 to 121 BCE.

The career of Yang Zhen may serve as an example of how an official could move from one post to another. In his youth he won a reputation for his scholarly ability. For some ten years he refused to answer a call that came to the provinces for the recommendation of persons suitable to hold office, and it was only when he was fifty years old that he held minor positions, perhaps no more than those of a low-grade clerk, in the provinces. However, Deng Zhi 鄧騭, general-in-chief and regent, had heard of his abilities and had him named as a man of flourishing talent; from that point he became, successively, regional inspector of Jingzhou and governor, first of Donglai (modern Shandong) and then of Zhuojun (modern Hebei). He was next translated to the central government as superintendent of transport (*taipu*) in 117 CE and then promoted superintendent of ceremonial (*taichang*); he rose to become chancellor (*situ*) in 120 and supreme commander (*taiwei*) in 123. A man of integrity and out-spokenness, he threatened to expose the malpractices that a rival had brought about during the absence of the emperor from the capital while on a tour. Paying the price of his rivals' animosity, he was dismissed to take his own life at the age of seventy.

Along with this system of offices a series of honorary or super-numerary titles conferred dignity with nominal authority and a position of respect without administrative responsibility or salary. These additional titles could be given *ad honorem* to officials who were already installed in a post. Those who held that of palace attendant (*shi zhong* 侍中) enjoyed the privilege of free access to the palace, with opportunities to act as intermediaries or negotiators between high-ranking parties. They might be undertaking missions of a confidential nature, perhaps one in which an emperor, heir apparent or empress dowager was involved; at times they might exploit their positions of trust to spread innuendo or introduce insinuation in the court.

Additional benefits other than salaries could come the way of an official, but it cannot be known whether these were regular or exceptional. Officials were allowed a regular day of rest from work in their office, perhaps one in six, and they could take leave for sickness. According to an old rule that pre-dated the empires, if a parent or wife died when an official was on duty he was entitled to thirty days of mourning leave, with fifteen for the death of a grandparent or half-brother or half-sister. In imperial times there was an assumption that senior officials took three years off duty for mourning, but this principle was often in question, and the period may at times have been set at thirty-six days.

Some officials may have received an allowance of clothing on arrival at their posts in the central government, possibly in sufficient supply to allow for seasonal changes. They may likewise have received one special meal every five days, inferior only to those served to emperors, and attendants, male and female, may have looked to their creature comforts. When travelling on business officials could pass the night at a postal station, where their servants could borrow equipment for cooking. If they were not accompanied by servants, the staff of the station provided cooked meals. In all cases they were supplied with water and other stores. Such facilities were evidently available to a low-level official of a county on the east coast, who set out in 11 BCE to visit some of his colleagues in neighbouring counties. Fortunately the notes that he made of where he spent the night have survived.

From an incident that is dated circa 58 CE we learn of the distribution of chattels to officials. This was material that had been confiscated from a high-ranking official, no less than a governor of a commandery, who was guilty of embezzlement. Zhongli Yi 鍾離意, who was serving in the Secretariat, refused the pearls and jewels that he was offered, quoting precedent and objecting to contamination with something that was tainted.

Officials earned the praise of their emperor or their immediate superiors if their conduct was seen to be honest and the judgement with which they settled human problems fair, and if the efficiency and speed with which they faced practical problems was effective. They could be criticised for oppression or extortion or for being open to corruption. Popular approbation of those who served well in the provinces could take the form of a public demonstration asking for their retention rather than their transfer elsewhere, or hindering an official who faced a criminal charge from obeying the summons (see p. 42 above). Occasionally the people of a region might establish religious rites to keep the memory of a loved governor green, as was done for Wen Weng 文翁 (governor of Shu; modern Sichuan). From the point of view of the government, successful and praiseworthy administration would lead to an increase of revenue, for, as more and more vagrants and displaced persons were found and identified and their names placed on the registers, so did their contributions increase the amount of tax that was raised. Officials anxious to demonstrate their efficiency might therefore make a point of reporting the numbers of persons newly entered in their records. Suppression of crime and the firm maintenance of security counted high on the credit side for an official who was hoping for promotion.

Officials might also earn merit by raising the cultural standard of living. They could do so by setting up schools, as did Wen Weng in Chengdu, circa 150 BCE. Or they could attend to the improvement of human habits in areas that, unlike those of the centre, had not enjoyed the benefits of a few centuries of civilised government. Shortly after the close of Eastern Han officials in modern Hainan and along the Vietnamese coast were introducing marriage arrangements where they were not known, and prevailing upon men and women to wear clothing rather than run around naked. As the influence of the educated officials was brought to bear on outlying districts, it became possible to suppress some of the religious customs that were of a questionable or pernicious habit. Perhaps as early as around 400 BCE the local magistrate of one of the kingdoms had used his ingenuity to stamp out the custom of floating girls down the Yangzi River, where they would drown, as a sacrificial tribute to its Count (He bo 河伯). About 60 CE Diwu Lun 第五倫, governor of Kuaiji (modern Zhejiang), eliminated the habit of sacrificing cattle, which had caused considerable poverty. Another such official (Zong Jun 宗均; d. 76 CE) stopped the practice of some religious rites and of services paid to two mountains named Tang 唐and Hou 后 in Lujiang commandery (modern Anhui), circa 56 CE.

Some officials such as Zhang Tang 張湯 (suicide 115 BCE) were known for the rigorous severity with which they saw that the laws were obeyed and its infringements punished. Others were still ready to carry out humble work when they reached senior positions, as was seen in the way that Diwu Lun used to feed the horses when he was governor of a commandery. At times of weak government there were some officials who were said to receive 'pay as for a corpse'; they simply pocketed their salaries, acquiescing in other persons' actions and taking no steps to check unworthy conduct or wicked activities.

We read much of the advice proffered and the decisions taken by the highest ranking officials which determined matters of state policy in principle or in general terms. Before reaching such eminent positions many of those officials had probably served at lower levels, and it was the steady work of administration that they undertook, their control of the land and the population, that made the operation of imperial government possible. They may have been senior enough already to offer advice as gentlemen or counsellors (*dafu* 大夫); they may have been director of a specialist office of the central government; or else, whatever the offices they held, they may have been able to bring their influence to bear as palace attendants.

A sense of hierarchy ran through the civil service. As the framework laid down the distinctions of seniority and the degree of independence or responsibility that pertained to each level, the scope for initiative could well be limited. There was a danger that by actions that lay beyond the bounds of his authority an official might find himself liable to indictment and punishment; however should he fail to take the action needed to avert danger, such as that of defence against invading enemies, he would be equally culpable, even though in strict terms he did not possess the necessary authority. To lead others into taking such steps, he might feel tempted to forge a document, such as an imperial decree, that would serve his purpose, but he would likewise be courting danger. In 36 BCE Chen Tang 陳湯 and Gan Yanshou 甘延壽 took precisely such steps to enable them to engage in battle with an enemy beyond the border. To the fortune of the empire they succeeded in their enterprise, but on return to Chang'an they faced legal and disciplinary trouble. A different case may be cited for a century or so later. As an official of the central government, Zong Jun forged a decree which enabled him to bring about the surrender of rebel tribesmen in Wuling (modern Hunan); he was lucky enough to receive a reward.

Many senior officials had received a scholarly training at the hands of distinguished academicians. In the course of their careers they may have faced specialised problems for which they had had no such preparation, such as handling floods, taking emergency measures at a time of plague, distributing staple goods in times of need or defending a frontier against marauders or a sea front against pirates. For some matters, they might have been able to seek guidance in technical manuals that concerned mathematics, astronomy, medicine or military tactics, and had they the patience to wade through forbidding volumes of documentation, they could consult legal records in the search for precedents. Probably a copy of the imperial decrees would be available for reference, but although a provincial official might well be familiar with the oral mythological accounts of the past he would not have had written historical records of his own dynasty at hand.

Despite all this we find officials handling technical problems. Floods that broke out in 29 BCE wrought widespread havoc. No less a person than the superintendent of agriculture, one of the nine ministers, took energetic steps to organise relief; a colonel serving in the army set to work to repair the breaches of the Yellow River banks by laying loads of stone to dam the flow. Diwu Lun at one time was responsible for inspecting the minting of cash and checking for fair practice in the markets of Chang'an. Circa 51 CE he was appointed chief of the physicians in Huaiyang kingdom. We do not know whether he had acquired a knowledge of medical matters or any personal experience or skills therein.

Reasons for promotion would have varied widely. Records of government at county level of circa 15 BCE which derive from a coastal area in the east (modern Jiangsu) usually give little more than integrity or meritorious service as the reason; in a few specific instances promotion was due to arrest of a robber gang or of escaped convicts.

At the higher levels of the civil service officials could find themselves demoted or dismissed for a variety of reasons. It was relatively easy to have a prominent official charged on grounds of impropriety, failure to observe the laws or downright crime. Should his involvement in the politics of state, the councils of the palace or the intrigues of the women's palaces provoke disagreement or enmity, an adversary could easily take action to accomplish his downfall. Disgrace could take the form of dismissal or punishment for crime, the latter even including sentences to death, flogging or castration. Rather than face such an humiliation, senior officials often preferred suicide.

A live case which might have involved flogging an official arose shortly before 60 CE. A decree had ordered that a son of one of the non-Han leaders who had made over to the empire should receive a gift of fine silk; in implementing the order the Secretariat had mistakenly delivered the gift in hundreds rather than tens of bales. When Mingdi saw the accounts he angrily summoned one of the gentlemen with the intention of having him beaten. However Zhongli Yi, deputy director of the Secretariat (*Shangshu puye* 尚書 僕射), intervened. 'Everyone makes mistakes', he said; 'when an error is due to indolence or carelessness, it is a major crime for senior officials but a minor one for those of lower status. This mistake was of my making, and it is I who should be the first to be charged'. Zhongli Yi thereupon took off his clothing and made his way forward to be flogged. Mingdi relaxed, told him to resume his headdress and pardoned the gentleman who had been concerned.

A less painful form of demotion took the form of transfer from a post in the central government to one in the provinces, where the style of living lacked the high culture and material luxuries of the capital city. Such transfers also made it possible to remove outspoken or awkwardly minded critics away from the centre, where they might achieve a hearing, and direct them to a remote part of the empire where protest would fall on deaf ears or where the critics might themselves fall victim to a vicious or cruel local governor. Shortly after 124 BCE Gongsun Hong 公孫弘 the Chancellor was able to have Dong Zhongshu 董仲舒, whom he had grown to hate, appointed to a position in the kingdom of Jiaoxi (modern Shandong), whose king was known to inflict cruelties on those who served him. In 125 CE Chen Zhong 陳忠, who had incurred anger by his attempts to control the families of imperial consorts, was moved from his powerful position as director of the Secretariat (*Shangshu ling* 尚書令) to become governor of Jiangxia commandery (modern Hubei), at a safe distance from Luoyang.

By 5 BCE the number of officials in post had risen to over 130,000. Unfortunately we have no figures to show how this number had risen since the foundation of Qin and Han or how far it had changed by the time Eastern Han came to an end. Of the 130,000 officials it may be estimated that 100,000 served in the provinces and some 30,000 in the capital city of Chang'an, where they would not form an unduly disproportionate element in a population of at least a quarter of a million registered persons. Those few who reached the highest points of eminence or power, such as Liang Ji, may have lived in grand mansions in the outskirts of Luoyang, thereby exciting envy. The salaries and grades of their posts marked their social status, which could be enhanced in other ways, such as conferment of one of the highest of the orders of honour, that of noble, that are to be described below (see p. 136). Many of the chancellors of Western Han received this mark of recognition with its attendant emoluments.

Notes for Further Reading

See primary sources as follows: for Diwu Lun (*HHS* 41, pp. 1395–1402); his criticism of senior officials' request for appointment of persons to posts (*HHS* 41, p. 1399); mourning leave (Zhangjia shan, 'Zou yan shu', strip nos. 180–81); popular protest in favour of a governor (*HHS* 41, p. 1397); provision of food and clothing for officials (*HHS* 41, p. 1411 note and Zhangjia shan [Statutes], strip no. 267); Zhang Heng's memorial of 133 CE (*Hou Han ji* 18, p. 513); Zhongli Yi (*HHS* 41, pp. 1406–10); his refusal of stolen goods (*HHS* 41, p. 1407); and the gift of silk (*HHS* 41, p. 1409); and Zong Jun (*HHS* 41, pp. 1411–14).

See Bielenstein, *Bureaucracy,* for the academy (pp. 138–40); the number of officials (pp. 156–57); recruitment of officials (pp. 132–41); Nylan, for Wen Weng (p. 313); *Crisis and Conflict,* for repairs needed in the emergency of 29 BCE (p. 191); *Men who Governed,* for claims for registering vagrants (p. 61); a junior official's diary (pp. 53–59); the numbers of officials (pp. 70, 113); records of promotion, (pp. 71–74); and recruitment of officials (Chapter 4). For the suppression of religious rites and the spread of culture, see Loewe, 'He Bo Count of the River, Feng Yi and Li Bing', and 'Guang-zhou: the Evidence of the Standard Histories from the *Shi ji* to the *Chen shu,* A Preliminary Survey'.

6

Major Decisions of Government: Decrees and Memorials

There are no simple or universal answers to the questions which arise from the foregoing chapters of who was responsible for taking major decisions of policy and what processes were involved in doing so. It can only be assumed that very different conditions affected these matters over the four hundred years that saw on the one hand the steady development of the organs of government and growing intensity with which officials conducted their business and on the other the curtailment of official controls owing to a loss of discipline, the outbreak of insurrection, the rise of separatist leaders or the onset of local emergency.

Often enough the histories present major decisions in terms that are ascribed to the emperor, such as 'the emperor followed this advice' or 'the emperor had no leisure to take such action'. Sometimes we read of a less precise indication of an emperor's part, in terms such as 'the emperor was pleased' or 'the emperor was angry', or there may be a more formal decision in the form of 'an edict which granted approval'. Very occasionally we may be told that an emperor took a personal part in government, as is recorded for Xuandi from 68 BCE; until then it had been in the hands of Huo Guang 霍光 and a few others.

Recognition that it was the emperor who took a decision tends to occur when controversial matters were in question. This is not generally recorded for the many routine decisions taken in governing the empire, but events such as the appointment of men to the senior posts of state receive special treatment. By inclusion in the 'Imperial Annals' chapters of the histories it is at least implied or claimed that they depended directly on an emperor's choice, or at least his acceptance of the will of others, coupled with his own authority. The histories do not record obedience to the imperial will over all matters that were of high importance, such as the adoption of far-reaching schemes to control the daily lives and work of the population or the choice of a moment for embarking on territorial expansion or military action.

There were others who took part in pondering major questions of policy, insisting on compliance with their own intentions or tendering advice and warnings in view of the consequences and dangers that they foresaw. The emperor himself, particularly if he was under age, might be subject to cajolement, persuasion or pressure from one of his consorts. On occasion a consort would be anxious to advance her family's interests by seeing that a close relative was situated in high office. The chancellor held the highest of those offices, but his powers were by no means free of constraint. To take a decision that was of practical importance he must secure the agreement of his colleague, the imperial counsellor; for it was he who exercised a more direct control over those officials of the civil service who would be due to implement a chancellor's conclusions, and for their part they required direct authorisation before they would take any action. The nine ministers of state would participate in discussions at the highest level, appending their concurrence or support to a proposal that the chancellor put forward. At times senior officials in the provinces, such as the governors or commandants of the commanderies, had no option but to take immediate action to meet a crisis or emergency, such as the occurrence of a natural disaster of flood or drought, incursion by raiding parties or the outbreak of insurrection. Similarly, only military officers who were on the march or encamped in the field could decide when it was judicious to advance or to retreat, whether it would be wise to act in a way that might harden an adversary's will for further activities or to secure a peaceful agreement by compromise.

Ideally the choice of appointment to the most highly responsible posts of imperial government would rely on knowledge of an official's record with an assessment of his merits and weaknesses, his special capabilities and his family affiliations. But despite the submission of reports on officials and the maintenance of records, precise and accurate information of this type was not necessarily available. Some officials enjoyed a high reputation thanks to hearsay, or to overstatement by a relative who stood in a high place in public life, and this would suffice to secure appointment; alternatively a decision to withhold an appointment might arise from the calculated calumny of a rival.

Officials of the lower ranks who served, perhaps, under the superintendents of ceremonial, agriculture or the lesser treasury, or those posted in the provinces, were indeed responsible for decisions of a lower order and for implementing those taken by their superiors. Several factors limited their degree of freedom, such as their relative position in the hierarchy, restriction within the bounds of their authority and the obligation to report to their seniors at the next higher level. But whether senior or junior officials were concerned, one overriding set of conditions tempered the scope of their activities; this was the shortage of precise or up-to-date information.

Officials of the central government required a well-grounded knowledge of the circumstances and causes of a problem that faced them, and this was by no means always forthcoming. They could not necessarily call on sufficient information with which to gauge the effort needed or expense involved in practical schemes, such as the distribution of supplies to areas in distress or the repair of communications or defence lines. In military matters in particular, a government that was intent on saving unnecessary expenditure might well fail to understand the size of a problem and to determine correctly the extent of the effort or the strength of the armed forces needed to set a situation right. There were few ways available with which to check the reports of disaffection in remote areas, of the disloyalty or wicked behaviour of one of the kings or of the oppressive and corrupt ways of an official. For bias and errors of exaggeration might well have entered into the reports of such matters.

Provincial governors and military commanders laboured under different types of difficulty from those that beset officials at the capital city, for they were working at a distance from the centre with no means of speedy consultation if an emergency arose. Aware of local conditions or the state of an enemy's fighting strength they might well wish to act on such a basis, irrespective of the declared will of the central government to whom such sources of information were not available. In this way a senior official could find himself on the horns of a dilemma—whether to take remedial action on his own initiative and eliminate all-too-present dangers, or whether to wait for the necessary authorisation before daring to move. In the first instance his decision could involve him in rebuke, demotion or punishment; in the second, delays could spell disaster to the commandery or for the troops in his charge. In addition he would not necessarily know of any changes of thought or policy that had taken place in Chang'an owing to changes of appointment in high places there.

Our sources tell of various ways in which decisions of policy were formulated and the necessary orders given. To all appearances an imperial decree proclaimed these as deriving from the emperor's will; at times they derived from the suggestions that an official had been required to submit or protests that he had sent in on his own initiative, perhaps with some daring. Traditionally such documents have been termed 'memorials', but not all officials were entitled to present expressions of their views without orders to do so.

Decrees commanded officials to give due consideration to the problems of the day, sometimes with wide terms of reference, sometimes with respect to a particular need; they might state a request for advice or enjoin action already deemed necessary. They were issued in the name of the emperor himself or at times that of an empress dowager, but it cannot be assumed that it was those high dignitaries who personally framed the decrees or other comparable documents, such as rescripts. It is unlikely, for example, that shortly after his accession in 141 BCE Wudi would have himself composed three famous rescripts. Written in the best style of measured prose, these asked for advice on the basic problems of governing an empire, and they elicited responses from Dong Zhongshu 董仲舒; at the time Wudi was aged no more than sixteen. Similarly some of the decrees of Eastern Han were issued during the reign of an infant emperor, as in 144 and 145 CE.

Some decrees may have been designed to call attention to a weakness or failure of government, thereby criticising those who were responsible. But thanks to a rhetorical device these avoid immediate blame or denunciation. In decrees written with this intention the emperor would blame himself for personal deficiencies which had allowed a sorry state of affairs to develop and to bring unhappiness to his people; he could then order officials to take adequate steps to meet the current difficulties. A further rhetorical device is seen in the deliberate evocation of times long, long ago when disorders were occurring and named persons could be seen as responsible; the warning note was clear for all to understand.

However they were formulated, the imperial decrees of which our sources now retain summaries conveyed decisions that concerned dynastic, administrative and religious matters. In his valedictory decree Wendi (d. 157 BCE) took the opportunity to reflect on the major destinies of life and death and to give orders that his obsequies should be restricted to a modest scale. Decrees frequently displayed a monarch's care for his people; they could grant bounties to groups of the population, such as a mark of increased social status (i.e., orders of honour; see p. 136 below), a gift of food for the needy or exemption from tax in areas badly affected by natural disasters. A decree of 72 BCE called for the payment of respects to Wudi, the current emperor's great-grandfather. Later on, a decree which is ascribed to the Grand Empress Dowager Wang ordered enquiries to be set afoot into the circumstances in which the recently deceased emperor (Chengdi) had met his end (7 BCE). It was in decrees under her name that ever more honorific titles were to be given to her nephew Wang Mang, as yet an adherent of the Han dynasty.

Decrees could convey decisions that affected domestic matters, such as a mitigation of punishments for crime or the establishment, or withdrawal, of a commandery. A decree of 52 BCE ordered officials to advise on the correct treatment and status to be accorded to the leader of the Xiongnu 匈奴, when he would visit Chang'an in the following year. In 117 CE a decree set up a commission to report on the need for relief in certain distressed areas; another of 110 CE ordered the migration of a section of the population away from the south-east coast to the interior, where they could be controlled more easily. From time to time decrees called for the presentation of candidates to fill official posts; less frequently they expressed an interest in finding or interpreting an old, and perhaps lost, text of literature.

Part, perhaps a major part, of an emperor's duties lay in the performance of religious rites of two sorts. These could be addressed to a series of deities, on behalf of the whole empire, or they could take the form of obeisances and offerings rendered at the shrines dedicated to earlier emperors. From time to time questions arose as to the identification of the deities who deserved these services, the manner in which the rites should be conducted or the number of the shrines to imperial ancestors that merited their expensive upkeep and offerings. Decisions rested on the highest levels of government and were initiated by means of decree.

Some of the decisions recorded in decrees followed representations made by officials, which the throne 'approved' and then adopted. On some occasions when a controversial matter arose decisions would follow a call for consultation, the expression of opposing views and a final choice that was left, reputedly, to the emperor. There were also some rare occasions of a special nature when a large number of officials acting in unison presented a proposal or expressed their views. There are no cases on record of reference of a question to a popular assembly whose conclusions carried authority and demanded action.

Both the memorials of officials and the decrees of emperors sought support for their contentions by citing approved texts such as those chosen for teaching, or for their inculcation of moral principles or the lessons of history. Memorials and decrees would refer to persons and incidents of history or mythology, either as examples of paragon conduct that should be emulated or, by way of warning, so as to avoid wicked actions and their dire consequences. Memorialists would, as it seemed, flatter an emperor by praising the qualities that he possessed; possibly they were indicating that he should strive to acquire them. Almost de rigueur they would praise the achievements of the founding emperor and his closest and most successful advisors. They could appeal to religious belief or cite the sayings of approved masters, such as Confucius or Laozi. They might refer to ancient precedent or to existing institutions and perhaps back up their propositions by calling on facts and figures of a practical nature.

Decrees could include rhetorical statements; their stately terms could couch unpleasant facts; their gracious grants of an order might be no more than a recognition and acceptance of practices that already existed; and there were times when an unauthenticated or forged decree played a part in imperial history. Posted in 36 BCE to serve in the Western Regions, Gan Yanshou 甘延壽 and Chen Tang 陳湯 were aware of the dangers that might arise from the moves of one of the leaders of the peoples of Central Asia. Whereas they realised that speedy action was necessary, they also knew that they needed written authority to take it, and they forged the decree that would allow them to call up the forces that they required. Such decisive action achieved the desired results, but back at Chang'an the two officials faced criminal charges from whose consequences they were lucky to escape. At a lower level, circa 123 CE two prominent men who carried honorary titles such as palace attendant (*shizhong* 侍中) forged a decree to call for cash, grain and building materials from the superintendent of agriculture and others; these supplies were to be used for building private houses, with their lakes and gardens. In 168 CE the eunuch Cao Jie 曹節, with the honorary title of regular palace attendant (*zhong changshi* 中常侍), contrived the elimination of Chen Fan 陳蕃 (senior tutor, *tai fu* 太傅) and Dou Wu 竇武 the Regent by means of an unauthenticated decree.

A few examples illustrate the ways in which these procedures worked out. Each one of those that are described here was *sui generis*, concerning a particular question or incident; none should be taken as an example of regular or normal practice. The cases quoted here, mainly from Western Han, concern formal procedures by officials, charitable actions, military plans, the investiture of kings, economic controls, the deposal of an emperor and the respects due to the memory of deceased emperors.

The Statutes of 186 BCE, which will be described in Chapter 8, provide details of how some of these procedures could or should operate. If officials at county level had a request in mind that would require incorporation in imperial institutions, they were obliged to forward their ideas or suggestions to the senior official of the commandery, presumably the governor. He would then forward it for scrutiny by the highest ranking officials of the central government. Attempts by a county official to by-pass the intermediate stage and go directly to the chancellor of state or the imperial counsellor would be punished by a large fine.

Other legal documents of the same date illustrate how the senior officials of the central government, having approved the requests that had come to them from the provinces in this way, would duly transmit them for formal inclusion in a decree. It is evident and perhaps somewhat surprising that minor items, such as authority for the sale and purchase of a horse in one area and its transfer elsewhere, might be subject to these procedures and eventually require deliberation by no less a person than the Son of Heaven.

A decree of 179 BCE drew attention to the material needs of those in want, such as widows and orphans, and ordered officials to consider the means of alleviating such sufferings. A further statement of the time noted the occurrence of abuses whereby officials were drawing on stale, long-stocked supplies of grain for distribution to the needy. Officials duly put forward their requests for action to prevent this, and an order named the appropriate steps to rectify such practices. These specified the amounts of grain to be distributed, with variations according to age, and distribution was to be subject to inspection.

In 135 BCE there arose the question of the best policy to adopt when treating with the Xiongnu, the strong confederation of Central Asia that was potentially hostile and which could wreak severe damage on Chinese farmlands and settlements of the north. The Xiongnu had made overtures to secure the establishment of peaceful relations with Han, and their request for such was referred for consultation. The histories include a long account of an exchange of views between two senior officials who took opposing sides to the question. Wang Hui 王恢 (1), superintendent of state visits, argued against accepting the suggestion for a treaty of amity, on the grounds that the Xiongnu could not be trusted to keep to its terms. Han Anguo 韓安國 (1), the imperial counsellor, advised acceptance of the proposal as he saw no long term gains arising from the alternative policy, of a hostile attitude and military action.

The two men likewise disputed the value and effect of a deceptive plan devised by one of their colleagues, whereby the Xiongnu forces would be ambushed. Arguing against Han Anguo's point that military action against the Xiongnu would involve popular hardship and dangers and disrupt agricultural production, Wang Hui insisted that it was only brute force that would tell; and it was Wang Hui's view that prevailed. As proposed Han forces attempted to lure the Xiongnu into a trap, but the scheme failed in its purpose. Wang Hui was forced to suicide; Han Anguo died in 127 BCE after rendering further service, in both a military and a civil capacity. A discussion of comparable matters in strategic rather than tactical terms is seen below (p. 180).

Dynastic affairs came to the fore in 117 BCE. In a move that seems to have been contrary to the trend of the times whereby the kingdoms were being reduced in strength or even eliminated, three of Wudi's sons were nominated in that year to be kings of Qi (in modern Shandong), Yan (Hebei and Liaoning) and Guangling

(Jiangsu). It is apparent from some of the documents, preserved somewhat uniquely, that the decision to do so had not passed without discussion or even controversy as they record no less than fifteen stages whereby it was reached.

This question started with a request put forward by Huo Qubing 霍去病, a nephew of Wudi's empress Wei 衛 and a successful general of some renown, who bore the honorific title of marshal of state. He asked that consideration should be given to the status and rank that was fit for three of the emperor's sons, borne to secondary consorts. The request was passed to the chancellor and imperial counsellor who, along with other officials, proposed that the three men should be nominated kings, in accordance with ancient tradition. A decree ordered further consideration on the grounds that the three sons were commoners and of an immature age, and that it would be more appropriate to raise them to a rank that was no higher than that of noble (for this rank, see p. 49 above). The chancellor and imperial counsellor replied that nomination as nobles would run counter to the accepted ideas of precedence and that that rank was too low for the three sons. A decree next insisted that, in the bestowal of rank, merit was of greater importance than kinship and that the three men, or youths, should be raised to the rank of noble. The two senior officials rejoined that youth was no ban to nomination as kings, as had been apparent in recent Han practice, and that, with due regard to the difference between pre-imperial and imperial social structure, the rank of king was more suitable than that of noble.

A further memorial was now presented in the names of the chancellor, the acting imperial counsellor, the superintendent of ceremonial and the acting superintendent of the imperial household. They claimed to have acted after consultation with over twenty existing nobles. They recalled how Gaozu, founding emperor of the dynasty, had set up kingdoms for his sons, and they asked for nomination of Wudi's three sons as kings in accordance with that model. It was at this point that those whose views had been represented in the imperial decrees gave way. Twenty-one days after the matter had been raised, a decree ordered the installation of the three men as kings. After four further items of procedure and nine days, Liu Hong 劉鴻 (1), Liu Dan 劉旦 (1) and Liu Xu 劉胥 (2) were duly installed as the kings of Qi, Yan and Guangling on a day that corresponded with 9 June of 117 BCE and which had been chosen for its auspicious properties. The histories include the texts of three deeds of investiture, with due warnings of the results of disloyal behaviour. Sets of maps for presentation to the new kings probably accompanied these deeds.

A decree of 81 BCE ordered the chancellor and the imperial counsellor to hold discussions with candidates who had been recommended as being suitable for office and with the men of learning. They were to enquire into the state of suffering of the people and deliberate whether the government's monopolies of the salt and iron industries and of the trade in alcoholic liquors should be abolished. The monopolies had been instituted some forty years previously at a time when the Han government was initiating active steps to control the working lives of the population. By 81 BCE the strength of this resolve had ebbed and the value of the steps that had been taken at the time came into question.

We possess an independent account of the deliberations that was probably compiled some three or four decades subsequently. Cast in the form of a dialogue, its sixty chapters include argument and counter argument, thrust and counter thrust, with those who were opposed to the principle of the monopolies winning the argument. The discussions ranged over a whole variety of issues that the terms of reference evidently allowed. Apart from the advantages and disadvantages of the monopolies themselves, the disputants addressed other economic issues, such as the use and distribution of wealth; the advantages of a trader's occupation; the proper use of coins and the control of minting; and the imbalance seen between extravagance and poverty. The means of recruiting the right type of men to serve as officials and the prestige of the men of learning came into question. The expense of territorial expansion and of military expeditions featured in the debate along with the practical value of an export-import trade.

In very general terms, the parties to the debate criticised the methods of government that Shang Yang 商鞅 had practised in Qin in pre-imperial times, and they discussed the value or weaknesses of copying the social structure and institutional models that had been evolved for the very different conditions of those days. Some speakers espoused the cause of ethical values and social ideals; others looked to the realistic and practical conditions of governing an empire. Although the dialogue shows the critics of the monopolies reducing their opponents to silence, in the outcome of the talks their point of view went almost unheeded. By way of compromise no more than the iron agencies in the metropolitan area, and those set up for the sale of liquor in the provinces were closed.

Three emperors, two of them young men, took their place on the throne in Chang'an in the year that ran from 21 February 74 to 9 February 73 BCE. Liu Fuling 劉弗陵, posthumously entitled Zhaodi, had acceded at the age of about twenty-two in 87 BCE and died on 5 July 74 BCE, with no heir to his name. Liu He 劉賀 (4), aged eighteen, succeeded him on 18 July, to be deposed after twenty-seven days on 14 August. Liu Bingyi 劉病已, known as Xuandi, duly took his place at the age of eighteen on 10 September, to reign until he died of natural causes in 48 BCE. The *Han shu* recounts the formalities whereby these events took place or were contrived, together with the parts played by leading officials and the formulation of the documents that were required. Our sources do not reveal openly the disputes that lay behind or followed the occurrences of this *annus mirabilis*.

At the time of Zhaodi's death, control of the government lay in the experienced hands of Huo Guang 霍光, who held the office of general-in-chief and the honorific title of marshal of state. At the death of an emperor it was expected that the empress dowager would issue the necessary orders. On this occasion the empress dowager was none other than a granddaughter of Huo Guang, aged no more than fifteen. It would seem to have been unlikely that she would have been able to refuse him the authority needed to translate his decisions into imperial commands and then into action. For various reasons he excluded three surviving sons of Wudi, Zhaodi's father, from succeeding to the throne. He sent a commission to summon Liu He (4) to make his way from his kingdom of Changyi (modern Shandong) to Chang'an; as a grandson of Wudi the young man had a strong claim to succeed, and he proceeded on his way at breakneck speed.

Once Liu He was emperor, his unrestrained behaviour gave great cause for alarm. Huo Guang concluded that he was not fit for his position and contemplated the possibility of deposal. To bring this about he summoned a meeting of the most senior members of the government; under a threat of violence, he extracted their agreement to his conclusion that Liu He must be removed. Thanks to a decree of the empress dowager most of Liu He's personal attendants were prevented from waiting upon him in support, and the young man was ordered to listen to a memorial put forward under the names of Huo Guang, twenty-seven senior officials and eleven others. The document recounted Liu He's failure to conduct himself in a manner that befitted a mourner for the late emperor, his debauchery during his journey to Chang'an, his misuse of the emperor's seals, his indulgence in undue merriment and his sexual encounters with some of the women who had served in Zhaodi's palace.

These revelations, we read, so shocked the young empress dowager that she ordered Liu He, emperor though he was, to leave his place in the audience chamber and submit to punishment; but the memorialists had not yet finished. They added a tale of his seizure of valuable treasures such as gold and jade objects, and silks, that were held in the palace, of gross misbehaviour while in his cups, of the issue of decrees to give orders for all manner of things, of his punishment of those who dared to remonstrate, in short, of the way he was throwing Han institutions into disarray. Finally Huo Guang and his colleagues requested that sacrifice should be offered at the shrine dedicated to Gaozu and that a full account should be rendered there of the failure of the present incumbent of the throne to match the qualities suited to his august position. The empress dowager duly gave her assent, by decree. Liu He refused to accept that this act involved his removal from the throne; Huo Guang made it clear that it did so and personally loosed the imperial seal from Liu He's clothing for delivery to the empress dowager.

Nearly a month had to pass before a successor could be installed. Huo Guang's next step was to present a memorial which proposed that Liu Bingyi, a great-grandson of Wudi, aged eighteen, should succeed. Liu Bingyi had been saved from death during the course of the dynastic crisis of 91 to 90 BCE and had been brought up away from the capital city. With the approval of Huo Guang's memorial, a commission set out to bring Liu Bingyi to Chang'an with all the trappings that were suitable to the position that he was to occupy. As yet, however, he was no more than a commoner with no rank to his name, and as such he could not rise immediately to the highest position, that of emperor. On a day corresponding to 10 September the empress dowager received him and invested him with a nobility; officials could now deliver him the seals of an emperor, and he could take his place on the throne.

The same pattern of memorial alternating with decree, with some memorials appearing over the names of a large number of senior officials, occurred when a controversy of a particularly sensitive nature arose. The question at issue was raised shortly after the accession of Yuandi, in 48 BCE, and it elicited opposing answers. The issues were so significant that at times the emperor was apparently unable to determine which points of view carried the greater powers of persuasion, and the question remained open for discussion until the close of the reign of his successor, and even subsequently until that of Aidi (r. 7–1 BCE). In this rather special case it does seem that the power of decision rested with the emperor. As will be seen, the problem varied from those already considered in that it was a matter of concern to the emperor's own family.

The point at issue was the retention or dismantlement of some of the shrines dedicated to the memory of deceased emperors. Built regularly as one of the edifices that accompanied the tombs, these shrines housed a deceased emperor's wooden memorial tablet and received the obeisances and offerings of his descendants. Some shrines were built to keep green the memory of an emperor's father who had not himself sat on the throne, such as the fathers of Gaozu and Xuandi. In addition to the shrines set up at the imperial tombs, others were built in the provinces to mark the occasions when Gaozu and Wendi had honoured the areas with visits.

As a result, early in Yuandi's reign no less that 176 shrines existed, each requiring guards for security, maintenance of the property and the provision of daily, monthly and seasonal offerings. These expenses had risen markedly over the years and the treasury now had to provide, as was estimated, for over twenty-four thousand offerings annually (including some at ancillary buildings), forty-five thousand servicemen and over twelve thousand prayer reciters, cooks and musicians, exclusive of those persons needed to rear the animals required for sacrifice. Money was short in Yuandi's time; public expenditure was under scrutiny and other items were subject to reduction.

The issue carried wide-ranging implications. Respect for ancestors lay at the heart of religious obligations, and failure to perform the rites could bring about not only a sense of shame but also reproaches and criticism. Dynastic authority and strength depended on continuity and unbroken links with the past. Moralists were proclaiming the demands to obey *xiao* 孝, the model of selfless conduct in the service of one's parents. Learned men of the day were teaching the texts of *li* 禮, those rules of deportment and ritual that would ensure social stability and discipline. There remained the overriding question of whether or not it was justifiable to abandon models of behaviour of the sacred past in order to accommodate to the exigent needs of the present.

As early as the time of the Empress Lü (effective ruler 187–180 BCE) discussion of this matter had become subject to a ban, which was re-imposed at a time during the reign of Chengdi (r. 33–7 BCE). It was perhaps for this reason that although the highest dignitaries in the land, including Wei Xuancheng 韋玄成 the Chancellor, expressed their views on the matter and did so in answer to a decree, they felt it necessary to seek safety in numbers, and there are records of memorials presented in this connection by seventy, forty-four, twenty-nine, eighteen or fifty-three signatory officials. The memorialists fastened on a limit to the number of shrines that it was proper to maintain; the choice of those to be singled out for services in perpetuity, thereby crediting an imperial ancestor with special honours; and the choice of which ones should be chosen for dismantlement. Two further issues arose that could perhaps arouse danger if voiced; whether a degree of kinship or one of merit should take priority in making these choices, and whether dismantlement of the shrines would affect the chances of the birth of an heir to the throne.

Argument swayed here and there, with protagonists on both sides drawing on past precedent and incident. At times the subject was deferred pending the further consideration that the emperor requested or ordered. Compromise rather than firm decision marked the course of the discussion over its forty years. Some of the shrines were actually dismantled in 38 BCE, but lying ill Yuandi grew afraid of the curses that his ancestors might bring about by way of punishment and ordered their restoration. It took courage to refuse to obey such an order, but this was not wanting in the person of Kuang Heng 匡衡, chancellor from 36 BCE. One long-lasting effect of the debate was the memorial penned by Liu Xin 劉歆 in 7 BCE, arguing the case for according the highest possible honour, that of maintenance in perpetuity, to the shrines of Wudi (r. 141–87 BCE). Wudi's reputation had been made to last (for further discussion of this issue, see Chapter 11, p. 176).

A decree followed the shock of an earthquake which was felt in Luoyang in 133 CE.

> Whereas, ungraced as We are with blessings We have received charge of Our awesome heritage, and possess no competence with which to accord with the rhythms of the hexagrams or to act in harmony with the cycle of Yin and Yang;
>
> And whereas along with frequent disasters that have brought their meed of suffering an earthquake has struck in Our capital city giving rise to fears whose end may not be known;
>
> We do hereby enjoin Our many ministers to inform us in what ways We can repair our deficiencies in answer to the warnings that We have received. Aware as We are that disasters do not occur without due reason, but in certain and determined response to other happenings, We command you each to search your minds and make plain where Our faults lie, being in no way bound to refrain from mentioning matters otherwise banned from discussion.

A slightly different version of the decree ordered the recommendation of men of unsullied qualities to submit their advice, which is duly recorded on the part of three famous men; Li Gu 李固, who called attention to scandals in the palace; the scholar Ma Rong 馬融, who discussed the workings of the universe; and Zhang Heng 張衡, mystic and scientist, who commented on the quality of the civil service.

Others besides Kuang Heng were responsible for taking decisions that affected public life and imperial policies. They did not all set forth their proposals in a memorial; some of them incurred grave risk or suffered grievous harm along with members of their families.

Xiao He 蕭何 (d. 193 BCE) has received full credit for his basic contribution to the foundation of the Han dynasty, and it is clear that it was his administrative skills that made it possible to re-form an imperial structure following the collapse of Qin and the subsequent attempts to re-establish a series of kingdoms. His foresight is seen in his collection or seizure of some of the legal and administrative documents whereby Qin had been governed. His reputation as an empire builder was recognised by some of the severest critics of later times, including the highly sceptical Wang Chong 王充 (27–ca. 100 CE).

Chao Cuo 鼂錯, who had been appointed imperial counsellor in 155 BCE, was executed in 154. The memorials that he presented in Wendi's reign had shown him to be a far-sighted, resourceful states-man who rendered sound advice on matters such as the unity of the empire, the proper part of the sovereign, the duties of senior offi-cials, the control and promotion of economic effort and the practice of military tactics. He had warned against the growing powers of the kings; Jingdi is said to have ordered his execution as a means of appeasing them and staving off their rebellion.

Jingdi also treated Zhou Yafu 周亞夫, one of his most loyal sup-porters, with comparable cruelty. As supreme commander he had suppressed that rebellion and in the course of doing so had taken strategic decisions that led to his success, but at the cost of disobey-ing his emperor's instructions; for he had refused to divert his forces so as to relieve those of Liu Wu (2) 劉武, brother of Jingdi and king of Liang, who throughout had remained loyal to the imperial cause. Zhou Yafu became chancellor in 150 BCE. Unable to see his own views and decisions prevail against the will of the emperor, he aroused suspicion and was charged with complicity in a plot. Jingdi made no move to save him, and he died on hunger strike in prison in 143 BCE.

With an exceptionally deep understanding of economic needs, Sang Hongyang 桑弘羊 likewise ended his life as a criminal (80 BCE). He had taken a leading part in sponsoring the plans for the government's monopolies and the schemes for stabilising the prices and transport of essential commodities; it is usually suggested that it is his views that are recorded in the account of the debate of 81 BCE. His views depended on a keen ability to estimate the expenses and revenue of government, but his proposal to set up military colonies as a means of maintaining a Han presence in Central Asia was too premature for adoption. As imperial counsellor he was one of those trusted to guide the steps of the young Zhaodi when he succeeded his father (87 BCE). In the course of his career he had aroused enmity and perhaps jealousy of his successes; involved in a plot against his rivals, he paid the price by suffering execution and extermination of his family.

Huo Guang was one of those rivals, and as has been seen in the case of the deposal of Liu He in 74 BCE there can be little doubt of his ability to take decisions and see them implemented. Indeed, that had not been the first occasion on which he had manipulated the imperial succession; it had been he who had taken steps to persuade Wudi to nominate Liu Fuling (Zhaodi) as his heir. Huo Guang had retained his position of dominance during that young man's reign and well into that of his successor (Xuandi), and he had built up a close family relationship with those two emperors. Throughout his career he had taken care to watch his step, and strong enough to survive enmities he died of natural causes in 68 BCE. But within two years members of his family paid the price of his dominance, his widow and son by execution, two others by suicide. In these final events it was probably the emperor who had taken the decisions.

Irrespective of the formalities that official procedures required, the power of decision and possession of a cool head could serve the empire in a crisis. In 30 BCE it seemed that floods were about to destroy the capital city. Wang Feng 王鳳, general-in-chief, advised the emperor and his family to take to their boats, leaving other inhabitants to save themselves as best they could. With his calm advice Wang Shang 王商 (1), general of the left, had allayed the panic, steadying the nerves and saving the lives both of those accustomed to the safe life of the palace and of those who lived in other less exalted quarters in Chang'an. His services recognised, in 29 BCE he became chancellor; machinations of his rivals led to his dismissal four years later.

Notes for Further Reading

See primary sources as follows: the death of Zhaodi and accessions of Liu He (4) and Xuandi (*HS* 68, pp. 2937–46; *HS* 8, p. 238; also *CHOC*, pp. 183–84; and *Crisis and Conflict,* pp. 75–78); the decrees of 179 (*HS* 4, p. 113), of 72 (*HS* 8, p. 243), and of 7 BCE (*HS* 97B, p. 3990); the decree of 133 CE and its three responses (*Hou Han ji* 18, pp. 507–13, with a slightly different version in *HHS* 6, p. 262); Dong Zhongshu's responses (*HS* 56, pp. 2495–523); evil behaviour attributed to two kings (*HS* 53, pp. 2414–17, 2428–32); forged decrees (*HHS* 8, p. 329; *HHS* 54, p. 1764); investiture of Wudi's three sons in 117 BCE (*SJ* Chapter 60; see also *Men Who Governed*, Chapter 12); official procedures of 186 BCE (*Zhangjia shan* [Statutes], strip nos. 219, 220, 506–24); policy with regard to the Xiongnu in 135 BCE (*HS* 52, pp. 2398–403); retention or destruction of imperial shrines (*HS* Chapter 73; see also *DMM* Chapter 13); Xuandi's personal part in the government (*HS* 8, p. 247; *HS* 89, p. 3624); Gale gives translations of select chapters of the *Yan tie lun;* see also *Crisis and Conflict,* Chapter 3, and *CHOC,* p. 187.

7

Official Documents and Government Communications

The earliest examples of Chinese writing that have been identified with certainty are the records of divination practised during the latter part of the Shang kingdom (from ca. 1200 BCE); these are inscribed on the carapaces of turtles and the bones of animals. Inscriptions cast on bronze vessels appear from the same period and in greater profusion in Western Zhou (1045–771 BCE) and the following Spring and Autumn period (770–481 BCE). It may be surmised that silk was used for writing from the seventh or sixth centuries BCE, and narrow strips of wood from at least the Warring States period (480–221).

Documents of wood, including bamboo, were first found and recognised circa 1900, and they have appeared with increasing frequency thanks to the archaeological work reported since 1972. Major finds of documents date from the Warring States, Qin and Han periods, with one very large cache of the third century CE. Possibly a form of paper, or 'proto-paper', may have been used infrequently for writing from Western Han (206 BCE–9 CE), though the earliest record of its appearance in official circles is for 105 CE; it came into wider use from perhaps the second century CE, but the fragile nature of the material has precluded the discovery of many examples of this time.

It is perhaps surprising that any documents on silk survive from Han times or earlier, but a number of pieces have done so and are still in a state to be read. Buried in tombs or cast aside into rubbish pits or disused wells, wooden documents have had a better chance, given favourable conditions of climate and soil. As a result texts with a religious, mantic, philosophical, historical or literary content, particularly of the Han period, have been forthcoming from sites in growing abundance, together with treatises on astronomy, mathematics, medicine and military strategy. In addition there are remnants of a large number of official documents that derived from the hands of those who governed the empire and administered its peoples, and it is with those latter types of text that this chapter is concerned.

Wood was cut to different shapes and sizes depending on the size of a document, on the purpose for which it had been compiled and on the mode of its delivery to a destination. Lengthy reports, sometimes of a cumulative nature, were usually written on narrow strips, each of which carried one column of characters written on one side only. The strips were bound together with two or three horizontal strings, such that they could be rolled together to form a scroll, i.e., a *juan* 卷 or a *volumen*; such scrolls might consist of as many as seventy-seven or as few as three strips.

Documents of this form were fragile; one strip, or several strips, could slip out of the roll all too easily. Or, if the strings broke, the strips could be dislocated, and re-assembly in the correct order might not be immediately possible, any more than it is today. Such risks did not attend the use of wooden stationery of a somewhat different type; this consisted of larger boards, perhaps measuring up to 6 centimetres wide, which could accommodate the complete text of a document, in two or as many as twenty columns.

As is to be expected in an ordered, hierarchical society such as that of imperial China, regulations prescribed the length of the strips or boards that were in use. Normally, clerks would be wielding their brushes over strips the length of 1 Han foot (23 centimetres), but for certain purposes, perhaps for documents emanating from the higher ranges of office, they would use slightly longer strips of 1.1 feet. For very special cases, such as copies of imperial decrees or codes of the laws, they could be authorised or instructed to use lengths of 2.2 or 3 feet. Strips of those lengths were also used for copies of special literary texts. The title or note of the contents of a rolled document could appear in one of two ways. It might be seen immediately, being inscribed on the verso side of one of the strips that formed an integral part of the document when it had been rolled up. For this purpose the clerk would be writing on the upper and visible surface of a strip that took its place at the outset of the scroll. Alternatively the title could be written on a small label that was tied to the scroll in such a way that it would hang down from the shelf where the scroll was stored. Two or three strings ran laterally from the beginning to the end of the document retaining the strips in their positions and holding them tight when they were rolled together. Outside the scroll thus formed the strings were held fast in a block of clay that was within a wooden frame some three centimetres square and baked hard. The clay bore the impression of the seal of the official who had originated the document.

Pieces of wood of other shapes or sizes served other purposes. These included labels that displayed in large writing the destination to which a document or collection of documents was addressed. Passports that travellers carried to obtain permission to proceed on their way through official controls were of a different size. Express couriers might carry long pieces of wood, so shaped and planed as to be able to carry columns of writing on perhaps four surfaces. These may have been designed for safe transport on horseback in times of emergency. When presenting themselves to pay respects to their superiors, junior officials took with them a large board or 'visiting card' with which to identify themselves and obey the courtesies. These had been inscribed with some care to calligraphic style.

The material finds at our disposal include documents that originated from officials of various levels in the central government and in the provinces. Along with some complete, undamaged boards, there are a few examples of scrolls which have survived with their binding strings still attached and still serving to keep the strips in their correct order. But the great majority of the finds consist of the individual strips of dismembered documents, and these pieces themselves may be either whole or fragmentary. Rough estimates of the size of the archives made out in these various forms and deposited at different sites amount to 1,000 pieces (Han period; from Dunhuang 敦煌 in Gansu); 10,000, and a further 20,000 (Han period; at Juyan 居延 in Gansu); 36,000 (Warring States and Qin; from Liye 里耶 in Hunan); and over 100,000 from Zoumalou 走馬樓 (third century CE and later; near Changsha). In addition 115 pieces have been found at the site of one of the imperial palaces of Western Han at Chang'an, and 57,000 small fragments of inscribed bones were unearthed from another site there.

The seals used to secure the strings that bound a document together were of considerable importance and value, as they conveyed authority from one official to another. Depending on the status or degree of seniority of the holder, seals were made of jade, gold, silver, bronze and possibly wood; numerous examples of bronze seals that were buried in tombs are now seen in museums. Seals of jade, of which very few examples are known, were reserved for emperors, empresses and a few other very high personalities. Emperors in fact had to choose among several seals, each of which was used for a slightly different purpose. On the one occasion when an emperor was deposed, it was necessary to remove the seal or seals from his person, thereby depriving him of the means of exercising his authority.

Seals held by officials were engraved with the title of their office and perhaps their title as a noble (see pp. 49, 146) and their name; a number of examples of the clay tablets on which these were impressed survive. Unauthorised manufacture of seals engraved with the titles of officials could be a dangerously serious matter, for such an act was taken as presumptive evidence that whoever had ordered it was contemplating a coup d'état and preparing seals for the officials whom he would appoint to hold office in his regime. Accuracy in the inscription was a matter of importance, as seen circa 43 CE when the renowned general Ma Yuan 馬援 pointed out some inconsistencies and errors. The name of the county in which three officials were serving was given in different forms.

Some matters and their documents, such as calendars, affected administration throughout the empire; multiple copies were distributed to the commanderies and thence to offices at lower levels. There exist a few incomplete examples of reports, such as those of the stores held in a granary, that were made out in duplicate for a different reason. Either we have parts of a rough draft and a final copy, or one copy was drawn up for retention in the office which originated it and one was intended for delivery elsewhere.

Prior to the discoveries of manuscript copies of documents, our knowledge of official procedures depended on the evidence of the histories and a few other texts. Different conditions affected and perhaps constrained the freedom with which the histories were compiled. In some instances the compiler may have received permission to draw directly on material in the form in which officials had submitted it and to reproduce it in full; in other cases he may for various reasons have been limited to a summary. Examples of documents compiled in these various ways, and comparison with some of the manuscripts show wide differences both in the ways in which documents were actually penned and in the choice of the language and formulae to be adopted.

As has been observed, stationery of different shapes and lengths suited different types of document, at times perhaps reflecting the respect or dignity that was their due. Differences in calligraphic style perhaps arose from the differing skills of the writer, be he a well-trained official or a clerk relegated to low-level duties. Parts of a collection of imperial decrees are carefully written, with an eye to the proper formation of the characters, their spacing and their balance in the column, and it may be suggested that it was officials in the capital city who insisted on attaining such a professional finish. Rough and ready scrawls, nonetheless legible, characterise reports of stores on hand at local depots, or in military outposts on the frontier; those ordered to write them may well have lacked the benefit of a sustained training and may have been free of the supervision of a punctilious superior officer. One particular feature occurs somewhat rarely. Reference to the emperor or to actions that he took personally obliged the clerks to ensure that it would appear at the head of a column of writing rather than take a secondary place in the lower reaches of the strip.

There are considerable differences in the choice of language and vocabulary and in literary style. At the lowest levels reports would follow a pattern from which an ignorant or ill-trained clerk would be neither willing nor able to deviate. Nevertheless, at one point in the process of drawing up a report some officials had had to determine the model to follow, for example, as between 'Millet: 3 litres on hand' and 'Retained in store: millet, 3 litres'. Such minuscule and seemingly unimportant details can be of considerable value today in identifying members of one and the same report and discriminating between several reports of a similar content.

At a higher level the use of certain formulae or clichés was de rigueur. When submitting a report to his superior, an official would write *gan yan zhi* 敢言之, that is, 'I beg leave to state'; statements sent down the line would be introduced with *gao* 告, that is, 'You are hereby informed'; and certain instructions would conclude *ji ru ling* 急如令, 'to be treated with the urgency due to the ordinances'.

Other differences may be seen. Memorialists offering advice or proposing a scheme of action to the throne would in all probability assert in all modesty that they realised that, in so doing, they stood in danger of a sentence of death. An emperor's decree could protest his own ignorance, weaknesses or errors and go on to seek guidance and consultation within the context of the whole way in which the universe operated or the empire was governed. A legal dossier that passed from one official to another would repeat perhaps for several times the statements of evidence or of action taken throughout the different stages of the case. Citations which accompanied or explained the conferment of noble rank named the services rendered by the honorand in the terse terms of a court gazette.

Enriched as we are by discoveries at a few sites of parts of manuscripts that derived from administration of the empire, we must nonetheless recognise that we are seeing no more than a fraction of the documentation produced in the process of government. Amid this, the wooden pieces left behind in the command posts of the armed forces in the north-west tell us something of the system of communications as practised from office to office. Copies of parts of the laws that have been found in the interior lay down the ways in which that system was to be organised, right from the outset of the empires.

Ideally postal stations that might comprise over twenty houses were set up at intervals of 10 or 20 *li*. It seems likely that they came under the direct control of officials in the commandery, and for that reason some of the postal stations may have been situated at the external points of a commandery, for ease of contact with those of the neighbouring units. Depending on their own wells, the stations were equipped with mills and furnishings, such as mattresses and cooking utensils, with which to accommodate and feed officials who were travelling on business, together with their attendants. The stations seem to have acted as inns for their use, without charge.

The normal, regular postal service conveyed routine and non-urgent documents from one postal office to another. An express service, on horseback, carried those items whose transit required speed. Some mail was delivered in a different way, stage by stage, as in the defence lines of the north-west. Regulations prescribed that couriers carrying normal deliveries should cover 200 *li* in a day and night; failure to do so, with its consequent delays (as might occur in legal proceedings), could incur punishment by flogging or the payment of fines, as did breakage of the seals attached to the items of mail.

The Statutes of 217 BCE ordered that notes should be appended to all documents, incoming and outgoing, with the date and time of receipt and despatch. Due acknowledgement should follow receipt; loss of a document should be reported without delay. Evidence for compliance with this procedure comes from the defence lines of the north-west. Here officials maintained registers of the items that they despatched or received, recording the name of the originator as seen in the seal, the contents or subject of the item, its date, the time taken for delivery and the names of the servicemen who had handled the process. Labels attached to a postal package might bear a secondary inscription that gave the time of receipt. It may be presumed that records of this type were also kept in the offices of the kingdoms, commanderies and counties.

The postal service conveyed copies of decrees, whether authentic or forged, memorials if these were being submitted in writing, calendars, legal documents, routine reports from the provinces and records that derived from the workings of the armed forces. Some of these documents were in the form of ledgers, with day-to-day entries; some were of cumulative items of business that covered several months; and some took the form of a table. In addition to the documents made for general distribution, offices of the central government drew up records that were intended for no more than one addressee. We do not know of any instructions that ordered the retention of these bundles of wooden strips or of any records that show how long they might be kept. We learn, however, that when the capital city was set up at Luoyang for the Eastern Han emperors, two thousand wagons conveyed written material there from Chang'an. We do not know how far those wagons were loaded with government documents or how far with the works of literature that had been collected for the imperial library shortly before the change of the capital.

For all the postal arrangements and sanctions that legal orders prescribed, it could well have happened that not all the mail reached its destination in the allotted time or as was needed for purposes of administration. Circulation of the incoming year's calendar could be just such a case (see p. 111 below). Officials of the central government were responsible for adjusting the luni-solar calendar as was needed from time to time and for determining how it should be kept in working order. Such work involved deciding which of the months were to be long, with thirty days, and which short, with twenty-nine, and at which point in every three years or so it was necessary to include a thirteenth, intercalary month. Exceptionally, a major decision affected the calendar in the choice of the month wherein the year was deemed to start. Originally this was fixed at the tenth month, but with effect from 103 BCE this was changed to the first month.

Of more regular occurrence were changes in the way in which years were enumerated. For much of Western, and all of Eastern, Han, they were counted from the first year of a regnal title, which was phrased perhaps as a prayer or as a mark of gratitude for auspicious times, or to display the virtues of the emperor and the successful achievements of his government. Such titles might be changed every five years or so, as in Western Han, but they tended to last for longer periods in Eastern Han. Thus the years 61 to 58 BCE were known as years one to four of 'The Supernatural Sparrows'; 57 to 54 as one to four of 'The Five Phoenixes'; and 58 to 75 CE as years one to eighteen of 'Perpetual Peace'. A few documents bear dates which refer to a year by a title that had been superseded, thus suggesting either that the change had been put in hand with insufficient foresight or that the mail had failed to get through in time for its adoption.

As will be seen in detail below (Chapter 8) manuscripts found recently include parts of legal documents of three types that passed through the hands of the couriers; there were the texts of the statutes and ordinances; records of legal cases whose issues were in doubt and required decision at a high level; and dossiers of cases that been settled after making their way through levels of officialdom, low and high.

A group of 202 strips that measured 27 centimetres (1.2 feet) in length carried the text of eighteen statutes of the Qin empire that are dated to 217 BCE, with titles that denoted their contents, such as 'Agriculture' and 'Currency'. A further group that is dated 186 BCE is somewhat larger, running to 520 slightly longer strips of 31 centimetres (1.4 feet) in length. These give the texts of twenty-seven statutes and one ordinance, some of their titles corresponding with those of the earlier group of 217 BCE and some of the prescriptions being comparable. Neither of these sets of strips carries a complete set of laws, and those that are represented may be defective. For example, the one ordinance of which we possess parts includes numbered clauses of which the highest is twenty-three, but portions of the text of no more than eighteen are present.

There are also two groups of strips that record incidents in which the law had been invoked but no decision had been reached. These could concern disputes regarding the ownership of property, bodily damage inflicted by one person on another, investigation into the theft of documents or action taken by officials such as the examination of bodily remains or the arrest of criminals. One such case concerns the retention of official mail for eight days, with the inclusion therein of fraudulent entries therein.

A complete dossier of a case that arose in 28 CE runs to thirty-eight strips (1 foot in length). This arose from the sale of a load of fish in the north-west, during the winter, and the ensuing financial transactions, which involved a question of accountancy or honesty.

When Shi Rao 師饒, a comparatively junior but highly responsible official, was buried at a site in Yinwan 尹灣, Jiangsu province, his grave included a series of documents that derived from the administration of Donghai commandery in which he himself had taken part. They can be dated to 16 to 11 BCE and may well have been of the types of reports rendered to the central government each year as an account of how effectively the officials of the commandery had performed their tasks. All of the documents that are mentioned below except for the first are in the form of a wide wooden board (6 by 23 centimetres; 0.25 by 1 Han foot) inscribed on both sides.

Seventy-six wooden strips found in the tomb had been parts of a calendar on which the holder had entered a personal record of some of his activities, almost in the form of a diary. Shi Rao gives the dates and locations of the journeys that he undertook, staying once at the postal station of Lanling 蘭陵, which was probably a centre of scholarly learning. At one time he journeyed in the company of the governor of the commandery; on a later occasion he may have been visiting neighbouring offices to report that the latter had just died. We read of Shi Rao's activities in arresting criminals and alternatively of him repairing to the hills of the countryside for a few days' vacation. He had held office in the Bureau of Merit, and in that capacity he may have acted as personal assistant and confidant of the governor. Among his colleagues he may have earned deference and careful treatment, for it was through the Bureau of Merit that the procedure for assessing officials' performance passed with the possible consequences of promotion.

Situated on the east coast (in southern modern Shandong), Donghai was one of the largest commanderies of Western Han with no less than thirty-eight sub-units of counties, nobilities and two estates made over for the upkeep of female members of the imperial family. A document which is entitled 'Collected Reports' provides a wealth of detailed information that could be forthcoming only from careful and efficient administration and record keeping, unless it had been invented fraudulently. We read of a total of 2,203 officials, ranging from the governor to clerks at the lowest level who were in post in the commandery, and of its measured territory and its registered population, numbered in terms of households and individuals. The document gives the extent of land under the plough and of that made over for orchards; there are accounts of the quantity of grain that had been distributed and of money received and spent. The figures for the population give a breakdown between the sexes and distinguish between certain age groups, and they give a figure of the number of vagrant persons whom officials had been able to reclaim and thus render liable for the statutory burdens of tax and service.

A second report gives a breakdown of the officials and junior staff serving in the headquarters of the commandery, its thirty-eight sub-units and in five agencies responsible for the production and distribution of salt and iron. The total figure of officials here is 2,202, almost identical with that of the 'Collected Reports' and perhaps deriving from a slightly different time. The counties and nobilities are listed in descending order according to the official rank or status of their magistrates and administrators (for details see p. 47 above and Chapter 3, Table 2). The numbers of their assistant staff members varied accordingly, corresponding with differences in the extent of the population. Thus magistrates with the title of *ling* 令 controlled 60 to 107 subordinates; those entitled *zhang* between 27 and 86. Junior staff members included prison officers, overseers, patrol leaders and village heads.

Two reports account for the promotion of 122 of the officials in the commandery. Promotion may have been granted in recognition of meritorious or special service, such as that of apprehending criminals or deserters, or it may have been due to length of service. Details include the place of original domicile of these officials, many of whom came from commanderies or kingdoms close to Donghai, but the distribution among the different provincial units is anything but random.

A further document sets out the reasons why certain named officials had been absent from their posts during the year in question. Some had been carrying money to the capital city or escorting men who had been sentenced to service at the frontier on their way to their destination. Others were absent owing to legal charges that they faced; some had been granted compassionate leave on the death of a close relative. Some had simply failed to take up duties at their post.

The finds from Yinwan also include a report that was entitled 'Collected Records of Arms, Vehicles and Equipment Held in the Arsenal in the Fourth Year of *Yongshi* 永始 [13 BCE]'. The list of items is formidable, as is seen above (Chapter 4, p. 65). The document poses the major question of whether it refers to a local arsenal situated in an area near the coast that would appear to have been free of threat, or to the major arsenal at Chang'an which has been subject to excavation. It seems difficult to explain why such a large stock of arms and armour should have been maintained in Donghai commandery.

From shortly before 100 BCE the expansionist policies of Wudi's reign saw the extension of the defence lines to the west, the growth of a line of communications and trade route that led into Central Asia and the establishment of organs of government in the present provinces of Gansu and beyond. The strength of the Chinese presence depended on the control that the armed forces could exercise over these remote regions and the protection that they could afford to travellers. Their ability to control and protect varied considerably over the decades, according to the strength and initiative of the home government and the degree of freedom from interference by the communities who lived beyond the pale. Although modelled partly on the administrative organs of the commanderies of the interior, those established here were not entirely normal, responding as they did to the possibility of threats from non-assimilated peoples and the need to maintain military preparations in good trim. Such conditions produced the documents of which we now have remnants. These were left by the armed forces in the barracks, storehouses and rubbish pits of the armed forces in the lines of Dunhuang and Juyan.

These military units were controlled by the commandants of the commanderies that were set up there in perhaps 111 or 104 BCE. The great majority of the documents were those needed to keep the armed forces in readiness for action and the sparse population of those parts under surveillance. The forces must be well disciplined, effectively organised and supplied with their needs, and they must be able to keep a watch for suspicious activities and inspect individuals who were active in the area. As a result, many of the types of report of which we have but fragments are not witnessed elsewhere; nor are they comparable with those found, for example, in Donghai commandery.

However, there is evidence to show that the officers and officials of the north-west were in contact with the central government and subject to its orders. Documents found at Juyan included texts or parts of texts of imperial decrees. There are also parts of an incomplete calendar which appears to have been a copy made locally but discarded by the clerk at an early stage owing to his inclusion of mistakes. It is likely that this was intended to be a copy of a calendar sent from the central government. There was also a formal report addressed to the central government of action taken against a potentially hostile leader of one of the unassimilated groups; it is drawn up with an eye to the niceties of reporting to the throne. The maintenance of records of mail (see p. 110 above) may likewise show the importance attached to keeping contact with neighbouring units and perhaps with authorities in the capital city.

The forces drew up or received lists of officers with details of their age, place of domicile and social status. Some such lists showed how the system of conscription operated, with men from the interior coming to serve their time on the frontier. The orderly rooms kept registers of military equipment such as javelins, or flags issued to named individuals, or of cattle kept in official charge. Other registers recorded the amounts of grain and salt distributed to officers, men and their families according to a scale of rations that varied with age and sex; one item refers to the issue of horse fodder. There are carefully kept records of the amounts of grain received and distributed as rations for servicemen by one of the major centres of supply.

There are also records of the issue of clothing to servicemen and of financial matters. Such lists recorded payments made as salaries to officials and officers, receipts of certain monies that were due and the purchase of consumable stores such as glue. One report lists the sums due to officers for salaries that were overdue; some strips refer to matters of taxation.

One report from Juyan shows that officers could face tests in archery every year according to carefully prescribed regulations. As was the case with officials posted to the commanderies of the interior, so here they were subject to assessment of their merits and the performance of their duties. Records give details of their length of service, and accomplishments such as an ability to write or to handle accounts. At the front line of defence, the small units of perhaps five men were subject to inspection of the equipment that they held, the state of the buildings that they occupied or guarded and their state of preparedness for action.

There are a number of reports of the activities and work to which the servicemen and their officers were put. They controlled passage through points of access to their lines, recording the names of travellers with their age, height and colouring and notes of any weapons that they carried and their horses and carriages. Details give the dates and times of entry or exit through the control points. A signals' log records the observation of flags or flares hoisted by neighbouring units up or down the line of defence posts, and one complete document lays down the code of signals to be followed. There are fragments of reports made after patrols had been ordered to inspect the area outside the immediate vicinity for signs of unaccountable or suspicious activities, and of the action that they took in response.

In one document, some officers needed to explain the circumstances in which they had injured and arrested one of two armed men whom they had encountered. A tantalisingly fragmentary account of an officer named Xi 熹 tells of how he observed some fires that required explanation; his report is couched in the terms used by junior officials in other reports, such as 'I fully realise that I stand in danger of a sentence of death'. On a more mundane level, reports tell of the regular and perhaps arduous work to which servicemen were put. They may have been out on patrol, or else they made and stacked sun-baked bricks, with a quota for their day's turn out. They worked as cooks for their units; they groomed horses; they tended gardens or orchards; or they may have been detailed for accountancy.

Attention has fastened hitherto on manuscript copies of documents found usually in parts and occasionally complete. In addition the three histories of the period, the *Shiji, Han shu* and *Hou Han shu,* include material that seems in all probability to have been drawn directly from archives held in the offices of the central government, subject to editorial change, greater or less as it might be.

One group of these chapters lists the kingdoms and nobilities of the empire with dates of their original foundation, their relationship to the imperial family, the reasons for the bestowal of the nobilities and the names of all those who succeeded to hold them, by way of hereditary transmission, with dates of tenure and closure. This information is set out in tabular form, together with notes of the circumstances in which these honours were brought to an end, and showing their history in chronological sequence. It seems likely that the historians who compiled the *Shiji* and the *Han shu* had at their disposal documents that an office of the central government maintained and kept up to date as an essential record of the privileges and obligations of many figures in public life.

A second group of chapters in the histories, which must surely draw from such archives, lists the major administrative units of kingdoms and commanderies with the titles of their constituent sub-units of county and nobility. The records chosen for inclusion date from 1–2 and 140 CE. They include figures for the registered population of each of the major units, both for the households and individuals. Notes appended to these lists at an early stage, possibly by the compiling historians themselves, provide further information. They tell of the history of these units, going back to pre-imperial times with circumstances in which they were founded or their status or titles changed; the notes include information of special features, such as the situation of an agency for salt, iron, clothing or orchards. Clearly such a record would have been of paramount importance to those who were organising and governing an empire.

The histories also include, again in tabular form, lists of those who held the senior offices of state from chancellor to the metropolitan superintendents with notes of the circumstances in which an office was vacated, be it by death, dismissal, suicide or punishment for crime. It is not certain whether these lists derived from documents drawn up by an office of the government or whether they were compiled at the initiative of the historians.

Notes for Further Reading

Tsuin-hsuin Tsien provides an account of the emergence of different types of written communications. Enno Giele maintains a database which lists all known wooden and silken manuscripts of the Han period (http://www. lehigh.edu/); see *RHA* for an explanation of some of these. Documents in tabular form have been transmitted as Chapters 13–22 of the *Shiji* and 13–20 of the *Han shu* (*Men Who Governed,* Chapters 7 and 8). For the postal service, see *Zhangjia shan* (Statutes), strip nos. 264–76; for the use of two thousand wagons to convey documents from Chang'an to Luoyang, see *HHS* 79A, p. 2548.

For facsimiles and annotated translations of wooden documents from Dunhuang and Juyan see Chavannes and *RHA*. Strips from Juyan refer to subjects that are mentioned in this chapter as follows (references are to strips as assembled in *RHA,* vol. 2): duplicate copies of reports (W 2); imperial decrees (UD 8); mail registers (MD 1–3; TD 1, 2; and X 1); special scribal treatment for references to the emperor (UD 9); Xi's report on the observation of wood fires (UD 6). For a code of signals, see the new finds from Juyan (EPF 16. 1–17). For delivery schedules, see *RHA,* vol. 1, pp. 43–44, and Hulsewé, *RCL,* p. 86; the latter book presents annotated versions of the legal documents of 217 BCE; for the dossier of a legal case of 28 CE, see the same author, 'A Lawsuit of A.D. 28'; for legal cases that were in doubt, see Shuihudi documents ('Feng zhen shi') and Zhangjia shan documents ('Zou yan shu'); for the records from Yinwan, see *Men Who Governed,* Chapter 2; for an incomplete, and faulty, calendar, see *RHA* (TD 10). For the manufacture of seals and its implications, see *SJ* 118, p. 3091; for Ma Yuan, *HHS* 24, p. 839 note 2.

8

The Laws of the Empire

Standing orders with which to regulate Qin and Han society and to deter and punish crime took the form of the statutes (*lü* 呂) and ordinances (*ling* 令), which were promulgated by imperial decree and circulated to provincial offices by the postal couriers. Of permanent application throughout the empire, these commands were the nearest equivalent to the laws that arose in other cultures, such as those of Israel, Athens, Sparta or Rome, but important conceptual differences separated those of China from those elsewhere.

The statutes and ordinances of the Qin and Han emperors were expedients designed to administer and control their populations; they derived from the experience, requests and decisions of officials, and they were intended to lay down the practical means of government and to solve problems that arose therein. For Israel, Greece and Rome the laws held a religious and intellectual authority of a higher order. The Torah conveyed God's commands to his people, revealing moral issues and prescribing the correct ways to seek holiness, perform rituals and conduct oneself in daily life. In Greece, some would say that the laws had sprung from the will or whim of the gods or from the intellectual achievement of a man such as Solon the Wise. Citizens of Rome looked back to the Twelve Tables inherited from the past but lost since 386 BCE, and they saw these as binding arrangements agreed between the two classes of society, the patricians and the plebeians.

In the West laws may have emerged from assemblies of the people, subject as these occasions were to the persuasions of the orators and the manipulations of the politicians. Emperors and officials of Qin and Han laboured under no such constraints of obedience to the voice or will of others, let alone that of a *demos*. Nor did those rulers enjoy the benefits of theoretical or analytical writings such as those of Plato, Aristotle or Cicero. And it cannot be conceived that, like the President of the United States of America or the sovereign constitutional monarch of the United Kingdom, a

Chinese emperor would have been content to bind himself to rule in accordance with the laws of the land.

It is thus hard, or even impossible, to discern an abstract concept of law in China's early empires in the way that this had been emerging elsewhere. We would look in vain for statements of the rights, obligations or privileges of either those who governed or those who were governed; nor can we find a theoretical discussion or definition of what Western cultures term 'justice'. There is also an important usage of terminology. 'Statutes' and 'ordinances' denote particular types of order or document; the term *fa* 法, meaning originally 'model', later came to be used in legal terminology, even to denote a 'law', but it is not used in this way in the early empires.

The statutes and ordinances of Qin and Han did not set out to protect men and women from the oppression of officials, though such intentions are sometimes visible in their provisions. Their purpose was to maintain law and order and to control the people and their work on the land. Carefully regulated sanctions and punishments instructed officials how to eliminate crime. Other rules distinguished between individuals on the basis of kinship or privilege and set out the means of collecting revenue. Insofar as the statutes and ordinances included punitive measures for failure to obey, they differed from the provisions of *li* 禮, those recognised conventions of behaviour that were designed to maintain the stability of a community with its inbuilt social relationships and hierarchies.

Couriers of the postal service conveyed copies of these laws up and down the empire; written as they were on long strips (see p. 105 above), safe carriage without breakage may at times have been hazardous. Until quite recently our knowledge of these texts was severely limited, depending on citations that may have been of no more than fragments preserved fortuitously. These appear in writings of later times, and they do not note the date when a law was formulated or when it operated. This situation changed radically, for the better, with the discovery of two sets of wooden documents that carried the texts of Statutes and Ordinances of Qin in 217 BCE, and of Han in 186 BCE.

Later records show that these sets were no more than small selections of the laws already formulated in those early days of imperial rule. Some had indeed derived from the kingdoms of pre-imperial times, and, although officials of Han claimed that they had simplified the complex rules of their immediate and as alleged cruel predecessors, it is only too likely that the Han dynasty inherited and practised them with little change or mitigation of the severities with which the Qin emperors were charged. Several identical or near identical titles appear in the Statutes of 217 and 186 BCE, such as the statutes on agriculture, the establishment of officials, statutory service, currency, checking and the issue of rations from staging posts. Certainly some modifications of Qin's punishments were introduced later, and as will be seen many accretions developed. Some of the Qin and Han statutes and ordinances survived with full authority for some four hundred years.

The new finds give the texts of eighteen statutes of Qin, with selections from some others (217 BCE), and twenty-seven statutes and one ordinance of Han (186 BCE). Both in these manuscripts and in citations known from other sources, a title defines the broad content or subject; in some cases there is a serial notation, such as 'Ordinance A'. Both the statutes and the ordinances could include several items or clauses that were of a related nature and might themselves be numbered. Sixteen such items survive of the twenty-three at least that were included in the single ordinance of which we have a manuscript text, 'Ordinance on Points of Control at Waterways and Passes'.

The two categories of statutes and ordinances do not seem to differ in respect of the subjects that they cover but there may have been a formal distinction, at least in some cases. The statutes lay down procedures to be followed and penalties for failure to do so, and they write with the assured authority of a command that cannot be questioned. The ordinance of which we have parts included accounts of the steps that preceded the formulation of a new set of orders; its items record a request made by a provincial official for authority to act in a certain way, the transmission of such a request to higher authorities and the grant of imperial permission to proceed, in the form of a decree. It cannot be known whether such was the regular form of other ordinances, of which we possess no more than fragmentary citations.

From Qin the Han empire inherited six chapters of statutes and ordinances which may have been adopted earlier by Shang Yang 商鞅 (ca. 385–338 BCE) as part of his work in strengthening the discipline of the kingdom of Qin. Xiao He 蕭何 (chancellor of state 198 BCE; d. 193 BCE), who is often described as one of the founding fathers of the Han empire, added three chapters to this nucleus; his near contemporary Shusun Tong 叔孫通 (superintendent of cere-monial 195 BCE; d. before 188 BCE), who was responsible for for-malising court procedure and state rituals, added a further eighteen. By the middle of Western Han there existed a total of sixty chapters, nearly half of which had come from the hand of Zhang Tang 張湯, a well-known specialist in legal matters who held the post of superintendent of trials from 126 to 120 BCE.

At the same time legal documents of other types were taking shape in ever increasing volume. There were dossiers of individual cases, recording how they had passed from one level of authority to another until a decision was granted. Officials who found themselves in a quandary would submit a detailed account of an incident and the steps already taken, asking for guidance or a definite instruction on how to proceed. There were also voluminous writings by schol-ars who set out to explain the meaning of some of the basic docu-ments, word-by-word and sentence-by-sentence. By Eastern Han this latter category of writings amounted, as it was said, to over twenty-six thousand items.

Administration of the laws and the conduct of criminal cases could thus present an official with a need to consult a large and cumbersome body of material, which may or may not have been easily available. In addition precedents and legal decisions had often resulted from incidents that had arisen at different times and in a variety of circumstances. Attempts to reduce this volume of writing from time to time apparently brought little improvement to a diffi-cult situation; rules that concerned one and the same subject could lie dispersed in different documents, or they could be duplicated or appear in inconsistent form.

Nevertheless some attempts were made, perhaps at the initiative of an official who had himself faced such problems. Perhaps circa 75 CE Chen Chong 陳寵 or Bao Yu 鮑昱 produced a treatise, in seven sections, in which he tried to set up categories whereby judi-cial decisions could or should be taken. Shortly after 220 CE officials of Wei 魏, one of the three kingdoms that exercised control over parts of the Han empire, set up a commission of six men who were to produce a new corpus of statutes and ordinances, judiciously selecting items from existing documents. Their labours did little to decrease the bulk of the documentation or ease the work of their colleagues; these officials were now faced with four categories of laws: New Statutes (18 chapters), Ordinances for Provincial Units (45 chapters), Ordinances of the Secretariat and Ordinances for Military Purposes, in all more than 180 chapters.

In general the laws were concerned with the safety of the realm, taking note of the dangers of defection, and with the operation of government as seen in the establishment and grades of officials and the scope of their authority, and in matters of security, fraud and the authenticity of documents. The laws affected the daily, working lives of the population, as seen in agricultural practice, schedules for marketing, the transport of goods, minting of coins, allocation and tenure of land, the scale of taxation and cases of exemption from such burdens and control of travel within the empire. They specified punishments for crimes of violence, such as murder, armed robbery, injury inflicted on human beings and livestock, rape and kidnapping. They also laid down punishments for theft, for desertion so as to evade tax and service and for the export of gold and contraband goods. The statutes brought out the effect of social distinctions, such as the privileges attached to the orders of honour (see Chapter 9 below), and the rules for the inheritance of property. They also laid down some of the procedure, such as for denunciations and the conduct of trials in criminal cases.

Particular subjects in which these laws were concerned varied considerably, from false denunciation of a person for crime to the manufacture and use of poison, or from the limits of an official's jurisdiction to rewards for the arrest of criminals. Material matters also featured, including the delivery of tax paid in kind, such as hay or straw; a ban on felling trees at certain times of the year; taxation levied from traders; and the distribution of food to those in need. The following examples of the items mentioned in the Statutes and Ordinances of 186 BCE may give an idea of the variety of subjects that could be included under each one. They also show that the process of dispersal of legal orders under different headings and duplication had already set in.

> *Dao lü* 盜律, Statute on Robbery, in twenty-six strips: penalties for stolen goods; connivance at robbery; bribery; theft by a

person from outside the frontier; robbery by a group; infliction of bodily harm; anonymous accusations; threats to seize money or goods; grave robbery; impersonation of an official; awareness of kidnapping; removal of goods outside the border; export of gold.

Jun shu lü 均輸律, Statute of the Transport of Goods, in three strips: transport of goods through points of control by wagon or boat.

Jin guan ling 津關令, Ordinance on Points of Control at Waterways and Passes, in thirty-eight strips: unauthorised transit at points of control; passports; export of gold; permitted transit through points of control; marks on property; deaths outside the frontier; possession, control of the movement, registration, purchase of horses and their allocation for official purposes; movement of conscript servicemen between counties or commanderies; request to set up a point of control.

The following examples, of which the first two date from 217 BCE and the other three from 186 BCE, show how the laws might be formulated.

(a) From the Statutes on Artisans: When making accounts, items that are not of the same norm must not be listed in the same way.

(b) From the Statutes for the Establishment of Officials: When prefectures, general offices or the twelve commanderies dismiss or appoint officials as well as assistants and subordinates of the multitude of offices, they dismiss and appoint them as from the first day of the twelfth month, ceasing to do so at the end of the third month. In case of death or abscondence as well as when there are old vacancies, in order to fill these, one should not wait for the time (mentioned above).

(c) From the Statute on Violence: Fraudulent manufacture of some of the emperor's personal seals is punishable by execution at the waist by way of warning.

(d) From the Statute on Arrests: Outbreaks of robbery by a group or of violence perpetrated by robbers are to be reported to officials. If officials conceal such reports without informing the authorities of the county, or if thanks to a delay of a full day in so doing the criminals are not caught, those who are responsible are to be brought to trial by means of prosecution.

(e) From the Statute on Coinage: Those who, being aware that others are counterfeiting coins, buy copper or charcoal for them, or circulate coins thus newly made, are guilty of the same crime as the counterfeiters.

The manuscripts of 217 and 186 BCE each include documents of a different type, being accounts of actual cases in which complexities had arisen and an official felt it necessary to submit a report, perhaps seeking authority to take action. The twenty-five cases of 217 are varied. A father requests permission to have his son banished to distant Shu (modern Sichuan) for reasons that are not stated. In another instance a father denounces his son for failure to carry out his filial duties and requests that he be put to death. Other reports concern a suspected case of leprosy and the examination of the corpse of a suicide, brought about by hanging. A daring feat by thieves who dug a tunnel to stage a robbery in a house drew a detailed report of which any police officer might feel be proud. A man who stole 1,000 cash gave himself up and denounced his accomplice, who had failed to do so. Two men disputed ownership of a cow; a villager brought in a female slave said to be obstreperous, with a request that she be punished by tattooing and amputation of her nose. A commoner brought in a man and a woman whom he had arrested and fettered on the grounds that he had seen them fornicating. Attention to the cases reported for 186 BCE will follow later (see p. 130).

Wilful neglect of the provisions of the statutes and ordinances and criminal offences could incur punishment, usually of a severe type. There were several ways of inflicting the death penalty; hard labour sentences ran for varying periods of time; and different parts of the body could suffer disfigurement or mutilation. Criminals could face fines of differing sums of money, reduction of social status or banishment to distant places in the empire. Even if they were officials they could be flogged mercilessly, or they could be banned from holding further office.

These punishments were designed to put an end to further criminal activity outright or to provide men to work under compulsion at official behest. They could bring discredit or shame to a wrongdoer and his family, or they could make a criminal immediately identifiable by a glance at his or her body. Some of these punishments could be combined, such as hard labour service and mutilation, though it is difficult to see how such convicts could provide valuable forms of labour, if hampered, for example, by the loss of a leg or a foot. Close relatives of a criminal might be subject to punishment; payment of large sums of money could secure redemption.

A choice of different ways of carrying out the death penalty may have depended on the type of crime committed, but it is difficult to discern any fixed principles that discriminated between execution with display of the body, decapitation with display of the head, execution in public and execution at the waist. The Statutes of 186 BCE prescribe these punishments for murder and crimes of various degrees, including parricide, violence, counterfeiting the seals of the emperor or his officials and marriage, or sexual relations, between a slave and his master's wife.

Sentences to hard labour ran from one to five, and exceptionally six, years. Such convicts might be held under close watch or detention; they might be shackled or fettered; and some might suffer amputation of a foot or a leg. These punishments were given for plotting murder or violence without causing death and for injury wrought on others or self-inflicted with a view to evading statutory service. The documents record cases of a sentence of five years' hard labour for striking one's superiors, the sale or purchase of human beings, forgery of documents and adultery. A boatman who carelessly allowed his passengers to drown was liable to the same punishment, as were wives who beat their husbands. Theft or abandonment of documents and officials seals, and entry of false returns of age in the official registers, carried the same penalty. Technical terms which denoted these sentences refer to types of work to which the convicts were put, such as *cheng dan* 城旦 for men and *chong* 舂 for women. These were sentences of five years spent 'building walls and standing guard duty from early dawn' and 'grain pounding'. It is unlikely that convicts were restricted to the work that is specified in this way.

Mutilation ran from tattooing, removal of the hair, amputation of the nose or of one or two feet to castration. Slaves, whether male or female, could suffer tattooing on the cheeks or the forehead. According to an anecdote it was thanks to an appeal launched by the daughter of a well-known physician that mutilating punishments were abolished in 167 BCE. There are nonetheless attested cases of castration thereafter, including that of the historian Sima Qian 司馬遷 (d. ca. 90 BCE). A plea for its abolition that an official entered in about 100 CE indicates that it was still in practice.

By contrast with the documents of 217 BCE which laid down fines in terms of a suit of armour or a shield, those of 186 BCE specify fines in units of gold, which range from 1 *liang* 兩 (15.24 grams; valued at 625 cash coins) to 1 *jin* 斤 (244 grams; 10,000 coins). It cannot be told how realistic these sums were or whether it was realistic to expect those that are stated to be actually paid and collected. For purposes of comparison one strip in the documents gives a price of 15 cash for a *shi* 石 (30 kilograms) of hay and 5 cash for that quantity of straw. A further reference to sums needed for redemption from punishments will be seen below.

The great majority of the fines that are mentioned were of 4 or 2 *liang* (2,500 or 1,250 coins). Four *liang* was the fine set for crimes such as accidentally caused fires, inaccurate reports of crime and striking persons of superior social status. Women who wilfully engaged in fighting and thereby suffered a miscarriage paid the same penalty, as did those persons who levied taxation without due authority, or either altered or damaged an official building. A fine of 2 *liang* was charged for striking a person of equal social status, loss of documents, interference with the city's gates and their locks and for each day of delay in registering the sale and purchase of land.

In 186 BCE the scale of the sums which could secure redemption from punishment ran to higher figures, for example, 10,000 cash for amputation of the nose or tattooing and 25,000 cash for the death penalty. The laws of that year provided for redemption both for those sentences and others, such as hard labour, and other forms of mutilation. In case of inability to find the ready cash, it was possible to fulfil these obligations, or at least part of them, by personal labour. This was reckoned at different rates, according to the type of punishment being redeemed, at perhaps 6 or 8 cash for each day's work; it is unlikely that many criminals could free themselves from dire punishments in this way.

Convicts on hard labour might also suffer flogging, which could extend to up to five hundred strokes, if we may believe our sources, and if we can further believe that survival after such harsh treatment was possible. Some sources specify a sentence of one hundred strokes, and regulations specified the length of the birch and the manner of administering this punishment. A hundred strokes awaited slaves who returned to their masters after making a bid for freedom. Fifty strokes was the lot of civilians or officials who likewise returned of their own volition after flight from their place of domicile or duty; payment of 1 *liang* secured exemption.

Some crimes were punished by forced service of two years at the garrisons of the north-west. That same penalty could apply to false or unreliable sponsorship of a person to be an official, or falsification of the ownership of land or residences. As will be seen below (Chapter 9) certain privileges such as mitigation of punishments were attached to the grant of some of the orders of honour and their attendant social status. Some punishments could take the form of a reduction of that status. Banishment could be added to some sentences, and it could be applied by decree to some of the highest in the land whose activities had rendered their presence at court or in the capital undesirable. Criminals sentenced to hard labour were at times subjected to further misery; their nearest relatives, women and children alike, might be detained under custody and put to work as officials might direct.

Criminal trials, which were conducted at various levels of the government, followed the receipt of information that any man or woman could bring to notice regarding the activities or suspicious conduct of anyone else. Members of the responsibility groups to be described below (Chapter 9) were in fact obliged to make such denunciations; in some cases criminals would denounce themselves voluntarily in the belief that such confessions would allow a reduction of the sentence that was their due. In such a way accomplices to some crimes, such as kidnapping, were not brought to face a charge if they had denounced their colleagues. Some types of written denunciation, perhaps those delivered anonymously, were ignored. Denunciations could be made verbally or in writing and they might be accompanied by a certificate of the truth of what was stated therein. Manifestly false denunciations were punishable. In addition to these ways in which a criminal case could start, commoners could apprehend and bring in suspects for investigation by officials.

The carefully staged and lengthy procedures that followed might be subject to delay owing to the sickness or absence on duty of any one of the parties concerned, and no official business took place on statutory days of rest. There was a lapse of 469 days before the conclusion of one somewhat complex case to be summarised below (p. 131); the actual hearing took place on no more than eighteen days.

Criminal trials could involve up to four stages, some of these being repeated. Initially an accused person faced an interrogation in which he or she was required to give an account of what had taken place. Next, officials would press the accused, asking for an explanation of the actions taken. Such an examination could lead to a confession of criminal activity and an indictment. In a third stage officials would question other parties to obtain corroboration from an external source of what had been stated; once satisfied they could conclude that the case was proven. The final, fourth, type of enquiry concerned the legal aspects. In this stage officials needed to know which, if any, of the statutes or ordinances applied to the case in question, so that they could take the right action and pronounce the correct sentence without fear of prosecution themselves.

The documents of 217 BCE provide a few instructions that cover the conduct of these trials. Identification of persons was necessary, with their names, status, place of domicile and reasons for the charge. In their efforts to obtain statements from a defendant, officials should not resort to flogging, for flogging could throw a case into disarray; such is indeed shown in one of the cases cited below (pp. 131–33). Even when it was clear that a defendant had been lying, officials should refrain from exerting undue pressure. But repeated lying or changes of a statement warranted flogging, provided both that the statutes allowed it and that a report was entered of the action taken.

Declared guilty, a criminal could lodge an appeal, but if this was not upheld the rating of the crime and its punishment would be increased by one degree. Those facing the death penalty could not themselves appeal but their close relatives were entitled to do so on their behalf, to be tattooed and sent down for hard labour in case of failure. Appeals made by children under ten would not be heard, nor those that were lodged a full year after a decision had been given. Starting at county level this process would be referred to the higher authority of the commandery and perhaps to officials of the central government.

The documents of 186 BCE include reports of twenty-two incidents or cases where application of the laws may have been in doubt. As distinct from those of 217 BCE, where neither dates nor names are given for the individuals who committed an outrage, suffered harm or faced a charge and a sentence, those who feature in the reports of 186 BCE are all identified and dates are provided. A number of these cases are concerned with misdemeanours of officials or their failure to fulfil their duties, such behaviour being taken as prima facie evidence for crime.

The subordinate officials of Shu commandery (modern Sichuan) faced charges of misuse for their own private purposes of the work of criminals who were serving sentences of hard labour. In Nanjun (modern Hubei) no less a person than a magistrate of a county was involved in the theft of grain that was in official ownership. A local official of Huaiyang (modern Henan) entered into a conspiracy to have a man killed who might otherwise have incriminated him. A prison official of the metropolitan area misused another person's passport to allow a woman illegal passage through a point of control; on another occasion conscript servicemen and officials in Beidi (modern Shaanxi) failed to prevent a slave from escaping through such a point. Another prison official concealed the presence of a deserter. A postal official, in Hedong (modern Shanxi), had retained mail for eight days, making a fraudulent entry in a document during the process. Bribery featured at least once in Hedong, when a criminal who had stolen documents escaped from arrest; his mother had been imprisoned in his place, to be released on the timely appearance of a pig and some measures of alcoholic drink. In one case, which dates from pre-imperial times, the ruler of Lu (modern Shandong) confirmed the judicial sentence proposed for theft and deception.

Activities of women and men who were not officials occur in some of the other cases. One of these centred round a woman's flight from her home and place of registration (in the metropolitan area) to accept service in some form of bondage. Her master had her married to a man without informing him that she had been a deserter. The laws, however, provided that marriage to a deserter was an offence which incurred tattooing and a sentence of five years' hard labour. The husband's plea of ignorance did not save him from a sentence. Deceit entered into another case, in Shu. This involved a plot to steal a licence for a privately owned horse and to forge the brand marks that would identify the animal. Elsewhere, a man who had been accused of entering into a conspiracy to steal an ox protested his innocence. On appeal he was exonerated when another party to the case was shown to have been lying. Fear of flogging, perhaps for a second time, had induced some of these parties to make false statements.

The documents of 186 BCE include a long account, which runs to thirty-seven strips, of a criminal case that had come up for review. As may be seen in the following summary, it was a case of considerable complexity, involving many of the procedural steps that have been mentioned. Insofar as the magistrate of a county was under accusation it was not a run-of-the-mill case.

By written orders of the imperial counsellor dated on a day corresponding with 1 April 220 BCE officials of Nanjun commandery re-opened a case in which accusations had been raised against Tui, magistrate of You 攸 county, which was presumably a constituent county of Nanjun. For various reasons which included the sickness of one of the officials concerned, the case was not concluded until 24 November 219 BCE. The case followed incidents of unrest in which some of the local inhabitants of lands newly acquired from Chu (taken over by Qin by 223 BCE) had been called out to suppress dissidents and bandits but had failed to bring them to heel. Altogether three attempts had been made to do so without success and at the cost of some casualties, including that of a man named Yi 義 who had been killed. Fearing punishment for their failure, the local inhabitants had fled with the arms that they had been lent and remained concealed in the hills.

Although lists had been drawn up with the names of those local inhabitants who had been defeated in the fighting and were due for arrest, such lists had been confused, with the result that it had not been possible to identify those who should have been arrested. Attempts to induce those who had sought refuge in the hills to come out had failed.

The case concerned a number of matters that were subject to criminal proceedings: allegations that a colleague of the magistrate had warned Tui that he could not hope to suppress the dissidents, thereby giving rise to suspicion of cowardice or even treachery; suppression of facts in the reports of the incidents; discrepancies in the statements made by officials; an intention to release suspect criminals without proceeding to judgement; loss or abandonment of official documents; failure to go to the assistance of one's own side during fighting; a show of cowardice and refusal to fight in the face of an enemy; and failure to make a reconnaissance when confronting an enemy. A number of these actions are defined as criminal in the Qin Statutes of 217 BCE or the Han Statutes of 186 BCE.

The dossier does not include the terms of the original accusation made against Tui, but it covers all stages of the review of the case. This started with statements made by Tui and others, including Shi 氏, officer in charge of criminal cases in You county, whose evidence was to be of prime importance. There followed:

1. Indictment of Shi, including a reference to his interrogation by officials, with a demand for an explanation of his actions; Shi succeeded in clearing himself.
2. Indictment of Tui, with his denial that he had released criminals without trial.
3. A second indictment of Tui, with his admission that he had in fact behaved criminally.
4. Investigation of the case to procure evidence with which to corroborate or deny the statements already made; this concerned the failure to maintain correct records whereby the criminals could be identified and the preparation of an accusation against the magistrate's clerk who had been responsible for handling records.
5. A legal enquiry; this determined that certain facts were to be accepted as proven, cited an ordinance and a statute that had a bearing on the case, gave the decision that these applied to Tui and declared the punishment to which he was sentenced.

The ordinance that was cited provided that officials who took to flight when encountering one of the many robber bands who operated in the newly acquired territories should be tried according to the Statute for Cowardice and failure to engage in battle. That statute laid down the punishment of execution for cowardice, and that of tattooing with five years' hard labour for setting incarcerated prisoners free; those who were of a status of two degrees higher than commoners would suffer removal of the hair and hard labour for three years. Such regulations were judged to apply to the magistrate of You; he duly merited removal of the hair and three years' hard labour and was put under detention.

At least two discrepancies were under consideration: (1) Tui's statement that two colleagues, the acting magistrate of Cangwu and the commandant, had warned him of the possibilities of failure to suppress the rebels; these two officials denied this. (2) The first of Shi's two statements did not mention the difficulties due to the confusion in the registers.

Unfortunately we possess no documents that bear on the state of the law and practice of trials in Eastern Han and that are of the same type as those quoted here. The items of punishment set out so clearly for Qin and at the outset of Western Han were certainly severe enough, and it is probable that they were indeed put into practice, perhaps to a greater degree of rigor than Han memorialists would like to have mentioned. It can only remain open to question how effective these measures were over the centuries in eliminating crime and stabilising Chinese society. In all probability the degree of success varied from time to time and place to place, perhaps dependent on the character or efficiency of provincial and local officials. Much later, in Eastern Han, when social and political conditions were perhaps giving rise to some anxiety, we hear a voice complaining that the rules and sanctions of the laws as practised were insufficient to keep the peace of the realm. In expressing these views circa 150 CE, Cui Shi 崔寔 even insisted that 'severity ensures order, while indulgence ends in anarchy'. Some fifty years later Zhongchang Tong 仲長統 re-iterated this call for a return to the imposition of harsh sentences, maintaining that they were as necessary and valuable as medicaments and treatments are to the body; and he even claimed that in place of the mitigations that had been ascribed to the time of Wendi (r. 180–157 BCE) the measures taken then had actually added to the cruelties of the law rather than mitigated their severities.

Notes for Further Reading

For accounts of the statutes and ordinances of Qin and Han, see Hulsewé, *RCL* and *RHL*. Further information is available in *Jin shu,* Chapter 30, pp. 915–23. For a legal dossier, see Hulsewé, 'A Lawsuit of A.D. 28'. Extracts of statutes as quoted above, pp. 124–25, items (a) to (e), are from documents from Shuihudi (translated in Hulsewé, *Remnants of Ch'in Law* A 53, A 79), and Zhangjia shan (Statutes), strip nos. 9, 146, 203. For accounts of investigations or trials of cases that were subject to doubt, see documents from Shuihudi, 'Feng zhen shi' (Hulsewé, *RCL,* pp. 183–207), and Zhangjia shan, 'Zou yan shu' (for the case which concerned Nanjun, strips nos. 124–61, pp. 223–25). The plea by Chunyu Yi's daughter for the abolition of mutilating punishments is related in *SJ* 105, p. 2795. For the rules for flogging, see Hulsewé, *RHL,* p. 128; for Cui Shi and Zhongchang Tong, see Balazs, pp. 209, 222; and *CHOC,* pp. 292, 311. For Chen Chong's attempted reforms, see *HHS* 46, pp. 1548–49.

9

Management of the People

It would be inappropriate or even incorrect to apply the term 'citizen' to the men and women of the Qin and Han empires. Unlike some, but by no means all, of those who dwelt in Athens they did not take an active part in determining the decisions taken in the name of and on behalf of all the inhabitants of the city-state. They did not pride themselves on being identified as members of a great community, as did the *cives* of the Republic or Empire of Rome, enjoying certain definable rights for which their ancestors had fought. It is unlikely that they would have responded to a call addressed to *citoyens* to unite and fight in the face of a despotic oppression, under the slogan of *liberté, égalité, fraternité*. The practice of casting a vote to determine the opinion of a majority and thereby to convey authority for actions would have been quite alien, and the evidence at our disposal allows no hint of a principle of equal treatment under the law for all. First and foremost, those who lived in the empires of Qin and Han were subjects of their emperor, obliged to obey his commands, to carry out the orders of his officials, to accept the distinctions of social rank, and to comply with the sanctions of the laws imposed upon them. Such distinctions ranged from the kings, second only to the emperor, to commoners, convicts and slaves.

Emperors and officials kept the inhabitants of the land under control by means of three institutions which had emerged separately but had become interdependent. The gift of orders of honour (*jue* 爵) conferred and defined degrees of social status and with it a place on a scale of privileges. Organisation by the household (*hu* 戶) served to extract a poll tax and a tax on the land, and to mobilise labour for the welfare and work needed in the empire. The responsibility groups (*wu* 伍) acted as unofficial guardians of the law, keeping watch for crime and reporting it as it occurred. In all cases these three institutions operated over the smallest possible groups or units within a community.

Whatever the principles and practice may have been under the kings of Western Zhou (1045–771 BCE) and in the succeeding Spring and Autumn period (770–481), a recognised scale of social status came into existence in the kingdom of Qin and to some extent in some of the other kingdoms of the Warring States period (480–221 BCE). It was possibly, or even probably, due to Shang Yang 商鞅 (ca. 385–338 BCE), whose leadership gave Qin the discipline with which to muster its strength of human and other resources and the will to use that strength to expand its territories, that a system of social ranks was formulated and applied to the whole population. In its turn, the Han empire inherited the system from Qin, giving it a new force and adding new purposes to the institution.

Under Shang Yang and later a series of orders of honour, or orders of aristocratic rank (*jue*), comprised seventeen degrees. They were conferred on individuals as a reward for particular acts of military service; for example, the lowest order in the series was granted for putting to death one enemy soldier, the next highest for killing two soldiers. The orders might also be given for peaceful services, such as the provision of grain where it was needed. In the fighting that followed the collapse of Qin's imperial authority (210 BCE), a number of the men who had supported Liu Bang 劉邦 and helped him to found the Han dynasty received these marks of honour and status as rewards for their success in battle. Thus Fan Kuai 樊噲 received successive orders for putting to death fifteen, twenty-three and then sixteen men; in a later exploit he put fourteen men to death and captured eleven, thereby earning the ninth order, termed *wu dafu* 五大夫. Once the Han dynasty had been established, the system comprised twenty orders, of which the highest two, noble of the interior (*guannei hou* 館內侯) and noble (*hou* 侯), were in a distinctly higher category than the other eighteen.

In no way can the system of *jue* be equated with distinctions of class and ranks as seen in the European orders of chivalry or the distinctions between free and slave, landowner and peasant, or employer and employee. In a new development, of Han times, bestowal of the orders of honour came to fulfil another purpose, that of displaying the majesty of the emperor and the beneficent care with which he treated his people. Between 202 BCE and 168 CE decrees conferred one order of honour on a general basis to one member of each registered household, probably its head; these gifts marked events such as the accession of an emperor or the nomination of his heir apparent. The same type of bounty accompanied religious observances in 205, 113 and 110 BCE and the occurrence of a solar eclipse in 53 and 147 CE. The frequency with which these general bestowals of imperial gifts took place varied considerably, and they were by no means exceptional or rare, being staged sometimes in every second or third year. Such frequency had in no way rendered them meaningless, as it was possible to accumulate orders, reaching up the scale to the eighth, *gongcheng* 公乘. On some occasions a general declaration of an amnesty for criminals, or a distribution of food and drink, accompanied the gift of the orders.

In addition to the general bestowals there were times when localised groups of the population received these gifts, perhaps as a reward for special services, or by way of help in moments of suffering, or to induce disaffected persons to desert the cause of a rebel leader. In about 167 BCE it was proposed to offer high-ranking orders to tempt members of the general public to move from their homes with their families and go north, to set up agricultural colonies. Certain individuals who had rendered valuable services, such as suggesting means of achieving economic stability, could likewise receive these high honours, even extending to that of noble of the interior.

Members of the public were also able to enhance their social status by purchasing these marks of distinction with ready cash. The government would grant these marks of honour to the rich in return for relief supplied to those in want, for completing certain good works or simply for making contributions to a sorely depleted treasury. In 123 BCE this principle was extended by the establishment of a separate series of orders supposedly for military service or achievement; large sums of money were involved in obtaining these orders, about which information is scanty.

The orders were worth a price, in view of the benefits and privileges that they brought to recipients of the honour. In some ways the social prestige that they brought might be obvious for all to see, as in the provision that only those of the eighth order and above were entitled to wear the distinctive head-dress associated with the Han imperial family. The value of the *jue* also appears in a negative way in the punishments that could follow false claims to their possession. Parts of a document found in the garrison lines of Juyan which is dated up to 62 BCE show how registers sometimes recorded the receipt of these orders and the dates when they were conferred.

Both the theoretical and the practical significance of the orders is apparent in their regular inclusion in documents such as legal dossiers in which individuals were identified according to their place of domicile, orders that they held, age and perhaps bodily features. Notification of social status in this way was essential in some official transactions and legal cases, as the orders carried with them the right to privileged treatment, such as a mitigation of punishments to which criminals were sentenced. In this way long terms of hard labour could be reduced for those with the second order or for their wives, and elderly or young relatives of those with the first order might receive exemption from all punishment. By extension the principle could enable those who held the orders to surrender them in return for reducing the punishment imposed on their relatives.

In addition the orders carried one highly valuable material gift that could provide many with a livelihood; they entitled the holder to an allocation of land and dwellings. The extent of the allocation varied considerably according to status; holders of the nineteenth order received 95 *qing* 頃 of land, those of the first order 1.5 *qing,* where the *qing* corresponded to about 11 English acres. In this way the system of orders of honour acted as an incentive to promote agricultural work, and they came the way of a large number of members of the population. At the death of a holder, his heir was entitled to receive an order of lower rank by one degree, and this could even be given to sons borne posthumously. As a result youths of twelve or sixteen years are known in the records as holding the status of the second and fourth orders, and one of eighteen years had reached the eighth order. Exceptionally we hear of an orphaned child of seven years who received an official appointment and the nineteenth order of honour; these gifts acknowledged the services that his grandfather had paid to the reigning emperor (Xuandi; r. 74–48).

Small groups of men and women lived together as a family (*jia* 家), whose unity presumably depended on bonds of kinship. Such a unity and identity assumed a particularly important place in religious matters such as the rites of funerals and obligations for mourning, and the family might well include members of different generations, with widening degrees of relationship. In official and legal terms however the family was not a definable, recognised unit. From the point of view of the government, the population consisted of households. These may be regarded as units that existed for working purposes, and they were the basic units whereby the lives of individuals could be controlled and taxation raised. It seems that it was only in Han, and not before then, that the unit of the *hu* came to play this role. An old rule of Qin had penalised groups of inhabitants who lived together and included more than one able-bodied male, but it is not known how far this applied either to the families or to the households in the empires of Qin or Han or how far it forced such units to divide.

Membership of a household would often include parents and children, perhaps with a grandparent, and there could thus well be some measure of identity between the family and the household, but there was no reason why the households would necessarily include all members of a family. There was also a close relationship between the households and the occupation of land for productive work, but whereas something is known of the circumstances and conditions in which land was allocated to the households, much remains that is uncertain. In addition to receipt of an allocation of land in respect of the orders of honour, it was possible to acquire some acres by means of inheritance or purchase, or perhaps by unrestricted reclamation. But in all these cases little can be said regarding the conditions of tenure or legal rights of ownership.

Each year officials of the provincial units drew up counts of the population in their areas and forwarded them to the central government. To do so, they depended on registration of those who lived there, and, although it was incumbent on all individuals to ensure that their names and details were entered on such documents, these cannot be taken as providing a census of the whole population; they were counts of all those persons whom the officials had succeeded in finding and identifying and thereby rendering subject to statutory obligations. That severe penalties attended flight and avoidance of registration and its consequences argues that it may not have been an uncommon practice.

Officials of the districts and counties drew up registers of five types giving details of the dwellings, the extent of arable land, the ages of those living thereon and the sum of the land tax due; the documents may also have included notes of the quality of the land and its suitability for different purposes. Individuals were identified as members of the households that worked on the allocation of land that they had received or otherwise obtained, and these documents provided the information on which to base calculations of the land and poll taxes. The commandery forwarded these reports to the central government, whose officials could draw up a general report of the extent of the registered population and of the areas of arable land in the whole empire.

Summaries of these full-scale reports survive for the years 1–2 and 140 CE, giving figures of households and their individual members for each of the commanderies and kingdoms of the day. The great variety in the size of the population in these units is due to a number of causes. Differences of climate and terrain were of considerable importance. Close to the centre, the degree of administration was likely to be more intense than at the perimeter, with the result that although the commanderies may well have been of smaller size, their inhabitants were liable to more energetic official activities. At the edge of the empire, commanderies were more widespread and subject to a far looser scrutiny. Examples of some of the counts that have been preserved in the Standard Histories follow.

	(a)	(b)	(c)	(d)	(e)	(f)
		FOR 1–2 BCE				
Runan	461,587	2,596,148	5.6	37	12,475	70,167
Donghai	358,414	1,559,357	4.3	38	9,431	41,035
Kuaiji	223,038	1,032,604	4.6	26	8,578	39,715
Qijun	154,826	554,444	3.5	12	12,902	46,203
Lujiang	124,383	457,323	3.6	12	10,365	38,110
Shangdang	73,798	337,766	4.5	14	5,271	24,126
Changsha guo	43,470	235,825	4.4	13	3,343	18,140
Wu guo	36,773	140,772	3.8	4	9,193	35,193
Liang guo	38,709	106,752	2.7	8	4,838	13,334
Nanhai	19,613	94,253	4.8	6	3,368	15,708
Dunhuang	11,200	38,335	3.4	6	1,866	6,389

	(a)	(b)	(c)	(d)	(e)	(f)
		FOR 1–2 CE				
Nanyang	528,551	2,439,610	4.6	37	14,285	65,935
Runan	404,440	2,100,788	5.1	37	10,930	56,778
Changsha guo	255,854	1,509,372	5.8	13	19,681	116,105
Yingchuan	263,440	1,436,513	5.4	17	15,496	84,500
Henei	159,770	801,558	5.0	18	8,876	44,531
Donghai	148,784	706,416	4.7	13	11,444	54,339
Guiyang	135,029	501,403	3.7	11	12,275	45,582
Nanhai	71,477	250,282	3.5	7	10,211	35,754
Hongnong	46,815	199,113	4.2	9	5,201	22,123
Rencheng guo	36,442	194,156	5.3	3	12,147	64,718
Hepu	23,121	86,617	3.7	5	4,624	17,323

(a) Households; (b) individuals; (c) average number of members of the household; (d) number of counties; (e) average numbers of households in a county; (f) average number of individuals in a county.

From these figures, it is clear that the households usually consisted of four, five or six members, and this conclusion is confirmed in the finds of documents for the commandery of Donghai of circa 16 to 11 BCE. Emanating from the headquarters of the commandery for transmission to the capital city, such documents were themselves summaries of the information supplied originally from the districts, but no examples have yet been found of the basic lists of households and registers that units of that level drew up. It is however likely that these would have included the same sort of detail as that seen in registers of a different type. These were the ones found in the rubbish pits of the garrison forces of the north-west, recording the rations distributed to men on active service there, accompanied by their wives and immediate kinsfolk. As may be seen in the following example, these records included the ages of all members of these groups, which one may perhaps term 'families', under the categories of adult (aged fifteen years and above; *da nan, nü* 大男女), serviceable (seven to fourteen; *shi* 使) and infant (six and below; *wei shi* 未使):

Sun Qingjian 孫青肩, private, of Wucheng 武成 unit: wife, Xie 謝, adult, aged 34, grain consumed 2.16 *shi;* eldest

daughter, Yu 於, serviceable, aged 10, grain consumed 1.6 *shi;*
daughter Nüzu 女足, infant, aged 6, grain consumed 1.6 *shi;*
total of grain consumed: 5 *shi.*

It was according to such basic registers that officials could calculate and extract the tax on the land and the poll tax. Land tax was payable in kind, usually grain but also hay or straw; other items, such as rare or exotic products, were sometimes acceptable, especially from the south. Calculated according to the yield, the land tax varied from one thirtieth to one fifteenth part of the harvest of cereal crops. On certain occasions a bounteous emperor granted exemption from tax to a locality, perhaps one that he had favoured with a visit thereby imposing considerable expense and labour on the inhabitants. The poll tax may have been fixed at 120 cash coins for each person, with variations at times of up to 190 or down to 40 cash; at times when it was levied on children it stood at 23 cash.

In addition to registering the population, officials of the districts and counties provided figures for the extent of the land under their control, and examples in an early textbook on algebra were perhaps chosen as a means of instructing officials how to calculate the acreage of irregularly shaped fields. Records preserved in the Standard Histories and in some recently found archive material provide an idea of the tasks that these officials accomplished. Empire-wide figures follow.

	1–2 CE	140 CE
Households	12,233,062	9,689,630
Individuals	59,594,978	49,150,220
Individual : household	4.7:1	5.1:1
Demarcated land	145,136,405 *qing*	—
Uncultivated land	102,528,589 *qing*	—
Potentially arable land	32,290,947 *qing*	—
Specified arable land	8,270,536 *qing*	—

Figures for the population are the totals given in the Han shu *and* Hou Han shu; *addition of the figures given there separately for each commandery and kingdom corrects these to 12.4 and 57.7 million for 1–2* CE *and 9.5 and 48 million for 140* CE. *No figures are available for the land in 140* CE.

The collected reports submitted by the governor of Donghai commandery circa 10 BCE include the following figures:

Households	266,290
Individuals	1,397,343
[Individuals: household, 5.2 : 1]	
Demarcated land	512,092 *qing*
Uncultivated land	211,652 *qing*

Armed with registers of the households and their members, officials were able to exact a further form of tax that was rendered as service. Normally, able-bodied males aged between 23 and 56 were required to spend two periods, each to last one year, as members of the armed forces. Part of this time may have been spent in training, part in manning the defence lines of the north-west, and they could be recalled to the colours in times of emergency. In addition these men served for one month every year as labourers under the direction of officials of their own counties; they could also be sent to work in adjoining commanderies.

The tasks to which they were put may well have included the transport of grain from where it had been delivered, as tax, to an officially manned granary, or they may have worked at the upkeep and repair of roads, waterways and bridges. Some of these conscripts may have been detailed to work in the salt and iron mines and their manufactures, or to build a city's walls, an emperor's palace or mausoleum or a king's tomb. In statements that may not be entirely accurate, we are told that no less than 146,000 men and women were called up to build the walls of Chang'an in 192 BCE and a further 145,000 in 190 CE and that the general gift of one order of honour marked the completion of the enterprise. What is not clear is how far this force depended on the regular supply of conscripts and how far it brought in other persons, including women, so as to proceed with the work as speedily as was possible. In 29 BCE the Yellow River burst its banks causing widespread inundation. In the emergency conscript labourers worked to seal the breaches, and the engineer who supervised the project was appointed counsellor of the palace and awarded the nineteenth order, noble of the interior.

At the death of the head of a household, responsibility for its work and its dues passed to his son; if he had no son to one of his close relatives, including his parents, widow, daughter or grandson; and it could even pass to one of his former slaves, now manumitted. Widows who did not inherit from a husband might themselves receive an allocation of land with which to set up their own household. Existing households could be divided, presumably among 'family' members, either by agreement or in accordance with the terms of a will. We are not told who bore responsibility for a household when the head was away on conscript service; this may have fallen to his wife or his son.

It is possible to see how the households of the countryside, firmly attached to the land as they were, were subject to control by officials and liable to render their dues to the government. But it is not so easy to see how the institution worked for those households which were registered in the towns, where individual men and women may well have lived independently, earning their living as servants, craftsmen or artisans. Such persons may well have included the younger sons of men who held an order of honour; unlike their elder brothers they did not inherit such a mark of status with its benefits.

The statutes and ordinances prescribed ways in which the households were required to pay their dues and laid down the penalties imposed for dereliction of these duties; in addition they regulated how possession of the orders of honour could affect the way in which government of the people operated. These laws also prescribed punishments for specified crimes, with allowance for privileged treatment of some offenders. At the same time officials of the towns and countryside kept a close watch to check evasion of the regulations and the serious crime of flight from the areas where tax and service were due. It is possible that some of the junior officials of the counties held posts whose duties lay in watching for cases of disobedience and apprehending those who had sought escape from their obligations.

Such a search for criminals and absconders and the full implementation of the rules that governed human conduct depended also on the third institution of early imperial times, that of the corporate responsibility group. As had the orders of honour, this institution had arisen in pre-imperial times, and it may well have been Shang

Yang, again, who set it firmly in operation in the kingdom of Qin. These groups consisted of five or perhaps ten members, members being taken variously as individuals or as families (*jia*). All members were in duty bound to denounce any one of their fellow members for crimes or suspicious activities; such reports could merit the reward of one order of honour, whereas failure to report a case could result in execution at the waist.

One of the statutes of 186 BCE laid down the function of the responsibility group. According to this, those persons who held up to the ninth order of honour and lived in each other's vicinity formed the unit of five, possibly exchanging tallies which bound them together in trust. The members kept watch on one another in their dwellings, observing their movements and immediately presenting themselves to report to the responsible officials in cases of robbery, acts of violence and flight. The officials then set up a strict control of passage through the gates of the wards.

In slightly earlier times however the provision may not have applied as widely as it did in 186 BCE. According to the documents of that year those who held the ninth order, *wu dafu* 五大夫 and above, were not included in the groups, and officials were not always implicated in proceedings taken against their fellow members. Later on however it may have been taken to an even wider degree than in 186 BCE. In an account of the debate that took place in 81 BCE, which was probably composed some thirty years later, a senior official of the government who was concerned about the prevalence of crime cited parts of the text of this statute, verbatim. In this version the membership of the group was extended almost to the top of the scale, reaching as far as the nineteenth order, noble of the interior.

The documents of 217 BCE tell something of the operation of the system. An official who was investigating a case claimed to have interrogated the members of the group that was concerned in order to obtain information, and he claimed possibly to have threatened them with punishment for concealment. In another case the members of a group responded to such questioning by giving evidence regarding stolen property (clothing). Other statutes, of 186 BCE, set fines of 4 *liang* 兩 of gold (2,500 cash; 50 grams) and 1 *jin* 斤 of gold (10,000 cash; 244 grams) for members of a group who failed to denounce their fellows for counterfeiting coin, or for not registering themselves as tradesmen. A false or incomplete denunciation however warranted punishment. For all this, in 81 BCE, as we are told, a critic of the government objected that the institution set family members against one another and brought it about that there were few persons who were left without a stain of criminality.

With the help of these three institutions, the orders of honour, the households and the responsibility groups, imperial Han officials possessed the means of controlling the population in minuscule groups of four or five persons and bringing laws to bear on all, except for members of the imperial family, including kings and princesses. It may be asked when governments of the empires or states of Europe first succeeded in setting up a scheme of organisation at such a small level. However, the Han institutions did not apply with equal force to those placed at either the upper or the lower reaches of the social scale.

The twentieth order of the series, that of the nobilities, conferred rank but did not require the same sort of obligations as those that fell to those of the other nineteen orders. Thanks to the preservation of lists which show how the nobilities of Western Han passed from father to son it is possible to trace much of the way in which the nobles took their place in society and played their part in public life.

The nobles stood outside the scope of the households and the responsibility groups. Instead of the allocated number of *qing* of land with which to work for a living, they were invested with responsibility for administering large areas which were worked by a specified number of households. They collected dues from those households, retaining a small part for themselves, and in return they maintained law and order there. The nobles are nowhere named as being members of the responsibility groups or as being subject to those groups. The number of households over whom they held some authority was carefully specified, and there were wide differences in the extent of this privilege. The dues that a noble retained from a thousand households was sometimes taken as a norm against which the profits of those of other occupations might be set.

The records of over eight hundred nobilities, stretching from the earliest days of the kingdom of Han until those of Wang Mang's empire, list entries for nobilities of several types. Over four hundred were granted to the sons of kings. Nearly three hundred were given as rewards for services by civil officials and military officers, and from 124 BCE it became customary to confer a nobility on an incoming chancellor. In a third category, something like an hundred of an emperor's favourites or the relatives of one of his consorts received nobilities; surrendered leaders of a non-Han community or group would receive the same honour, both to confirm acceptance of their expressions of loyalty for Han and to induce them to retain that sense of loyalty despite other temptations. Passed on from father to son, exceptionally a nobility might last for nine generations, but most of them died out perhaps after the death of the original holder without a son, or after one or two successors. Many were brought to an end as a result of the holder's crime or alleged crime. Some of the most successful officials who had already been ennobled might receive substantial increases in the number of households made over to their estates, as their work merited. Small nobilities would extend to less than five hundred households; the largest, such as that of the descendants of Xiao He 蕭何 (died as chancellor of state in 193 BCE) or that of Huo Guang 霍光 (died as marshal of state in 68 BCE) to nearly twenty thousand.

Second in title, rank and dignity only to the emperor, and ranged high above the twenty orders of honour, as seen in Chapter 3 above the kings were entrusted with responsibilities for governing wide areas of land and for administering their realms in accordance with the three institutions described above. But the kings, along with the princesses and empresses dowager, were subject to no less a rigorous scrutiny than that exercised by officials who were implementing the statutes and ordinances in the commanderies. The central government appointed the most senior advisors and officials of the royal governments, with orders and opportunities to report directly back to the throne if there was reason to doubt a king's loyalty or question his behaviour; a king could be impeached and summarily punished at imperial command. In a notorious incident, Liu An 劉安 (2), king of Huainan since 164 BCE, was accused of plotting a rebellion and died by his own hand in 122. Liu An is best known by the book that bears the name of his kingdom (*Huainanzi* 淮南子) and sets forth to explain the nature of the universe and mankind's place therein. References to the evil deeds of Liu Qu 劉去 and Liu Jian 劉建 (3), kings of Guangchuan and Jiangdu, are seen above (see p. 46).

At the lower end of the social scale, and without the benefits of the orders of honour and the households' allotments of land, were the commoners (*shu ren* 庶人). Either they had not received any of the orders, or they had been deprived of them by way of punishment. Convicts who had served sentences of hard labour and had been fortunate enough to survive such rigors presumably reverted to commoner status after their return, with none of the orders that they had held before their sentences had been pronounced.

Slaves, male and female, could be bought or sold, owned privately or made over to serve officials and work in their offices; surrendered enemy soldiers could be made into slaves. The powers that a slave owner was entitled to wield over his slaves does not appear to have been limited, except that he needed permission to put them to death. Otherwise he could maltreat them and beat them, male or female, and whatever a master's actions were his slaves were not entitled to denounce him. We hear of one instance of a commoner who denounced his slave for bad behaviour, refusal to work and disobedience, and of his hopes of selling him to the government to be sentenced to five years' hard labour. Slaves who injured a commoner or person of higher rank suffered tattooing, to be handed back to their masters; if they fled, officials might institute a search to apprehend them. If a slave put his own child to death he could be sentenced to five years' hard labour and tattooing before return to his master. For murder of a master, a slave was put to death with exposure of the severed head. Execution followed a slave's marriage or sexual relations with his mistress, mistress' mother, master's wife or daughter, such women themselves being punished.

If a commoner woman bore a child to a slave, ownership of the child reverted to his master, who was entitled to take over children borne to his female slaves and make them into his own slaves. Children of a male slave and a commoner became commoners. A slave owner could manumit male slaves who had performed well or meritoriously, and these would become commoners, as they also would if, in other circumstances, they inherited their masters' property. Female slaves who bore a child to their masters attained their freedom at his death.

On occasion, but as far as we know not regularly, convicts were assigned to join military forces engaged in a campaign, but they did not form a significantly large element under a general's command.

They are not known to have acted as garrison troops in the north-west, or as guards in the cities of the interior. They took part in the suppression of rebel leaders in Nan Yue (Vietnam) in 112 and Wudu (Gansu) in 80 and fought against Qiang 羌 tribes in the west in 61 BCE. In 18 CE Wang Mang used convicts in a fight against the Red Eyebrows.

Convicts took part in civilian works. A graveyard which was dug within the park set aside for Jingdi's burial has revealed the remains of perhaps ten thousand such persons who had presumably been allocated there for construction of the tomb and its shrine. Others toiled at repairing breaches in the banks of the Yellow River in 132 BCE and in building fortifications in Liaodong (Liaoning) and Xuantu (Liaoning, North Korea) in 75. In 22 BCE a band of convicts broke out in revolt in the iron agency in Yingchuan (Henan) where they had been assigned to work. A surviving inscription records how a force of 2,690 convicts was once employed in 63 CE. They were working on a project to build part of a road which led from the former metropolitan area to Shu commandery (Sichuan), running through somewhat difficult types of land. They built a stretch of road for 258 *li,* constructing five major bridges and 643 structures or supports for bridges, with the use of 766,800 tiles or bricks.

Notes for Further Reading

T'ung-tsu Ch'ü presents translations of primary material to illustrate his theme. The titles of the orders of honour are given in *HS* 19A, pp. 739–40, and in Loewe, 'The Orders of Aristocratic Rank in Han China', p. 99; for fragments of a register, see *RHA,* vol. 2, pp. 365–71 (document X 2), and p. 208 (nos. 5, 7) for tenure of orders by the young; for rewards gained by forfeiting these orders, see *RCL,* p. 83, and Zhangjia shan (Statutes), strip no. 204.

For the responsibility groups, see Shuihudi (Questions and Answers), strip nos. 96–97, 155–56 (*RCL,* pp. 145, 163); Shuihudi, 'Feng zhen shi', strip nos. 10, 82 (*RCL,* pp. 185, 203); *Zhangjia shan* (Statutes), strip nos. 201, 260, 304–5; *Yan tie lun* 10 (57 'Zhou Qin'), p. 584; and *Crisis and Conflict,* p. 110. For figures of the population, see *Han shu* 28B, p. 1640, *CHOC,* p. 485 and, for corrections, Bielenstein, 'Census', pp. 128, 139; for figures of population and land in Donghai commandery, see *Yinwan*

Han mu jiandu, transcriptions pp. 77–78, and *Men Who Governed,* pp. 60–63.

Swann discusses conditions of taxation, pp. 366–76. For age classifications and the distribution of rations as cited from Juyan, see *RHA,* vol. 2, pp. 87–91. Figures for the labour forces used to build Chang'an's walls are given in *HS* 2, pp. 89, 90, and Dubs, *History of the Former Han Dynasty,* vol. 1, pp. 181, 183. For the floods of 29 BCE, see *HS* 29, p. 1688, and *Crisis and Conflict,* p. 191. For the case of Liu An, see Vankeerberghen; a translation of the *Huainanzi* is available in Le Blanc and Mathieu. For nobilities, see *Men Who Governed,* Chapter 9. Sources on slaves carefully assembled by Wilbur may be supplemented by a number of strips from Shuihudi and Zhangjia shan, e.g.: Shuihudi, 'Feng zhen shi', strips no. 37–41 (*RCL,* p. 193, E 15), (Questions and Answers), strips no. 73, 104 (*RCL,* pp. 140, 148); *Zhangjia shan* (Statutes), strip nos. 30, 34, 36, 160, 162, 188–90, 382–83, 385. The inscription of convicts' work in 63 CE appears in *Shodō zenshū,* nos. 64, 65 (transcription p. 179).

10

Control of the Farmer, Artisan, Tradesman and Traveller

Encouragement by imperial decree, regulations of the statutes and the establishment of government offices testify to the means whereby imperial government strove both to promote the productive work of the fields and the workshops of the artisans and to control the working lives and commercial dealings of the emperor's subjects. Records kept by officials and inscriptions seen on manufactured items reveal some of the results of this interest while the occasional voice of protest points to weaknesses and failures. A few personalities stand out, of men who tried to understand the needs and ways of economic issues of the empire as a whole and succeeded in doing so, at least partly. Material evidence tells of the standards reached in the living conditions of the highest in the land; occasionally we learn of a man who was responsible for an important technical innovation.

Perhaps nine tenths of the population worked in the fields, many in the loess country of the north-west. Nature's disasters of flood and drought could render their lives precarious, sometimes suddenly; the lie of the land could all but sever contact between adjacent communities. Great differences lay between the work of the farmer in the rich, well-irrigated fields of modern Henan and that of those who built and tended the terraced plots that clung to the mountainsides in Sichuan. To all who worked in these conditions and to the officials who overlooked them, an emperor would from time to time declare in grandiloquent terms that the empire depended on the results of their labours. 'It is agriculture that is the basis of the world', a decree would run; perhaps calling on the traditions of a remote past, emperor and empress might perform a ritual gesture of taking a hand to the plough personally, and standing by, to work in the mulberry groves. From 114 BCE onwards the emperor planned to attend frequently at the newly opened cult addressed to Hou tu,

Sovereign of the Earth; such devotions ran in parallel with those that lesser mortals might offer to the gods of the soil and the hearth.

Statutes with the titles of 'Agriculture', 'Granaries' and 'Stables and Parks' take their place in the documents of 217 and 186 BCE. They required reports on the state of the weather and its effect on the crops and the harvest. The provisions of Wei 魏, a kingdom of pre-imperial days, had laid down the correct measurements for dividing off working plots of land (309 BCE). These are likely to have been adopted in the empires, whose officials were obliged to report by the eighth month of each year how much land had been reclaimed. Orders fixed the times for certain work such as clearing extraneous vegetation from the lanes or repairing the dykes between the fields, or the bridges, so that it would be completed in season; other orders banned work such as cutting timber from taking place out of season. The farmers of Qin were instructed how liberally or sparsely they were to sow their land for their different crops of rice, hemp, wheat, barley, millet, beans and peas. Regulations concerned the stacking and storage of these crops.

Some of the statutes referred to the care and feeding of oxen used in agricultural work. Losses of government-owned horses and cattle by death or other causes must be reported; horses in the care of couriers must be fed according to the regulations. Other rules covered the rearing of chickens, pigs and dogs and the disposal of newly borne, unwanted animals. A ban prevented the sale of beer directly from the farms, and a statute of 186 BCE laid down punishments for careless digging of wells and pits, and the use of devices that might be liable to injure animals or human beings.

Chao Cuo 鼂錯, who held high office during the reign of Wendi and suffered an undeserved death of a criminal in 154 BCE, had tried to increase the production of grain by promises of orders of honour and their privileges in return for the delivery of supplies. Problems could arise in providing for the armies and officials of Han who extended their activities and penetrated into the remote areas, particularly of the north-west and Central Asia. The government came to respond by encouraging the growth of agricultural colonies in those parts, sometimes staffed by conscript servicemen and their families. Circa 110 BCE Sang Hongyang 桑弘羊, an official blessed by rare gifts who was capable of taking a long-term view of the needs of the empire and the dangers it might face, suggested that such colonies should be set up at Luntai 輪臺 (in the modern Uighur Autonomous Zone, Xinjiang), but no action followed. Quite soon, however, his proposal bore fruit, with the establishment of the garrison lines in the north-west (ca. 100 BCE) where conscripts were assigned to the production of food and the necessary work of irrigation (at Juyan 居延, in modern Gansu). At a later stage colonies were set up, probably without conscript labour, in the area of Jushi 車師 (possibly modern Turfan) which did not lie directly within Han control; these were under the general supervision of the newly appointed post of protector general of the Western Regions, held by Zheng Ji 鄭吉 from 60 BCE. We also learn of agencies of agriculture that existed, and of the commandants of agriculture who worked in them, near the borders from time to time.

Increased production of cereal crops in some areas may have followed the technical innovations advocated by Zhao Guo 趙過 circa 90 BCE and thereafter adopted in part by some of those who worked the fields under official supervision. He had shown how effectively oxen could be used in ploughing, and how a system of parallel furrows and ridges, in place of a broadcast scatter of seed over a wide plot, would increase the yield. Han governments also promoted production of another type; we know of two agencies for fruit orchards that were established in Ba commandery (Sichuan). It is not known to what extent an increasing supply of iron tools helped the farmer.

Documents from the garrison forces at Juyan show Zhao Guo's methods in official use with the existence of granaries that bore its name (*dai tian* 代田). Other documents, from Yinwan 尹灣 (Jiangsu; dated ca. 10 BCE), include examples of the annual reports of provincial officials whose detailed figures show how the government's rules were working. These reports included figures for the areas of arable land and land actually sown with cereal crops, the extent of orchard land and the area occupied by tree plantations, together with the receipts of grain in the counties and the amounts that the officials distributed. In some cases these figures were shown to compare favourably with those of the previous year.

A chapter of the histories of Western Han sets out how some families of enterprise had built up large fortunes both then and in the earlier days of the Warring States. To place these achievements in their context, the account presents a list of the ways whereby it had become possible to earn a sizeable annual income. The standard of 200,000 cash that was taken for comparison was the income that a noble of a small estate of one thousand households could expect, by retaining 200 cash of the sums that he extracted from each one. Stockbreeders of horses, cattle, sheep or pigs and fish farmers could attain a comparable degree of wealth if their business was sufficiently large. Forestry of rare timber such as catalpa, the care of fruit trees, lacquer orchards or bamboo or market gardening could lead to the same results.

A second list gives thirty-two ways in which traders in the cities and the market centres could acquire large fortunes. They dealt in animals (horses, cattle, pigs), fish and slaves; slaughtered animals; animal products (skins, furs and horns); natural materials (lacquer, fruit, grain and timber); made-up foods (alcoholic drinks, sauces and so forth); textiles (silks and felts); carriages and carts; and manufactured items of bronze, iron and lacquered or plain wood. Earthenwares and potteries are conspicuous by their absence from the list.

In all cases these occupations lay largely beyond the direct control that officials could exercise over the households of the countryside, and commercial and industrial undertakings are repeatedly denigrated as being of secondary (*mo* 末) rather than primary (*ben* 本) importance to the well-being of the land and its inhabitants. In many instances they served the needs and tastes of men and women of the highest social orders, providing extravagant furnishings, such as a highly decorated censer for an emperor's or a king's palace, fine raiment for his consorts to wear or rare delicacies for his table. In time we hear how the style of living was changing, and men whose only claim to fame was that of wealth were able to emulate these habits and acquire such luxuries.

Along with the craftsmen and artisans who turned out these products, artists worked to embellish choice pieces of equipment or to present an emperor or a king with their paintings. Some of the finished articles served religious purposes, bearing icons or symbols that it was hoped would bring a blessing to the fortunate man or woman whose eyes gazed upon them or whose fingers clasped them.

Some items, such as jade suits, were designed and fashioned for burial with the dead rather than for enjoyment by the living. The workshops and foundries also produced some rare objects needed by officials in the conduct of their duties. Astronomers working in the imperial observatory required vessels with carefully graduated scales to measure the movements of the heavenly bodies that they were obliged to report. Uniquely, perhaps, a foundry turned out a special instrument, such as that designed by a scientist and mystic named Zhang Heng 張衡 (78–139 CE). Made of bronze, this drum detected the occurrence of an earthquake, indicating the time and place where the blow had struck. Other workshops may have followed the lead of Cai Lun 蔡倫, a eunuch who is said to have presented the court with a formula for making a proto-paper 105 CE; in fact examples of such a substance now found predate that report.

By contrast, the workshops produced materials of a lower grade, as needed in the conduct of everyday life, such as the pots and pans of the kitchen, and the iron ploughshares that a farmer, if lucky, might be able to buy or to borrow from government sources. Foundries produced standard sets of authorised weights and measures of length and capacity and the equipment that lay stored in the arsenals of the armed forces. Production of these latter items could be very demanding; we know of one arsenal, in the east, where the total number of items amounted to over twenty-three million (see p. 65 above).

Government was not content to rest unconcerned with these occupations and activities. Ranking at the high grade of 2,000 *shi* 石 (for grades, see p. 78 above), the court architect was responsible for planning and constructing buildings such as the imperial palaces and preparing an emperor's tomb with its adjacent shrine and chamber of rest. His assistants took charge of the stoneyard and collected the timber needed for the work, and they presumably controlled the masons, carpenters and unskilled conscript servicemen that were needed. In addition subordinate officials of the superintendent of the lesser treasury (*shaofu* 少府) were responsible for providing for an emperor's needs and wants such as medical attention, feeding and musical performances. The same office supervised the work of those who prepared the emperor's robes and kept his garments in a state of good repair.

A special office, named the *Shangfang* 尚方, was entrusted with the manufacture of choice items of bronze and jade for use in the palace. Creation of some of the most beautiful and meaningful bronze mirrors is attributed to the artists and craftsmen of the *Shangfang,* who may also have been responsible for making the jade suits in which emperors, kings and a few others were encased before burial, and the circular jade discs that they and their consorts prized in their lives. Artists were once required to prepare a set of portraits of Han's heroes with which to impress the visiting lord of the Xiongnu 匈奴 (51 BCE). On another occasion an emperor needed likenesses of the leading members of his female entourage, so as to select one to be a bride for a non-Han chieftain. It may well have fallen to the *Shangfang* to commission the work.

As and where natural conditions, such as the proximity of raw materials or supplies of fuel for the furnaces, might suggest, the central government posted specialist agencies in the commanderies to be responsible for certain tasks, but little is known of the ways in which they were organised and staffed. Two agencies existed for textiles, one in Henan and one in Shandong, and there were altogether nine for industrial work. Known more generally, the agencies for salt and iron were set up circa 118 BCE as a move to divert the profits of these undertakings from private hands and to bring the production and distribution of these products under the exclusive control of the government. This change did not pass without comment and protest, and the monopolies did not exist with full force permanently. However the record of the major provincial units of the empire for 1–2 CE included notes of thirty-four agencies for salt and forty-eight for iron that were established at that time, and we know of others that had been set up previously and had been disbanded. Uniquely we learn how a few of these agencies that were situated in east China were staffed. Three of those for salt were each in the charge of a director with either twenty-six or thirty subordinates; the two for iron were served in the one case by five and the other by twenty junior officials. They relied mostly on conscript servicemen to do the work. The statutes of 217 BCE ordered that vessels of the same type should be made in uniform size and that armour and arms should be marked either by incision or branding, with the name of the office which had charge of the item. They also set schedules for the training of artisans, which might last for two years. Inscriptions seen on lacquer or bronze vessels may reveal that officials took some part in their manufacture. At times they name the owner of the item or the palace for which it was made. They may record the fact that it had been inspected, perhaps with the name of the inspector, the specified weight and measurements of the object and the date when the inspection took place.

The later statutes, of 186 BCE, laid down severe punishments for those who made counterfeit coins or assisted in such work and for members of a responsibility group and others who had failed to report such activities. Nevertheless private minting became permissible from time to time until it was banned circa 115 BCE. Nothing is known about the ways in which the officially controlled mints were set up or operated. Qin and Han coins, of copper, bore a simple inscription that declared their weight. They were not embellished in the fashion of Hellenistic coins, with a mounted rider, such as had intrigued Han travellers into Central Asia. Unlike Roman emperors, those of Han did not exploit the coinage as a means of circulating a propagandist claim for the virtues of their rule.

Bond servants were sometimes put to work as artisans, presumably in the workshops for iron, bronze and lacquer wares, and also as seamstresses. We are not told how, before the introduction of the monopolies for iron, private manufacturers of iron goods recruited a force to work at their behest; nor do we know how this was done for the lacquer shops or the potteries. Possibly the second and third sons of a country household, who could not hope to inherit their fathers' orders of honour and household, may have moved to the towns, the iron foundries or the salt mines to secure employment and a living—perhaps as hired labour.

Two distinct views of the merchant and his occupation stand revealed in official writings of Han times. Some took the view that, classed with the artisans, traders were to be seen as engaging in work that was of secondary importance to the empire, and such an attitude may have gained general acceptance in official quarters. By contrast those men who were of a practical frame of mind, such as Sang Hongyang whom we have already met, recognised that farmer, artisan and merchant all had their part to play in utilising or exploiting the resources of the empire and distributing them for general benefit. Sang Hongyang himself could speak with personal experience of these matters, son as he was of a merchant's house in Luoyang. As against the call heard sometimes for a life of thrift, and a reduction of extravagance, there may have been some attempt to promote trade by the consumption of luxurious products and articles of manufacture.

Nevertheless officials were encouraged not to soil their hands by acting as tradesmen and they were even punished for so doing. In arguing against the principles of the monopolies of state, Zhu Hui 朱暉 (ca. 85 CE) saw the transfer of management of the mines into government's hands as tantamount to ordering officials to undertake precisely that role. A further and perhaps more usual criticism of merchants lay in the disproportionately great profits that they might make at times when necessities were in short supply, thus adding to popular distress. Early in Western Han a number of measures had perhaps been intended to prevent merchants from attaining high social status, by banning them from sporting the obvious material symbols of wealth and from making their way into public life. For example they were forbidden to wear luxurious clothing and silks and to ride in carriages; their sons and grandsons were not allowed to serve as officials. Such restrictions were not maintained on a regular or permanent basis, as has just been seen in the case of Sang Hongyang. As a reward for his services he received the tenth order of honour; he finally held the post of imperial counsellor (87–80 BCE).

At times major schemes were introduced in an attempt to alleviate the difficulties that unrestricted trading might bring. These sought to stabilise the price paid for staple goods and to ease their transport. In face of the suffering that could follow either extra abundant harvests or crop failure, in the years 54 to 44 BCE the government set up experimental 'ever-level granaries'; in times of glut officials bought up stocks and helped the farmers by paying a higher price than that of the market; in years of famine they sold it at prices that were considerably lower than what a monopolist merchant might demand.

Merchants dealt in manufactured items, luxury foods, raw materials and perhaps jewellery and exotica, such as rare products of the fruits of the south. A ban prevented them from exporting certain goods such as iron wares and female livestock beyond the points of control at the border. At times, however, large consignments of silks made their way into Central Asia, there to persuade the leaders of potentially hostile groups to retain peaceful relations with Han and refrain from pillaging the homes, farms and settlements of the north. These deliveries were undertaken by the officials of the government, which also allowed or even promoted the growth of a large-scale export trade into Central Asia. It was partly to serve these caravans, numbering at times several hundred men and animals, that the protective routes that led to Dunhuang 敦煌 came into being, from circa 100 BCE. Chinese silks and perhaps bronze and pottery wares lay packed on the camels' backs for the outward journey; after perhaps two years or more they brought back home rare items such as livestock, furs, or raw jade, on which craftsmen would ply their skills, perhaps in the workshops of the *Shangfang*. The account of the debate on public issues that was held in 81 BCE records opposing views on these operations, some spokesmen doubting the value of an exchange of China's stocks of usable materials for luxurious baubles.

Han tombs included at least one tableau of an official performing his duty of supervising the activities of the markets, but as in other cases it cannot be known whether such controls were imposed on a regular or permanent basis. These officials were presumably required to prevent cheating and suppress any brawls that might break out; they would perhaps also ensure that transactions accorded with the standard sets of weights and measurements that the government had approved and distributed.

How far these officials could interfere over matters of pricing is not known. The documents of 217 BCE refer to a fixed market price for a slave and record the rule that except for items worth less than 1 cash prices must be attached by tags to commodities for sale. They also laid down rules for the safe stowage of cash and a ban on access to the markets by convicts. Attachment of tags for pricing carries with it an implication of another type, that is, that of a public whose standard of literacy was sufficient to understand the characters for numbers.

Stall holders in the markets were obliged to register themselves for tax. Those who failed to do so could face a charge of robbery of a sum equal to the tax that they had evaded, confiscation of their stock in trade and cash and removal of their right to hold a stall. A heavy fine awaited members of a responsibility group who failed to report such cases. In the course of their dealings, stall holders were not permitted to discriminate between coins that were of good and poor quality. At one time merchants paid a tax of 120 coins in respect of every 2,000 that went through their hands; craftsmen and metal workers paid tax at half that rate. The normal rate levied on possession of a light carriage was 120 cash, but merchants, whether settled in one place or travelling by land or water, paid double that as well as 120 cash for boats of 50 Han feet (11.5 metres) or more in length.

The statutes of 217 and 186 BCE included precise regulations for the scale of rations that the postal stations were authorised to provide for officials travelling in the course of their duties. As might be expected, the allowances of grain, salt, sauces and vegetables varied according to rank and social status; servants and horses also received their due allowances. Such comforts may have awaited Shi Rao 師饒, who left notes of the places where he had spent the night, almost in diary form, when he was on the road in 11 BCE. At times he was travelling in a private capacity, passing his nights with friends. He also visited official posts in other counties or commanderies than his own, and on occasion he stayed with the governor. His business included a search for and pursuit of criminals.

Regulations rather than comforts attended the travels of lesser mortals, as is brought out in the terms of the one ordinance found among the documents for 186 BCE. Finds from other sites show officials engaged in exercising the necessary restrictions. The twenty-three clauses of the Ordinance for Waterways and Passes (*Jin guan ling* 津關令) illustrate how points of control were set up at mountain passes and waterway crossings and how travellers were subject to scrutiny both in the interior and at the perimeter. Illegal entry and exit through these points could be punished, as was the loan or forgery of the 'passport' that every traveller must carry and present; children might be allowed through without the necessary documentation, as were babies nestling in their mothers' arms.

Officials at the passes were to keep a look-out not only for fugitives but also for attempts to conceal contraband goods, even to the point of searching in a coffin that was being escorted outside the territory where Han laws operated. Registers listed by name persons allowed through the points of control with their means of transport, and items that were due for return such as gold. At one of these posts, we learn, dutiful officials questioned whether they should allow passage to a party of convicts who had been assigned to work in the orchards of a neighbouring commandery; apparently their documents were not quite in order.

Elaborate rules governed the movement, purchase and transfer of horses through these points of control, particularly at the perimeter. Registers recorded how these animals moved from place to place, starting with the place of purchase; they gave bodily details such as height and the marks branded on their hides for purposes of identification. These detailed matters of administration of an empire could find their way into the offices of the metropolitan superintendent of the central government in Chang'an.

Passports, which measured 1 by 6 Han inches (2.3 by 13.5 centimetres), served as a means whereby officials at the passes could check for escaping deserters; disfigurements such as tattooing would alert them to the presence of a criminal or former criminal. The following examples of fragments of the documents found in the north-west show how these regulations were being implemented by controls at the Golden Gate and the Jade Gate, near Juyan and Dunhuang, respectively, from perhaps 100 BCE.

(A)   Juyan strip no. 15.19

Report submitted by Zhong 忠, overseer, northern district, on the day *Bingzi* of the intercalary month (first day *Jisi*) of the fifth year of *Yongshi* [4 March 12 BCE]:

Cui Zidang 崔自當, of Yicheng 義成 village, states that he is engaged in shopping for himself and his family at Juyan. I beg leave to report that there has been no incident in which Zidang has been summoned for judicial reasons and that he is qualified to be issued with a passport. For delivery, with respect, to the Jin 金 Pass, Jianshui 肩水, and the Suo 索 Pass, Juyan county.

Forwarded on the day *Bingzi* by Peng 彭, assistant to the magistrate, Lude 鱳得 county, to the Jin Pass, Jianshui, and the Suo Pass, Juyan county, for action in accordance with the statutes and ordinances.

[Signed] Yan 晏, clerical assistant, and Jian 建, senior clerk.

It may be noted that this document shows that communications between the central government and some of the commanderies, particularly those at the perimeter, could well be delayed. Orders had evidently been given for designation of the year in question not by the fourth year in the existing reign title (*Yongshi* 永始) but as the first year in a new one (*Yuanyan* 元延), but this change had evidently not been received in time for use in the intercalary month, which fell after the first month of the new year.

(B)   Juyan strip no. 29.1
Passport of Sun Shi 孫時, officer commanding Yanshou 延壽 Section, Tuotuo 彙佗 Company, dated *Jiyou,* first month, fourth year of *Yongguang* [4 March 40 BCE]; Sun Diqing 孫第卿, wife, adult, of Wansui 萬歲 village, Zhaowu 昭武 county, age 21; Wangnü 王女, daughter, non-adult, age 3 years; Er 耳, sister, non-adult, age 9 years—all with black colouring.

(C)   Juyan strips no. 505.12, 505.13 and 43.7 (incomplete)
Qiong Yang 瓊陽, of Yiwang 宜王 village, Xiaogu 效穀 county, Dunhuang commandery; age 28; one light vehicle, one horse; admitted south, inwards, on *Bingwu* of the intercalary month.

and

Wei Feng 衛豐, accountant's clerk, Juyan; son Wei Liang 衛良, of Ping 平 village, Juyan, age 13; one light vehicle, one horse; proceeded north, outwards, on *Wuzi* of the twelfth month.

and

Shi Cun 史存, of Beizhong 北中 village, Henan 河南 county, Henan commandery, eighth order of honour (*gongcheng* 公乘), age 32, height 7 [Han] feet 2 inches, colouring black. . . .

It has been seen that imperial officials were engaged in maintaining law and order, judging criminal cases, collecting revenue, organising the work of the population and seeking to increase the produce of the land and to distribute it for general use. They also attended to other tasks such as the repair and maintenance of communications and the provision of relief in times of hardship and affliction by natural disasters. Ideally they were seen as promoting cultural standards by setting up schools of learning, as indeed Wen Weng 文翁 did in Chengdu circa 160 BCE. In practice they introduced some of the norms of civilised life in areas where these were as yet unknown. In this way as late as the third century CE, after the close of Han, officials posted in the extreme south (modern Guangxi and Vietnam) found it necessary to teach the propriety of wearing clothes to natives of both sexes and to set up arrangements for marriages.

The histories of Western and Eastern Han include biographical accounts of the officials who were known for the part they had taken in the government of the empire; whereas it is possible to discern typical or general ways in which their careers ran or they administered the land, there can be no way of setting up a norm of their achievements or the conduct of their duties. The records of three officials of the early decades of Eastern Han are cited here as examples of how officials could bring their character and their work to bear upon the people of the land. Some of their achievements and actions have been noted above in different contexts.

Zhongli Yi 鍾離意, who was a native of Kuaiji commandery (modern Zhejiang), is known for his integrity, kindnesses and charity. As inspector of posts in the commandery he once intervened to save a junior official from facing a criminal charge. At a time when many of the inhabitants were dying of plague (38 CE) he took a personal hand in bringing comforts and medicaments to those who were suffering. As yet he held no senior appointment, but attached soon to the office of the chancellor of the central government he ordered clothing to be sent to a band of convicts who were suffering from bitter cold while on the move and had them freed from their manacles. As magistrate of a county he once allowed a man who was on charge for avenging his father to go home to attend to his mother's funeral. In 58 CE the governor of Jiaozhi commandery (Vietnam) was charged with embezzlement; his property was confiscated and was to be distributed among officials. Zhongli Yi refused to accept his share of pearls on the grounds of propriety. Rewarded with cash and appointment as deputy director of the Secretariat, he reprimanded Mingdi for his callous indulgence in the pleasures of the hunt, and later for having a palace erected at a time of popular suffering due to drought (60 CE). Unsuccessful in his attempt to bring about a reduction of the severity with which cases were being tried, Zhongli Yi was demoted to be chancellor of Lu kingdom. It was said that he treated the population of the counties where he had been magistrate with the kindness due to a baby. Finding once that there were no buildings in the market, he took it upon himself to find the necessary resources from his own salary and gave a lead to others to supply materials to be used in their construction.

Zong Jun 宗均 was a man of Nanyang, a home of some of Han's most important iron foundries and a scene of considerable fighting in the confusion that preceded the restoration of the Han dynasty in 25 CE. Sponsored as a Gentleman (*lang* 郎) thanks to his father's position as an official, Zong Jun devoted himself to academic study, to be appointed magistrate of Chenyang 辰陽 county in Wuling commandery (modern Guizhou). In the face of a prevalent trust placed in shamans and in the presence of spirits, he set up schools and banned certain rites that were of a deleterious or unseemly nature. Involved in the outbreak of a rebellion staged by non-Han peoples, he took the questionable step of forging a decree with which he was able to bring about the surrender of the rebels; he received the emperor's pardon for his crime and congratulations on the successful outcome of his enterprise. He was governor of Jiujiang (Anhui) at a time when the inhabitants were suffering from the rampages of tigers and other wild beasts, and then from a plague of locusts (56 CE). Re-assuring his flock that the animals were part of the natural order, he suggested that they did not deserve trapping, and added that real oppression derived from the harsh and greedy behaviour of officials. Somehow he gained a reputation for ridding the area of these plagues. As previously, so here he suppressed some of the religious practices, such as those addressed to two mountains. These may have involved human sacrifice, as was likely to have been practised at other times.

Following a legal charge in 63 CE, Zong Jun was dismissed from his position as chancellor of Donghai kingdom (Shandong); the inhabitants staged a protest, voicing their longing for his return in a song. As director of the Secretariat he held steadfastly to what he believed to be right, irrespective of the anger that he had aroused on the part of the emperor (Mingdi); his subsequent appointments included those of colonel, internal security, and governor of Henei commandery (Hebei and Henan). The general appreciation of his administration and its effects and the love that he inspired in the population was seen in the widespread prayers expressed for his recovery from illness. Zong Jun retired owing to ill health and later refused appointment as chancellor, dying in 76.

Diwu Lun 第五倫 came from a family that was originally of East China but had long since been moved to Changling, where the tomb of Gaozu was to be built. Posted to inspect the production of coins at a time when trading in Chang'an was subject to counterfeiting, he took control of the markets and stamped out irregular practices, to the general satisfaction of the inhabitants. Raised to be a *xiaolian* 孝廉 that is, person of family responsibility and integrity and thus fit for appointment, in 51 CE he became leader of medical workers in Huaiyang kingdom; two years later he impressed Guangwudi with the advice that he gave him in audience. He soon became governor of Kuaiji commandery, but in that exalted position he would still cut the hay to feed his horses, and he sold off much of the salary that he received in kind, taking a cheap price so as to benefit the poor. At the time the commandery was much given to irregular and perhaps pernicious religious practices, and it was subject to the influence of diviners, and of shamans and the fears that they excited. Diwu Lun suppressed one rite that was particularly injurious, that of the sacrifice of cattle.

In 62 CE Diwu Lun was summoned to the capital to face a legal charge. Such was his popularity that crowds blocked his path, seizing hold of his carriage and horses, and it was only by means of a subterfuge that he was able to make his way to Luoyang, by water. Freed from legal proceedings by the emperor he retired to private life, to be appointed governor of Shu (Sichuan) in a few years' time. The commandery was endowed with rich resources and housed a number of officials and others who commanded great wealth. The governor set about suppressing the power of the rich in favour of poorer persons, whom he appointed to junior offices, thereby reducing the extent of corruption. Early in the reign of Zhangdi (acceded 76 CE) Diwu Lun was appointed imperial counsellor. He did his best to reduce the powers and influence of members of one of the imperial consorts' families. He found opportunity to protest at the severity with which government had been practised since the time of the first emperor of Eastern Han and to criticise the recommendation of unsuitable persons for office. Aged some eighty years, Diwu Lun died shortly after 86 CE.

Against these examples there should be set the accounts that the histories give of officials who were known for their improper or rigorous conduct of their duties. The following instances are from Western Han times.

As a young man, Zhuang Yannian 莊延年 (2) had been able to study the statutes of the empire at the office of the chancellor. At a very early stage in his career he denounced some of the highest and most powerful figures in the land, such as Huo Guang 霍光, marshal of state, and Tian Yannian 田延年, superintendent of agriculture (from 75 to 72 BCE), to be himself accused of crime. Subsequently he held a post that was concerned with the suppression of non-Han rebels in 61 BCE, and he later became governor of Zhuojun (Hebei). In the absence of effective governors hitherto, the commandery had been open to the unrestrained and unlawful behaviour of some of the local powerful families, who gave asylum to robbers and other men of violence; armed protection was needed for safe passage on the roads. Able to impose order, Zhuang Yannian was promoted governor of Henan commandery, where he again stamped out crime, breaking the power of the great families. Of a quick turn of mind and ruthless in ordering the death penalty, he became known as 'The Chief Butcher'. As a result of his methods stability returned to the commandery. However his record of oppression, with which his mother is said to have upbraided him, may have blocked his way to promotion. Charged on a number of counts he died at the hands of the executioner in 58 BCE.

In the course of a career as magistrate of various counties, Yin Shang 尹賞, of Julu (Hebei), became known for the successful way in which he quelled crime, but he was at one time dismissed on a charge of practising violence. However his qualities served well to countenance the unruly and lawless situation that had arisen in Chang'an in the closing years of Chengdi's reign (16–9 BCE). Deserters and fugitives were finding asylum there; powerful families of the north were carrying out their own acts of revenge and not stopping at the murder of all members of a family; and inside the city itself officials were liable to be killed by gangs of youngsters. Appointed magistrate of Chang'an, Yin Shang rounded up criminal elements of the population, including armed ruffians and merchants who were practising their trade without registration, by the hundred. He had them cast into pits that he had had dug and they were then covered by rubble and stone. Yin Shang subsequently served as governor of a commandery and finally as superintendent of the capital, to be held in fear by officials of the metropolitan area. He died in 2 CE.

Notes for Further Reading

Hsu Cho-yun gives a general account of the farmers' work with full citations from primary sources. Directions for the conduct of agriculture appear frequently in the statutes of 217 and 186 BCE, especially in Shuihudi (Statutes), strip nos. 1–12 (*RCL,* pp. 21–25), and *Zhangjia shan* (Statutes), strip nos. 239–56. For sponsored agricultural colonies, see Hulsewé, *CICA,* pp. 62–63, 78–79; for Zhao Guo's methods and the *dai tian,* see Swann, pp. 184–91, and *RHA,* vol. 2, p. 319.

For artisans, see Barbieri-Low, Wagner and Shuihudi (Statutes), strip nos. 98–114 (*RCL,* pp. 57–63). For excavations of ironwork sites, see Wagner, Chapter 6.

For commerce and the activities of the merchant, see *SJ,* Chapters 30, 129; *HS,* Chapters 24, 91; *Yan tie lun* 1 ('Ben yi'); Gale, pp. 1–11; Swann, *passim*; and Loewe, 'Attempts at Economic Co-ordination', pp. 258–60. Swann, pp. 377–84, sets out the specification for and changes in the coinage; Zhangjia shan (Statutes), strip nos. 200–8 give regulations for its control; see also 'Attempts at Economic Co-ordination', pp. 260–64; for taxation on merchants, see Swann, p. 281. For Chinese acquaintance with Greek coins, see Hulsewé, *CICA,* pp. 106, 115, 116.

Photographs of the strips from Juyan translated on p. 162 appear in *RHA,* vol. 1 Plate 4, no. 13, and vol. 2, Plate 33 (TD 8 nos. 1, 2) and Plate 32 (UD 5 no. 1). References to other subjects follow: the Ordinance for Waterways and Passes, *Zhangjia shan* (Statutes), strip nos. 488–526; passports and similar documents, *RHA,* vol. 1, pp. 107–114; the portrait of the ill-lucked princess, Loewe, *Biographical Dictionary,* p. 547 (s.v. Wang Qiang); and Shi Rao's diary, *Men Who Governed,* pp. 54–57. For Wen Weng's civilising influence in the west, see *HS* 89, p. 3625, and Nylan, p. 313; human sacrifice is graphically portrayed on bronzes found in southwest China dating ca. 108 BCE (see *The Chinese Bronzes of Yunnan*).

Shuihudi documents refer to subjects as follows: entitlements to rations, (Statutes), strip nos. 179–82 (*RCL,* pp. 83–85); the pricing of slaves, 'Feng zhen shi', strip nos. 37–41 (*RCL,* p. 193); the secure keeping of cash, (Statutes), strip no. 97 (*RCL,* p. 56); stall holders and use of cash, (Statutes), strip no. 68 (*RCL,* p. 53); see *Zhangjia shan* (Statutes), strip nos. 228–37 for entitlements to rations, and no. 260 for the registration of merchants.

References to persons mentioned above follow: Diwu Lun (*HHS* 41 pp. 1395–402); Sang Hongyang (Kroll); Yin Shang (*HHS* 90, pp. 3673–75); Zhongli Yi (*HHS* 41 pp. 1406–11); Zhu Hui (*HHS* 43, p. 1460); Zhuang (Yan) Yannian (*HS* 90, pp. 3667–72); Zong Jun (*HHS* 41, pp. 1411–14).

11

The Stability of Imperial Rule:
Controversial Issues

At the outset of the Han dynasty, the concept of empire was experimental and subject to question; at its close it was accepted as a regular way of life that brought a people unity, imparting to their institutions a continuity with the past and an outlook for the future. In Han's early decades memories of the practice of empire under Qin may not have been encouraging, for Qin had lasted less than twenty years and there were those who recalled harshness rather than charity as the hallmark of its government. Succession to Qin by another empire which boasted that its rule stood above all other authority and beyond all local loyalties was not necessarily the only way forward, as had been seen in the attempt of Xiang Yu 項羽 to set up a series of co-existent kingdoms; for in the fights that broke out among equally ambitious protagonists Xiang Yu's attempts to do so had failed. Victorious in these fights, Liu Bang and his supporters set up a regime that inherited and largely adopted the very institutions by which Qin had ruled.

On a number of occasions in Western Han the existence or continuity of empire came under threat. In 188 BCE the Empress Dowager Lü severed for a few years the authority vested in the house of Liu. In 154 BCE the newly acceded emperor stood in danger of removal thanks to the actions of some of his relatives. There were fears of a similar threat in 122 BCE, and from 90 to 91 BCE Chang'an city was beset by fighting between rival factions of the imperial family. The imperial succession caused grave problems in 74 BCE, to be followed by some decades that were relatively free from crisis. Some years later, when the leaders of the empire had been failing to display a commanding presence and authority worthy to rule, two specialists in esoteric matters and calendrical computation were bold enough to warn that the house of Han was approaching its allotted end and to call for a re-dedication of dynastic purpose and strength.

Credit may well be due to Wang Mang, founder and sole emperor of the Xin dynasty (9–23 CE), for re-asserting the value of united imperial rule and putting it into effect in such a way that the concept of empire could be seen as the norm. But his authority was short-lived, and throughout history he has become saddled with the reputation of an usurper. Only rarely in Eastern Han times did an emperor show himself to be master of his empire; others around the throne dominated public life and controlled major decisions of state. Nevertheless the existence of empire persisted. After some decades which saw a breakdown of imperial authority the Han dynasty came to an end with the abdication of the last of its emperors in 220 CE. There arose leaders of different houses in different parts of the land who set themselves up as rulers with every intention of restoring a united, single rule. By now the concept of empire as against the co-existence of several legitimate ruling authorities was not to be brought into question, however rarely it was successfully achieved in practice.

Successful empire required that those who were ruled therein recognised themselves as its members and accepted that empire had been created and was being practised legitimately; and here such a claim could not be sustained without reference to the past. A rich tradition and stock of mythology that had come into being and was fostered centuries before the Qin empire had been created contained elements and stories that could either support or subvert the idea and practice of a monarch's united rule. Accounts of the remote past, when human communities first came into being, called to mind paragon rulers of all civilised humanity; perhaps they were pictured in superhuman guise; their leadership brought a blessed way of life to all, and their teachings and orders commanded respect. But there were also examples of rulers of the world who were known for their wickedness or selfish indulgences, and whose excesses were to be execrated. With the passage of time, records of greater authenticity told of leaders and princes first of small and then of larger localised areas who developed the means of government; they brought burdens to bear on the inhabitants, perhaps in return for benefits such as security. In a further stage of development, for which our information is more reliable, the kings of the Warring States (480–221 BCE) imposed the force of government in a far more intensive way than had been seen previously. Despite intrigues and deceptive diplomacy said to have been practised at the highest levels, the inhabitants may well have developed a sense of loyalty to the ruling house where they lived, whether in the uplands of the west or the watered fields of the Huai River valley.

Empire rested on a more sophisticated style of political organs and social forms and a deeper administrative experience, and it posed a new set of demands whose fulfilment was necessary if the authority of government was to earn recognition and carry obedience. But if comparison may be allowed with the systems that were developing in the Western world a major contrast is apparent. Whereas Qin and Han China had no concept of a citizen or citizenship, individuals in some of the Greek cities and Rome had acquired a sense of active membership of their community and took some part in its government. They might act as members of an assembly, or as persons deputed by lot to hold some position of authority; or they might bear an acknowledged responsibility for representing the views of others and bringing them to notice. No organs of government or forms of social grouping of early imperial China could provide scope for such activities.

In Athens major decisions taken in the name of the whole free community and affecting others such as slaves would at times follow open discussion. Agreement to a decision might have depended on the skills of an orator in persuading those present to agree to a proposal or reject those of rivals. In Rome the views of the lower class of inhabitants might be presented for debate by the patricians of the senate. In Chang'an and Luoyang those who had risen to the highest ranks of the civil service could present their own views and counsel to their emperor in private audience, and appropriate decisions would follow. They could be called to account for the consequences of their actions and decisions to the same high authority; they were in no way responsible for explaining them to their critics and rivals.

The practice of Han government could depend on the heavy demands that officials might impose and the severe punishments that they might order. With little opportunity for those who received such treatment to question the basis on which such orders rested, it is difficult to see how voluntary support for a ruling authority could be expected. Bounties in the form of material gifts or privileged treatment would help to do so, but religious performances of the palace or intellectual argument of learned men might well fail to convey to the public the persuasive message of a link between majesty and the common man and woman. An emperor's word could indeed grant an amnesty or a distribution of food and drink and thereby engender some acknowledgment of his powers and his charitable goodness. He might make a public display of his devout services to higher beings, but such acts would not necessarily be seen to relate to his authority or to support a call for a general obedience to his officials.

Voluntary support for a ruling authority or enthusiastic loyalty to a dynasty may well depend on the persuasive or compulsive power of a religious or intellectual type. However, whereas the citizens of the Greek cities and Rome shared a belief in the same gods as those recognised by their rulers, neither nobles nor commoners of Han China took part in the rites to which an emperor subscribed. Appeals to superhuman powers for authority to rule had certainly been voiced in China long before the dawn of empire, but they seem to have carried little weight in the minds of those who founded the Qin and Han empires and formed their organs and means of government. It was only with the passage of years that the need to identify such sources of authority became apparent, to be sought either in the godhead of Heaven or in a universal, cosmological system. In intellectual terms, exercises in defining and explaining the values, needs and forms of government had reached a far more sophisticated level in the West than in the East, where a Plato, Aristotle or Cicero had yet to arise.

From early days in Han the question had arisen of the legitimacy whereby the dynasty had come into being and the morality of the incidents that had attended its creation. Tales of long ago, when hereditary kingdoms had come to an end, could be interpreted in one of two ways: either as acts whereby a champion of good behaviour had eliminated a regime that was notorious for its evil ways; or as incidents in which a man of violence had arisen, expelled a reigning monarch to whom he owed allegiance and taken his place on the throne. In the first case the change of ruler was to be applauded, as it delivered those who were ruled from oppression and perhaps cruelty; in the second case, the newly self-established monarchs should be seen as murderers. The histories of Han include a vivid description of an argument about these issues that took

place in the presence of Jingdi (r. 157–141 BCE) and which bore
on the reputation of his own house and forbears. The Han dynasty
had been founded after the elimination of Qin and the murder
of its nominal head, Zi ying 子嬰, and although no head of
the house of Liu had taken a personal part in such actions, the
manner in which they benefited therefrom allowed scope for question: was the founder of the dynasty in fact no better than a
murderer?

That Jingdi closed the discussion abruptly need occasion no sur-
prise. Open discussion of this issue could easily involve criticism of
the morality of the reigning dynasty and it would be a bold official
who would dare to risk it. But whether or not the question was
mentioned directly, it is likely that doubts regarding Han's right to
have acquired dominion gave rise to thought and the need to show
that it depended on valid authority. Writing shortly after the accession of a sixteen-year-old emperor, between 140 and 134 BCE Dong
Zhongshu 董仲舒 (ca. 179–ca. 104 BCE) may have shown considerable initiative. In responses addressed directly to the throne, he
asserted that imperial rule was dependent on a superhuman power.
This power was seen in Heaven, which was capable of two types
of action, depending on the conduct of the ruler and his officials.
Heaven might confer support for a ruling house or give warning
that it should be replaced. Dong Zhongshu showed considerable
courage in putting these views forward; he may well have been the
first person to do so in Han times, while drawing on opinion that
was so far unvoiced; and there were those at court such as the grand
empress dowager who disagreed basically.

Dong Zhongshu's ideas could only be controversial. Those who
had formed the Qin empire had relied on force, and there is little
to show that the two emperors or their advisors looked to religious
or intellectual authority to validate their actions. Nor is there evidence to show that the first emperors of Western Han regularly
relied on officials who proclaimed such a need. Dong Zhongshu
was in fact drawing attention to a major cleavage of opinion, between
those who looked to the traditions ascribed to the kings of Western
Zhou (1045–771 BCE) and those to whom the practices of the kings
and then the emperors of Qin appealed. By fastening on Heaven as
the source of the superhuman support that imperial government
needed, Dong Zhongshu was alluding to the beliefs of Zhou times

and the claim that the kings of Zhou were the sons of Heaven, placed in their position on earth at Heaven's command. Those who had practised imperial government under Qin had not looked beyond the need for human powers to maintain their strength and ruling authority.

Writings of Western Zhou times refer to the mandate whereby Heaven had conferred such authority on the kings. In his own time, Dong Zhongshu did not call directly on this doctrine to support his arguments, but it is clearly seen somewhat later in a memorial that was submitted by Kuang Heng 匡衡 (chancellor from 36–30 or 29) perhaps in 34 BCE. Even then however it seems that the time was not ripe for acceptance of the idea and its place in discussions of political theory. It is seen in full in the famous essay 'On the Destiny of Kings' that the historian Ban Biao 班彪 (3–54 CE) wrote at a time of dynastic uncertainty or even turmoil, when the survival of the house of Han was highly questionable. In stressing that rulership is the proper function of the man appointed thereto by Heaven, Ban Biao did his best to show how this had been true of Liu Bang 劉邦, the first of the Han emperors. Here was a rebuttal of the doubts raised by one speaker in front of Jingdi some hundred and fifty years previously.

Controversy also attended a search for support for dynastic authority from intellectual ideas of another type. This was the theory that all stages and changes of creation, of birth and death and of success and failure followed the pattern of a cycle of five phases. These changes occurred inexorably in the three estates of the universe. The pattern appeared in the heavens and the movements of their bodies, in the growth and decay of natural matter and in the lives and deaths of mankind and animals. Likewise the emergence, survival and replacement of a dynastic house could be explained in the same terms. But just as the mandate of heaven can have been of little appeal to the emperors of Qin or indeed for most of Western Han, this theory was basically flawed, for it carried with it the message that the existing dynasty was certain to reach its end in favour of another. There was however every reason to invoke it so as to validate the authority of Wang Mang. By founding his own short-lived dynasty of Xin, he had taken the place left by the imperial house of Han; it suited him very well to claim that the change had been part of the process of cosmic being.

A further difference of view lay in the formal religious occasions in which the Han emperors took part, supposedly on behalf of their realm and their subjects. From the outset of Western Han these took the form of worship addressed among others to five divine powers, but these are not to be confused with the five phases just mentioned. There is nothing to prove that such services necessarily included subservience to that theory, with its insistence on a cycle of their rise and fall or their correlation with natural objects, emotions, sovereign powers and spatial or temporal divisions as was to be asserted later. Emperors attended services to the five divine powers and to certain other deities with increasing frequency from 123 BCE, but not with the regularity that had been intended. Controversy arose with proposals to discontinue services to the five in favour of a new series that was to be offered to no less than heaven and earth. These suggestions arose at much the same time as some officials were re-introducing the idea of heaven's mandate. The formal change, which was inaugurated in 31 BCE, provoked considerable discussion and was in no way permanent; it was to be revoked and then restored on several occasions in the following years, finally to gain permanent acceptance. Possibly a dynastic motive may have affected the earlier uncertainty and caused change and change-about. The reigning emperor (Chengdi; r. 33–7 BCE) had not succeeded in producing an heir, and it was thought that failure to propitiate one of these sets of deities might have been responsible for the undeniable weakness of the throne.

Dynastic and religious issues entered into two other controversial matters, the construction and purpose of the *Ming tang* 明堂 and the care of the shrines dedicated to the services of deceased emperors. According to ancient tradition, a *Ming tang*, or Hall of Devotion (sometimes rendered, incorrectly, as 'Bright Hall'), had served as the solemn place of convocation where the highest in the land rendered their dues to the supreme power, termed 'god on high' (*shang di* 上帝). But when the question arose of constructing such a building, the information that was available to Wudi was by no means clear and consistent. At the beginning of his reign four officials proposed the erection of a *Ming tang* where the emperor would grant audience to and receive homage from his kings and nobles. Owing perhaps to the influence of the Grand Empress Dowager Dou 竇, no action followed; two of the officials concerned were dismissed, and two were driven to suicide.

Possibly the grand empress dowager had objected to the construction of a *Ming tang* that was intended to serve imperial purposes rather than act as a hall for religious ceremonies, but we cannot be certain of her mind and her motives. The idea rose again in 110 BCE, some twenty years after her death. Wudi performed his acts of worship to the five powers and Grand Unity at a *Ming tang* that lay away from Chang'an; certainly it was a hall with a religious purpose but probably not of the type that the grand empress dowager would have wished to see.

At the end of Western Han when the credit and reputation of the imperial house had reached a low ebb a *Ming tang* was erected at the capital city, but once again its purpose had changed. Seasonal services for the Han dynasty took place there in 5 CE; once Wang Mang had set up his own dynasty to replace Han, it was in the *Ming tang* that the services to the Han emperors, of the now defunct dynasty, took place. The new building served imperial purposes as a venue where Han emperors were relegated to the position of visiting guests rather than retaining that of lords of their realm. Along with other buildings the *Ming tang* was destroyed by fire at the close of Wang Mang's dynasty; a new one arose at the Eastern Han's capital of Luoyang, to witness an emperor's reverence for his father on at least one occasion (59 CE).

The second matter at issue was that of the appropriate services due to the memory of deceased emperors, as has been mentioned above (Chapter 6, p. 98). Rendered at the chambers of rest and the shrines that formed integral parts of the imperial mausoleums, by the time of Yuandi (r. 48–33) the daily, monthly and seasonal sacrifices had become demanding and expensive. At a time when various measures were being adopted to reduce expenditure, the question arose of the extent to which these rites should be maintained. But proposals to discontinue some of them aroused dispute on a number of grounds other than those of the material expenses, for example, points of ritual, the proper use of traditional ways and the choice of honours due to certain emperors.

The shrines and their services played a key role in maintaining the line of the imperial family with its correct sequences of generations and degrees of kinship. According to some sources it was correct to retain the shrines and services for seven generations in the case of the ruler of the land, and five or three for those of lower social ranks and status; there were also those who took the view that five was the correct number for the head of the imperial family. A further matter arose in the question of whether the provision of these services should be continued for some emperors even after seven generations, in perpetuity. This distinction was marked by the use of the special term *zu* 祖 'ancestor', or *zong* 宗 'forbear', rather than *di* 帝 in the posthumous, temple titles whereby emperors were to be known. The distinction may have disappeared in Eastern Han.

Maintenance or abandonment of some of these shrines became a live dynastic issue. Shortly after the death of Xuandi (48 BCE), Gong Yu (2), who became imperial counsellor in 44 BCE, put forward a proposal to abolish some of them, and the ensuing controversy continued until at least 5 CE. Some of the memorials that concerned the question bore the names of a number of officials, perhaps as many as seventy, who were acting in a group. Possibly some of them had remembered that as early as 180 BCE discussion of this sensitive issue had been banned, at the cost of the death penalty, and they may have sought safety in numbers. Particular points arose in connection with services dedicated to the fathers of two emperors, Gaozu and Xuandi, who had not themselves sat on the throne, and with the dues that were appropriate for an empress or empress dowager. Discussion also brought to the fore the distinction that derived solely from birth and position in a lineage as against that of personal merit.

The grant of a special title that brought with it services in perpetuity was not in question for Gaozu, the founding emperor, and it was generally accepted as right for Wendi; they therefore received the ancestral, or temple, titles of Taizu 太祖 and Taizong 太宗, respectively. A proposal of Yin Zhong 尹忠, superintendent of trials, circa 45 BCE, that Wudi should receive similar honours rested on the achievements of his reign such as the reform of the calendar and the stand taken against non-Han peoples. Subject to dispute as this suggestion was, it was finally agreed to confer such honours, largely owing to the persuasive arguments of Liu Xin 劉歆 (46 BCE–23 CE), one of Han's most talented scholars. In this way Wudi received the temple title of Shizong 世宗 and has subsequently received unquestioned adulation.

The establishment of Eastern Han's capital at Luoyang involved change, and it was no longer practical to carry out services at the imperial tombs that lay mainly to the north of Chang'an. A single shrine was set up with memorial tablets for the eleven emperors of Western Han. Guangwudi received the temple title of Shizu 世祖; the tombs of Eastern Han emperors were situated alternately to the south-east and north-west of Luoyang.

As has been shown above (Chapter 1) a number of considerations could bedevil succession to the imperial throne. The matrimonial system and its attendant rivalries or the degree of kinship could arouse dispute, as could the expedient of thrusting an infant on the throne so as to safeguard the interests of a family that was dominant in the palace. The accounts that we have of the succession, deposal and abdication of emperors may reveal differing attitudes towards an emperor's position.

In his initial declaration, the First Qin Emperor saw no need to refer to any other claims than that of his conquest of his potential rivals. Following the domination of the Empress Lü and an abortive attempt to make Liu Xiang 劉襄 (2) emperor, it was Liu Heng 劉恆, known as Wendi, who acceded (180 BCE). His protestations of reluctance to accept the position may ring somewhat hollow, but they perhaps suggest a real need, that of showing that he would subsequently claim full support from those who had persuaded him or insisted that he should comply with their wishes. As we are told, unseemly haste, disregard of the decencies of ritual and a concentration on personal ambitions and pleasures marked the reactions of Liu He 劉賀 (4), the eighteen-year-old king of Changyi who was called to take the place of Zhaodi in 74 BCE. Such behaviour disqualified him from that position, as it was argued in the palace, and he held it for no more than twenty-seven days before deposal (for details of these incidents, see Chapter 6, pp. 96–7).

There followed the proposal of Huo Guang 霍光, general-in-chief and marshal of state, that Liu Bingyi 劉病已, later known as Xuandi, should become emperor. He called to mind the need for a monarch to conform with the ordered conventional way of conduct (*li* 禮) and to show respect for his ancestry. Liu He had been found wanting in just these ways, but the new candidate had been properly trained in these matters. Zhaodi had not left a direct heir, and in the absence of such a one, Huo Guang wrote, it was right to choose a collateral descendant with intelligence and integrity to succeed to the throne. Such qualities could be expected in the eighteen-year-old youth whose name he put forward; he had been educated in traditional writings, his behaviour was moderate rather than rash and he was of a philanthropic frame of mind.

In establishing his own dynasty to replace the one in which he had served as a senior official and finally as regent for an infant emperor, Wang Mang drew on examples of mythology and history, and on ideas that had gained some acceptance in the immediately preceding decades. To counter arguments that might be raised against his action, he called on strange events as indications that it was the will of heaven that he should become emperor, and he adopted one of the five phases as his patron. It was the power symbolised by Earth and the colour of yellow that was controlling all manner of being, as Wang Mang claimed, and he gave out that he was ruling in correct sequence under just such protection. He traced his ancestry back to Shun, the legendary monarch seen as a splendid example of kings whom all should emulate; his initial proclamation drew attention to his part as a successor to the kings of Western Zhou.

In his turn Guangwudi, first emperor of Eastern Han, also drew on earlier precedents. Like Wendi he made a show of reluctance to accept the suggestion that he should reign as emperor. When, finally, he agreed to do so, he had taken note of references to heaven's mandate and the compelling necessity for the existence of an acknowledged ruler of mankind. In what was perhaps a new gesture he signified his subservience to Heaven by building an altar; the smoke that arose from the sacrifices thereon conveyed notification of his accession to heaven.

The Han dynasty came to its official and formal end in 220 CE when Xiandi, the reigning emperor, issued his instrument of abdication in favour of Cao Pi 曹丕, king of Wei. In doing so he recognised the realities of the situation in which he stood, as all support already lay with Cao Pi. He called on precedents for abdication set by the mythological kings Yao and Shun who had acted thus in favour of their chosen successors. The document also referred to the principle that the mandate of heaven does not remain constantly in one house but reverts to a recipient whose qualities are of sufficient merit to bear the burden of its charge.

The stability of empire rested also on the relations that the emperor maintained with his immediate relatives by blood, the kings. The revolt raised by seven of these in 154 BCE was perhaps the most dangerous moment in Western Han, when the emperor's position and authority were likely to succumb to the will of others and the concept of empire might have been called into question. Suppression of the revolt led to countermeasures to reduce the effective power that any of the kings might wield. Two incidents perhaps suggest the persistence of the underlying difficulties.

Liu Sheng 劉勝 (1), half-brother of Liu Che 劉徹 (Wudi), became king of Zhongshan in 154 BCE and is best known owing to one of the accidents of archaeology. It was in his tomb, at Mancheng 滿城, that material remains were first found to testify to the use of a suit of jade for burial of the highest in the land. In 138 BCE Liu Sheng found an opportunity to complain of the strict way in which the kings were being controlled by officials who had been posted from the centre to act as senior officials in the kingdom. The measures that followed were perhaps intended to re-assert the importance of kin relationships in the imperial family while at the same time enabling the central government to control the activities of the kings' sons; the kings themselves did not increase their powers.

It is difficult to determine the considerations and motives that lay behind a decision of 117 BCE which followed the views of officials but thwarted the stated will of the emperor (for details, see Chapter 6, p. 94). The question had arisen of the proper rank to be granted to three of Wudi's sons; whereas Wudi had himself declared that they should be no higher than nobles, he was eventually obliged to yield to the counsels of his ministers and invest them as kings. This outcome was quite contrary to the ways in which the kings and kingdoms had been treated in the immediately preceding decade. It would seem, perhaps somewhat surprisingly, that in this instance it was officials, rather than an emperor, who were anxious to uphold the dignity and position of the imperial house. Problems of this type do not appear to have arisen in Eastern Han.

An occasion on which senior officials discussed the best tactics with which to confront the Xiongnu 匈奴 is described above (Chapter 6, p. 93). We also have a record of a case of argument and counter-argument wherein strategic issues arose. This affected major political decisions of the steps to be taken over problems in

Central Asia, where the Northern Route along the Takla Makan desert had fallen out of Han control (119 CE). At a meeting summoned to discuss the problem, Ban Yong 班勇 spoke in opposition to some who advocated closure of contacts with the north-west. A younger son of the highly successful general Ban Chao 班超, who died in 102 CE, Ban Yong had learnt much from his father's guidance and experience of campaigning in Central Asia; Ban Yong himself had served as a major in the field circa 107. At the meeting he argued against granting a request to send out a force of five thousand men in response to an appeal from Shanshan 鄯善, on the Southern Route; he believed that it would be expensive, unlikely to be effective and unlikely to provide long-term results. He also argued against the view that Han should abandon the Western Regions, insofar as such a withdrawal would serve to strengthen the Xiongnu. He maintained, with some success, that re-establishment of a colonelcy at Dunhuang with the express purpose of 'Protecting the Western Regions' would suffice to maintain Han integrity and prestige without provoking hostile reactions.

Mention is made from time to time of a principle that was basic to the way in which the emperor was seen. Should he be an active ruler and leader who would determine policies and actions; should he take a personal hand in government? Or should he be seen as a figurehead, sitting with his arms folded and entrusting his ministers with full responsibilities and powers? Examples of both types of monarch are found in both Qin and Han times; protagonists for both types could call on precepts of old to support their arguments. In particular those who accepted or promoted the idea of an emperor who stood aloof from the cares of state could refer to sayings ascribed to teachers such as Zhuangzi and Laozi, to whom the Grand Empress Dou had been devoted. *Wu wei* 無爲 was the ideal (see Chapter 1, p. 11); government of mankind and the land would proceed best without positive initiative, and rulers who took an active part in the government could not be assured of success.

Wu wei was clearly the order of the day when an infant sat enthroned, and it doubtless appealed to an empress, high-ranking officials, courtiers or eunuchs who had brought about just that state of affairs. Ambitious officials could enjoy the duties that had been entrusted to them and could inaugurate such activities as suited their frame of mind or satisfied their love of power. Some of them may have remembered how a strong-minded and wilful emperor could be a menace, as those who lived during Jingdi's reign knew only too well. While still heir apparent he had beaten his cousin to death with the gaming board at which they were at play and contest; as emperor he had ruthlessly sent down Chao Cuo 鼂錯, one of his most able advisors, for execution. In addition he had not stirred to save another of his advisors from a humiliating death in prison; this was Zhou Yafu 周亞夫, to whom he owed the retention of his throne at a time of crisis. A little later Dong Zhongshu observed that in ideal conditions a monarch should refrain from active participation in the running of public life, but if his empire had fallen under the influence of evil men or needed radical reform it was his duty to bestir himself so as to save his people.

Notes for Further Reading

See *Crisis and Conflict* for: services to ancestors (pp. 179–82; also *DMM*, Chapter 13); the state cults (Chapter 5); a suggestion of dynastic re-dedication in 5 BCE (pp. 278–80). See *DMM* for: Ban Biao (pp. 109–10; also de Bary, *Sources of Chinese Tradition*, vol. 1, pp. 176–80); chambers of rest and shrines (pp. 282–83); the debate on dynastic legitimacy (p. 86); and *Men Who Governed*, Chapter 12, for the investiture of three kings in 117 BCE.

References to subjects in primary sources follow: Ban Yong (*HHS* 47, pp. 1587–89); Dong Zhongshu's responses (*HS* 56, pp. 2498–523); Guangwudi's reluctance to take the throne (*HHS* 1A, pp. 20–22); Han Xiandi (*SGZ* 2, p. 62); Huo Guang's support for the accession of Liu Bingyi (*HS* 8, p. 238); Kuang Heng (*HS* 81, p. 3338; also *Men Who Governed*, p. 443); Liu He (*HS* 68, pp. 2937–46); services to Guangwudi (*HHS* 2, p. 100); the title of Shizu for Guangwudi (*HHS* 2, p. 95; also *DMM*, pp. 282–99). For Liu Sheng's tomb at Mancheng, see *Mancheng Han mu fajue baogao*.

12

Weaknesses and Problems

Farmers of Qin and Han times, men and women alike, toiled in the fields to wrest a living from the soil; artisans and craftsmen sweated in the workshops to produce choice items of bronze and precious metals; conscripts were set to hump grain from the fields, to hew and stack timber, to build palaces or mausolea; convicts, perhaps maimed or disabled, dragged themselves to their appointed place of toil. In all these occupations and activities they were subject to the regulations of the laws and perhaps to the direct supervision of officials. The three social institutions marked their status, gave some an opportunity to work for a living and brought the force of government to bear on their lives. Only indirectly were these men and women affected by controversies that beset the decisions of the emperor and his officials or by discussions that arose at the higher reaches of the world in which they lived. Nor were they necessarily affected by all of the weaknesses and problems to be discussed below. The direct contacts between ordinary folk and officials took place mainly at village or district, or possibly county, levels. The choice of an heir to the throne, the performance and type of the state cults and the formulation of the laws were not their concern; they simply lived according to the decisions wished upon them.

The imperial system may perhaps be judged to have contained the seeds of its own weaknesses or even destruction. As in all hereditary monarchies, there can be no guarantee that the system will produce incumbents who are worthy of their position. In addition there is no certainty that competition among rivals to secure the highest position will eliminate those unfitted for the task; rather it may make it more likely for those with marked aspirations and ambitions to find opportunity to do so. Whereas the matrimonial practice of the emperors may have grown up in a desire to ensure the production of an heir, it could hardly avoid engendering rivalries that could lead to violence or civil fighting.

Some of the emperors, such as Chengdi (r. 33–7 BCE), were castigated for their idleness or lack of interest in the welfare of the empire, rather than praised for standing away from the mundane concerns of government; others, such as Mingdi (r. 57–75 CE), were seen to be narrow minded. Some were clearly kept in thrall under the domination of their womenfolk (e.g., Huidi and Andi). Some made a show of ordering savings in public expenditure, as did Wendi and Mingdi for the tombs to be constructed for their repose; some were blamed for extravagance in the plans that they laid for just such purposes, as was Chengdi for a project that was later abandoned. The personality, strength and behaviour of emperors varied widely. Opportunities could lie open for other persons to plan for the imperial succession in a way that would favour their own families or deny such a prize to others; such steps would not stop at Zhao Zhaoyi's 趙昭儀 murder of an infant son sired by Chengdi, or Huo Xian's 霍顯 murder of Xuandi's empress Xu while pregnant.

An emperor's extreme acts of favouritism could call for censure, as when Gong Yu 貢禹 (2), circa 44 BCE, protested at the way in which minor consorts were being buried in the grounds reserved for emperors. Perhaps in jest, Aidi (r. 7–1 BCE) had once suggested abdicating in favour of Dong Xian 董賢 (2), to receive a stern reminder of where his duties lay and of his lack of authority to dispose of the throne at whim. Aidi did, however, accord Dong Xian the privilege of burial in a jade suit, reserved in principle for some members of the imperial family. Chen Zhong 陳忠 did not dare to voice a direct reprimand at the grant of the honorary title of Ye Wang Jun 野王君 to Wang Sheng 王聖, foster-mother of Andi (r. 106–125 CE), but he expressed his criticism in a specially composed essay. The evil behaviour of her daughter Wang Borong 王伯榮 drew a severe protest from Yang Zhen 楊震, who became supreme commander in 123 CE. With open access to the palace she was able to exploit her position wantonly and contrived that the correct succession of a nobility was violated; by right this should have passed to a younger brother of Liu Hu 劉護, but it was Wang Borong's lover, and later husband, who received the honour. On at least one occasion, somewhat earlier, an emperor had been aware of the criticism that favouritism might incur. Feng Yewang 馮野王 was probably the obvious choice for appointment as imperial counsellor in 33 BCE; his sister was one of Yuandi's consorts and the emperor refused to countenance it.

The part played by the eunuchs in public life, principally in Eastern Han times, may also be seen as deriving from favouritism. Eunuchs are mentioned in various contexts from the time of Gaozu onwards, and they regularly filled positions in the palace and some of the established offices, such as those of the masters of writing, within the Secretariat. But as yet they were set at a comparatively junior level without direct powers, and it is only from the time of Yuandi (r. 48–33 BCE) that we hear of eunuchs who were able to exert a dominating influence on public affairs. Two, Hong Gong 弘恭 and Shi Xian 石顯, commanded sufficient power to force Xiao Wangzhi 蕭望之 to commit suicide (47 BCE); he had once been imperial counsellor.

It was by intervention in disputes between leading families of the palace in 92 CE that eunuchs attained a commanding position in government and at court. They formed a strong support for at least two emperors, Shundi and Huandi, one of whom they had assisted to reach the throne; in their own turn they aroused the resentment and jealousy of the officials who had risen to their positions by the normal stages of a career. After a bungled attempt to remove their influence in 168 CE they retained sufficient strength to secure the safety and continuity of the reigning dynasty, until they were finally eliminated in a massacre of 189.

Time and again an emperor's decree protested that his own failings were the cause of popular suffering or remarked on his inability to conform with the natural order of creation. He would seek counsel to see how he could comply with the cosmic order or how matters could be put right, as may be seen in the decree that followed an earthquake felt in Luoyang in 133 CE (see Chapter 6, p. 100). The text leads us to believe that at the age of eighteen Shundi was well aware of the gravity of his responsibilities. However, affirmations such as these did not necessarily derive from an emperor's personal heart searching. They may well have drawn from the protests or complaints that a high-ranking official was levelling at the ways of government and from that official's attempts to discredit those who had reached high and responsible positions of power.

A hope that a close tie of kinship would ensure the loyalty of the kings to the throne could hardly be sustained; for after the transmission of the imperial throne through two generations, a new emperor might find that some of the kings were his seniors by age, or that their relationship to the throne was now somewhat distant, perhaps as remote cousins of the monarch, sprung from different maternal lines of heredity. Some of the kings may even have harboured resentment, borne of antagonisms of the past in which their own immediate forebears had been involved; Liu An 劉安 (2), king of Huainan, had cause to remember how his father, Liu Chang 劉長 (1), had been treated. Perhaps the histories overstate the poor or evil behaviour on the part of some of the kings, but those accounts may reveal one real aspect of the situation; situated in remote areas away from the centre, a king was free of the restraints that would have limited his behaviour at court.

Political and social conditions and the appropriate means of organising and imposing government varied widely from those of the pre-imperial age. So too did the methods and aims of those who ruled the Qin and then the Han empire from the exemplary precepts enshrined in some of the writings of old. At their extreme points, the two attitudes to public life could be characterised the one as materialist and state-cantered, the other as idealistic and man-centered, but the issue was in no way simple; for in some instances, such as music, the examples left by the rulers of the past had not been identical. They had adopted different practices, and there could hardly be a set of immutable examples of conduct or policy upon which it was possible to draw.

A rescript issued generally to officials between 140 and 134 BCE invited their responses to the difficulties that these contradictory points of view caused; they should consider how far it was necessary to adhere to the institutions and principles of the past and how far these should be abandoned so as to take account of the immediate situation and its needs. In his reply Dong Zhongshu 董仲舒 (ca. 179–ca. 104 BCE) gave his view, that there is no clear-cut distinction whereby either of these attitudes to public life should be excluded. Those lessons and practices of the past that could lead to moral improvement should be retained, but the actual means of operating the government must be subject to revision as necessary, in the light of current needs. Indeed, it was certainly the case that there were differences in the ways that the monarchs of old had set about their task. These could be explained by the frank recognition that errors and faults had appeared in the practical application of their principles and that these required correction; but throughout such changes, the basic values and intentions remained unchallenged. Much the same answer is seen in the account of the arguments exchanged in the debate held at court in 81 BCE, the *Discourses on Salt and Iron.*

The presentation of arguments in China varied greatly from the ways that prevailed in Greece and Rome. For pre-imperial times we may read accounts of encounters between a sovereign and his advisors that are perhaps anecdotal and fictional rather than factual, but they are no less significant for that reason. They tell of incidents in which a roving man of affairs would exert his wits to impress on a ruler the great benefits that would accrue from certain types of action; the arguments that he deployed may not necessarily have been completely free of deception. Or, he might advise against undertaking steps that would appear to lead to immediate gains, but in reality concealed underlying dangers. These tales need not be accepted as veritable records of the ways in which the plans and policies of a kingdom were determined, or how kings might be gullible to persuasion by others, but they take their place in a tradition whereby arguments on the highest matters of state were presented face to face in the secluded safety of audience with a monarch. Neither in pre-imperial nor in early imperial times was there opportunity for the practice of oratory or public declamation either to advance or to denounce a proposed measure of state, as was seen in the assemblies of Athens and in the debates of Rome's senate. Chinese officials were not called upon to defend their decisions in public; nor was there any semblance of following the will expressed by a large number of people.

There was thus no presentation of opposing wills, ideas or arguments in public, and it may be thought that in this way China missed out when compared with the West. Arguments for or against a proposal were first advanced in the form of memorial and counter memorial, or they took place within the narrow confines of a hall in the palace. Exceptionally, the document to which reference has been made, the *Discourses on Salt and Iron,* provides an example of an oral exchange of views that had been expressly ordered by imperial decree. Biased as the account of that exchange is, it illustrates some of the difficulties that faced imperial governments, whether of a practical nature or as matters of principle. In this instance, as we are told, discussion ranged over the whole art of government, the call to increase material prosperity or to give priority to moral precepts.

Called specifically to give advice on the value of the government's monopolies of salt and iron production, spokesmen for the government and its critics argued the case for controlling the population or leaving its members to lead their own lives according to their own devices. They referred to a number of problems that were inherent in a major scheme of economic organisation and to the resulting weaknesses. As against the claim that the monopolies increased the revenue of the government, and that those sources of revenue would be used for the benefit of the people, it was countered that such profits derived from nothing but the people's own goods. The use of coinage, which had perhaps been increasing over the decades, also raised questions: Did the present system allow scope for economic oppression on the part of officials or merchants? Would advantage accrue from raising tax in the form of local products rather than in coin? Money, came the answer, serves to alleviate distress and to equalise prices. The critics of the government drew attention to the failures that could be noticed in the operation of the monopolies and their results; the quality of the iron wares was not necessarily of a high or an even standard, and the goods did not always reach the farmers, who could perhaps not afford to buy them. The spokesman for the government replied that it was the state that could provide a more regular service, with an assured supply of materials and labour, on which private iron masters and commercial magnates could not draw.

The parties to the debate considered the difficulties involved in relations with non-Han peoples. It was necessary to provide protection for those living close to the perimeter against the potential dangers of hostile groups; easy as it might seem to be to leave the non-Han peoples and their leaders to their own way of life, this would not necessarily be sufficient to ensure security. But if it was necessary to make a show of Han strength, short-term expeditions could hardly be of permanent value in deterring hostile activities. At the same time major campaigns could involve Han in great expense and the use of manpower; they could not be sustained for long and they would not necessarily succeed in reaching a definitive conclusion. The difficulty lay in finding and effectively defeating a highly mobile opponent who was greatly superior to the Chinese by virtue of a knowledge of the terrain, experience of its climate and use of the horse in warfare.

In addition, unlike Greece and Rome, imperial China did not call on a traditional ideal of military heroism. There was no regular and professional means of recruiting and training officers to serve in the armed forces; there was no attraction to do so in the same way as that seen in the *cursus honorum* and possibility of a career for officials. Furthermore, reluctance to entrust the overall command of a task force to a single general officer could lead to disputes and rivalries and prejudice the outcome of a military operation.

On a number of occasions the question arose of the most suitable way of handling potential enemies, to be seen mainly in various groups in the north. The choice lay between appeasement, with a show of friendship, or confrontation, with its dubious outcome. Friendship would be based on an acknowledged treaty of amity and an exchange of material goods that could cost the Chinese dear; perhaps the gift of a Han princess as a bride for one of the non-Han leaders would be matched by the retention in Chang'an of an heir to the leader of one such group. Wang Hui 王恢 (1) and Han Anguo 韓安國 (1) presented opposing arguments over these matters in 135 BCE (see Chapter 6, p. 93)

The highest point reached by those who sought a peaceful solution to these problems occurred in the state visit to Chang'an of Huhanye 呼韓邪, one of the leaders of the Xiongnu, in 51 BCE. That Han was ready to acknowledge the position of the visitor is seen in the treatment that he received and the mark of status with which he was honoured. Despite some opposition among the officials to such treatment of the visitor, these courtesies were of those of a higher rank than those accorded to the kings.

No agreed solution to these problems appeared during the four centuries of Han; the strength of each party varied from time to time. Han governments were not always able to maintain the defence lines in the north in a fully effective state, and the commanderies of the northern perimeter might lie open to penetration and disruption. Nor could a straight choice between a peaceful agreement or open hostility with the Xiongnu be taken free of other matters of policy. Some advisors to the throne saw the expansion of Han interests into ever wider territories as a means of consolidating imperial power and protecting imperial lands and peoples. Those territories themselves lay open to the influence of other leaders than those whose habitat lay in Chang'an or Luoyang, and advances there could hardly fail to involve Han in relations with communities or kingdoms situated deep in Central Asia, such as Wusun 烏孫 or Jushi 車師 (in the Ili River valley and Turfan). Other voices, of those who foresaw the difficulties and doubted the value of territorial expansion, would at times plead for retrenchment in the hope of retaining security on a narrower front. Nonetheless, it was in the initial decades of Wudi's reign (r. 141–87 BCE) that Chinese servicemen and officials, diplomats and travellers found their ways into the wide expanses of the north, north-west and north-east. There also arose the question of the extent to which comparable ventures should be undertaken in the south-west and south-east, which as yet lay outside the scope of imperial government. Advances in these directions were deferred while there lurked the danger of hostile activities in the north.

The establishment of organs of Han provincial government accompanied advances in the north and south, whether close to modern Burma or within modern Korea. But it could not be maintained that these wide stretches of territory came completely under the heavy hand of Han officials and the impact of intensive government. The headquarters of a commandery or the encampments of colonies might well remain isolated, bringing their influence to bear on no more than a narrow scale; such authority could in no way be pervasive in areas such as the near desert reaches of the north or the coastal strip of Vietnam. Officials had penetrated into these regions; Han forces had not occupied them.

Intervention in the south, particularly beyond the Ling range of mountains, could be perilous, as Li Gu 李固, a relatively junior official, appreciated circa 137 CE. Arguing against the idea of sending a force of forty thousand men to quell unrest and disorders in those parts (present-day Guangdong and Guangxi), he pointed to the difficulties of despatching a large force on a long and arduous journey and keeping it supplied. He added that such a force would be in no fit state to face an enemy after such an ordeal, and one could only expect that tropical diseases would have exacted their heavy toll of casualties.

Somewhat later (ca. 160 CE), a memorial submitted by another comparatively junior official, who rose to eminence and whom we shall meet below, shows up some of the failings of provincial government. While still no more than a member of the Secretariat Chen Fan 陳蕃 noted the harm wrought by bandits in the commanderies of Lingling and Guiyang (modern Guangxi and Hunan) and called for an examination of the success with which provincial officials, including the regional commissioners, were carrying out their work.

For all their hopes and intentions, Han imperial governments did not possess the means to organise economic production or extend their influences on a wide scale for long. Qin and Han governments had set up means to receive annual reports of the facts and figures from all parts of the empire and in doing so were far in advance of contemporary regimes elsewhere in the world. Nevertheless they were not in a position to plan policies on the basis of a budget, estimating the resources that were available and the expenses that they would have to meet. Some officials may have realised that the safety and success of imperial government rests on a careful maintenance of balance of the production of essential supplies, the use of labour to further works of general value and the avoidance of conditions that would provoke popular unrest, disobedience or even rebellion. The higher the proportion of manpower that officials took away from the farms to dig a canal or to campaign in the northwest, the less effort would be available for raising cereal crops or the hemp that the population needed for clothing. Dissident leaders could attract a following from various types of malcontent; there were the angry men and women who had been put to work too hard at projects from which they would receive no benefit, and there were those who were reduced to want owing to a shortage of food production. Such leaders might also attract deserters who, escaping from their obligations and facing the punishments of the Han laws, might welcome protection; folklore might tell of incidents of this type that featured in the collapse of Qin and the foundation of Han. In his forthright comments on current extravagance and the need for economies circa 44 BCE, Gong Yu (2) had perhaps realised the dangers.

Provincial officials would report to the central government on the conditions that they had witnessed in particular areas. They would doubtless bear these in mind when their own turn came to serve as senior officials of state who were responsible for initiating or suspending major projects. However their point of view may well have been somewhat narrow. Necessarily they would base their judgements on their own experiences and would have had little opportunity to compare their own conclusions with those of their colleagues who had served in other, no less significant, parts of the empire. Travellers such as Zhang Qian 張騫 (d. 113 BCE) could inform high-ranking officials in the capital of what they had seen and learnt in their wanderings far afield, perhaps into Central Asia; the few officials who were permanently posted in those parts, such as the protector general, might be able to supply comprehensive information about local conditions. But such possibilities were exceptional rather than regular, and it could hardly be expected that the central government could call on an overall account of geographical conditions for all parts of the empire; readers of these pages are in a far better situation to do so.

Imperial government rested on administration by officials of unquestioned loyalty, high intelligence and proven efficiency, but a combination of these qualities may not have been found as easily as might be hoped. Some officials had been appointed after an evaluation of their abilities; others had found their place thanks to the sponsorship of a relative or a senior servant of the empire. A fascinating text of the Qin period which is entitled 'How to Be a Good Official' (*Wei li zhi dao* 爲吏之道) enjoins attention to public rather than private interests and avoidance of oppression and decisions taken in anger. Officials should accept advice, take careful note of a situation, avoid excess and face up to danger. In a manner that is perhaps reminiscent of the exhortations of Chinese governments of the twentieth century, this document lists five good qualities for officials and five types of error into which an official might fall. They should be men of integrity and work with due care and respect for the people whom they were governing, encouraging them to overcome difficulties, and they were warned that disaffection arises from an official's pride, indolence and anger.

Dated some time later one of the documents found on the north-western perimeter writes of officials of three types; those of average or mediocre qualities; those who perhaps held sinecures and exploited their positions to their personal advantage; and those with a poor intelligence which could not be improved. In Eastern Han, Diwu Lun 第五倫 (d. after 86 CE) complained that there was no means of ensuring that officials who owed their place to sponsorship were of suitable ability. Circa 164 CE protests arose at the way in which eunuchs were sponsoring their own protégés for office.

Failure or inability to prevent actions deemed to be wrong or liable to lead to disaster might induce some men of high intellectual ability to forego the chance of public service and to seek a life of seclusion as a hermit. Alternatively, frustrated or angered by decisions that were being taken, an official might allow thoughts of dissidence to enter his mind; and should he be in contact with one of the kings who was himself dissatisfied with his position, he might even try to persuade him to launch a movement against the central government. The frequency whereby accusations of raising a plot gave grounds for the execution of senior men in public life perhaps reveals that fears of such an uprising were all too prevalent.

Imperial history did not lack examples to show how, all too easily, these treasonable attempts had taken place. From the point of view of Han loyalists of the house of Liu, and the historians who recounted the events, Wang Mang's establishment of the Xin (New) dynasty in 9 CE had been just such an example; they would conveniently forget or fail to bring to attention the thought that the Han empire itself owed its foundation to just such acts. Nor would they credit Wang Mang with any attempts to restore a sense of order to a troubled empire and land.

Constraints of various types may well have limited an official's scope for initiative. In general careers followed a well-trodden path, but occasionally an official could be promoted to a high-ranking position by-passing the usual stages. Throughout, officials were obliged to work directly to their seniors, and the need to conform with the hierarchical order might well have proven to be frustrating. They may well have been able to rely for guidance on an accumulated knowledge of earlier decisions, but the silent force of precedent and fears of taking an action that ran against its warnings may well have deterred experiment. Compromise may at times have been unavoidable, as when service to the ideals of public life would conflict with the will and determination of those who took the major decisions of policy.

In practical terms, retirement from office for the maximum period of three years to complete the mourning services due to a parent could have had a major effect on the continuity of government and the maintenance of a policy, but records do not show how rigidly this requirement was observed. Instruction in technical or even practical matters formed no part of an official's training, with the result that a newly appointed governor would have received no guidance on how to handle an emergency. If fortunate, he could depend on the skills and experience of junior officials and local inhabitants. Such help could be invaluable if he found himself responsible for repairing the breaches of a river's bank, stemming the spread of plague or alleviating distress caused by earthquake.

As in the United Kingdom, so in early imperial China there was no written constitution. Nevertheless, far from being arbitrary, constitutional practice was subject to rules of precedent, as is seen in the cases when an empress dowager took a leading part in settling the dynastic succession. As far as may be determined from the fraction of legal material that is available, the statutes and ordinances seem to have been drawn up on *ad hoc* basis rather than after deliberate examination of a major subject, such as agrarian management and its problems. The growing volume of legal documentation could well have added to the difficulties of a provincial official when faced with a case whose issues were far from clear and where a questionable decision on his part that lacked a precedent might lead to enquiry, dismissal or punishment. Referral of legal decisions to higher authorities, stage by stage, may have afforded some protection against this type of danger. The conduct of criminal cases allowed little or no leeway for presentation of two sides, one for the prosecutor and one for defending counsel.

Some officials were bold enough to express their condemnation of an emperor's personal behaviour which was seen as leading to the ruin of the empire. In 29 BCE Gu Yong 谷永, as yet a junior official, fearlessly attributed the coincidence of a solar eclipse and an earthquake to Chengdi's disregard of his duties and indulgence in the pleasures of the flesh; Du Qin 杜欽 had already entered his pleas for restraint in such matters. In commenting on the distress of the times, Chen Zhong 陳忠 pointed to the 'filial piety' of Andi, apparently in sarcasm. On rare occasions we hear of a clash of wills between the emperor and his officials, as has been seen in the investiture of Wudi's sons as kings in 117 BCE. Zong Jun 宗均, director of the Secretariat, stood apart from most of his colleagues, who consistently agreed with Mingdi's opinion over controversial matters. For disputing such conclusions (ca. 65 CE) he aroused his emperor's suspicions and anger, but by standing his ground he succeeded in regaining his confidence.

Circa 160 CE Chen Fan delivered a stern rebuke to Huandi in which he singled out the ruinous expenses of maintaining a large number of women in the palace. 'There is no robbery worse than having five women in the house' ran the proverb that he quoted, to be supported by references to the disasters brought about in this way in the past. As a result some five hundred women, as we are told, were removed from the palace. But his protest of 163 CE against the thirty-year-old emperor's taste for the hunt, thereby diverting labour away from the fields, fell on deaf ears. In an even more direct and dangerous way Chen Fan even questioned the legitimacy of Huandi's position on the throne, being no more than successor to a nobility. He was in fact alluding to the way in which Huandi had reached that position, at the will and choice of the Empress Dowager Liang 梁 and the Regent Liang Ji 梁冀.

Some subjects recur remorselessly in memorials submitted by officials who were brave enough to risk the consequences of straight speaking. The consorts, or dowager consorts, of an emperor were exerting undue influence, perverting the course of public life and leading to the ruin of the empire. The punishments of the laws were unduly severe, leading to grave distress. Officials were guilty of oppressive behaviour and subject to corruption, or perhaps too lazy to fulfil their obligations. Such strictures may very well have resulted from observation of official misbehaviour and popular suffering, or they may have derived from the rhetorical devices of those seeking power; it cannot be said how widely these complaints could be justified.

Two practical difficulties could affect the efficiency of an official's work. Communications might be delayed, thus preventing an exchange of information and subsequent orders in sufficient time for these to be fully operative. Secondly, confidentiality of sensitive items was by no means certain. There were times when disclosure of information or secret activities that told of a dissident's plans enabled the government to take precautionary steps. But there were also occasions when officials were charged with just such leaks of information from government documents, to suffer the punishment that was their due. In 66 BCE Su Chang 蘇昌, superintendent of ceremonial since 77, was dismissed for revealing secret matters to Huo Shan 霍山. Involved in the downfall of the Huo family, Huo Shan committed suicide; Su Chang was shortly re-appointed to an official post. Writing in 133 CE, Zhang Heng 張衡 complained that the current methods of selecting officials were superficial and failed to take account of their real, innermost qualities or defects. He added that once some of these men had obtained access to secret documents of the principal offices of state their contents could become public property, bribery would follow, and confusion between what was true and false in public life would ensue.

There may have been many weaknesses and faults in the system of government initiated by Qin and practised under the emperors of Han. Nevertheless in many ways the officials and the system that they operated led to successful results in governing a large number of people over wide expanses of country. As did other regimes, the early empires suffered their moments of failure, humiliation and scandal, but Han, whatever its failings, stood as an example to which monarchs and public servants of a later age looked back with nostalgia.

Notes for Further Reading

References to persons and subjects follow: Chen Fan (*HHS* 66, pp. 2159–71; *CHOC*, p. 313); confidentiality (*HS* 19B, p. 797); the decree of 133 CE (*Hou Han ji* 18, p. 507, with a slightly different version in *HHS* 6, p. 262); the *Discourses on Salt and Iron* (Gale; and *Crisis and Conflict,* Chapter 3); Diwu Lun (*HHS* 41, p. 1399); eunuchs' sponsorship of officials (*HHS* 54, p. 1772); Gong Yu (*HS* 72, pp. 3069–72); Li Gu (*HHS* 86, p. 2838); Huandi's accession (*CHOC*, pp. 261, 286); life as a hermit (Vervoorn); imperial favouritism (*HS* 72, p. 3071; *HHS* 46, p. 1558, 54, p. 1761); the rise of rebel leaders at the end of Han and Liu Bang's leadership of deserters (*CHOC*, pp. 110–19); types of officials, as seen in a document from the north-west (*Kaogu* 2005.9, 78–81); *Wei li zhi dao* (*Shuihudi,* pp. 165–76); and Zhang Heng's criticism (*Hou Han ji* 18, p. 513).

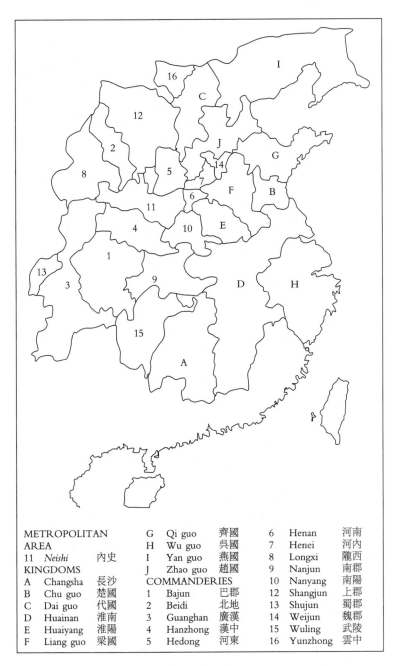

METROPOLITAN		G	Qi guo	齊國	6	Henan	河南
AREA		H	Wu guo	吳國	7	Henei	河內
11	*Neishi* 內史	I	Yan guo	燕國	8	Longxi	隴西
KINGDOMS		J	Zhao guo	趙國	9	Nanjun	南郡
A	Changsha 長沙	COMMANDERIES			10	Nanyang	南陽
B	Chu guo 楚國	1	Bajun	巴郡	12	Shangjun	上郡
C	Dai guo 代國	2	Beidi	北地	13	Shujun	蜀郡
D	Huainan 淮南	3	Guanghan	廣漢	14	Weijun	魏郡
E	Huaiyang 淮陽	4	Hanzhong	漢中	15	Wuling	武陵
F	Liang guo 梁國	5	Hedong	河東	16	Yunzhong	雲中

Administrative Units of the Han Empire, 195 BCE

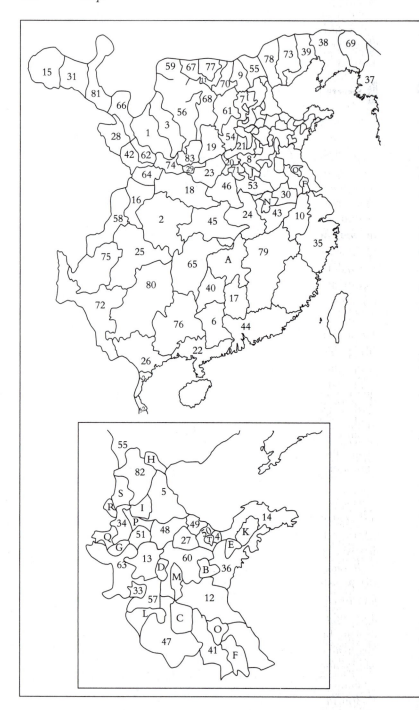

Administrative Units of the Han Empire, 1–2 CE

METROPOLITAN AREA

29	*Jingzhao yin*	京兆尹
74	*You Fufeng*	右扶風
83	*Zuo Pingyi*	左馮翊

KINGDOMS

A	Changsha	長沙
B	Chengyang	城陽
C	Chu guo	楚
D	Dongping	東平
E	Gaomi	高密
F	Guangling	廣陵
G	Guangping	廣平
H	Guangyang	廣陽
I	Hejian	河間
J	Huaiyang	淮陽
K	Jiaodong	膠東
L	Liang guo	梁
M	Lu guo	魯
N	Lu'an	六安
O	Sishui	泗水
P	Xindu	信都
Q	Zhao guo	趙
R	Zhending	真定
S	Zhongshan	中山
T	Zichuan	甾川

COMMANDERIES

1	Anding	安定
2	Bajun	巴郡
3	Beidi	北地
4	Beihai	北海
5	Bohai	勃海
6	Cangwu	蒼梧
7	Changshan	常山
8	Chenliu	陳留
9	Daijun	代郡
10	Danyang	丹揚
11	Dingxiang	定襄
12	Donghai	東海
13	Dongjun	東郡
14	Donglai	東萊
15	Dunhuang	敦煌
16	Guanghan	廣漢
17	Guiyang	桂陽
18	Hanzhong	漢中
19	Hedong	河東
20	Henan	河南
21	Henei	河內
22	Hepu	合浦
23	Hongnong	弘農
24	Jiangxia	江夏
25	Jianwei	犍爲
26	Jiaozhi	交趾
27	Jinan	濟南
28	Jincheng	金城
30	Jiujiang	九江
31	Jiuquan	酒泉
32	Jiuzhen	九真
33	Jiyin	濟陰
34	Julu	鉅鹿
35	Kuaiji	會稽
36	Langye	琅邪
37	Lelang	樂浪
38	Liaodong	遼東
39	Liaoxi	遼西
40	Lingling	零陵
41	Linhuai	臨淮
42	Longxi	隴西
43	Lujiang	廬江
44	Nanhai	南海
45	Nanjun	南郡
46	Nanyang	南陽
47	Peijun	沛郡
48	Pingyuan	平原
49	Qiancheng	千乘
50	Qijun	齊郡
51	Qinghe	清河
52	Rinan	日南
53	Runan	汝南
54	Shangdang	上黨
55	Shanggu	上谷
56	Shangjun	上郡
57	Shanyang	山陽
58	Shujun	蜀郡
59	Shuofang	朔方
60	Taishan	泰山
61	Taiyuan	太原
62	Tianshui	天水
63	Weijun	魏郡
64	Wudu	武都
65	Wuling	武陵
66	Wuwei	武威
67	Wuyuan	五原
68	Xihe	西河
69	Xuantu	玄菟
70	Yanmen	鴈門
71	Yingchuan	潁川
72	Yizhou	益州
73	Youbeiping	右北平
75	Yuesui	越巂
76	Yulin	鬱林
77	Yunzhong	雲中
78	Yuyang	漁陽
79	Yuzhang	豫章
80	Zangke	牂柯
81	Zhangye	張掖
82	Zhuojun	涿郡

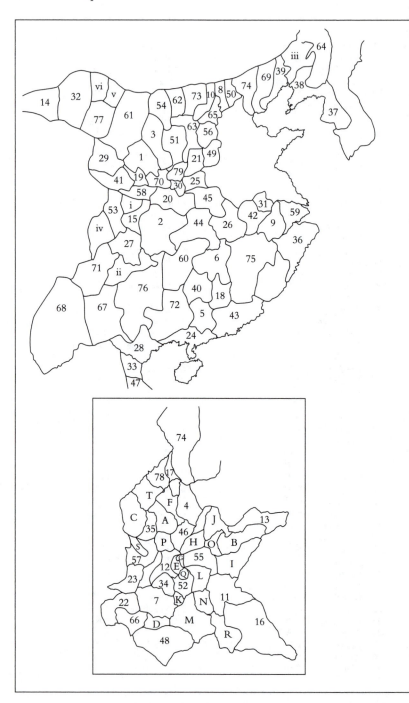

Administrative Units of the Han Empire, 140 CE
(after Lao Kan)

COMMANDERIES

1	Anding	安定
2	Bajun	巴郡
3	Beidi	北地
4	Bohai	勃海
5	Cangwu	蒼梧
6	Changsha	長沙
7	Chenliu	陳留
8	Daijun	代郡
9	Danyang	丹陽
10	Dingxiang	定襄
11	Donghai	東海
12	Dongjun	東郡
13	Donglai	東萊
14	Dunhuang	敦煌
15	Guanghan	廣漢
16	Guangling	廣陵
17	Guangyang	廣陽
18	Guiyang	桂陽
19	Hanyang	漢陽
20	Hanzhong	漢中
21	Hedong	河東
22	Henan	河南
23	Henei	河內
24	Hepu	合浦
25	Hongnong	弘農
26	Jiangxia	江夏
27	Jianwei	犍爲
28	Jiaozhi	交趾
29	Jincheng	金城
31	Jiujiang	九江
32	Jiuquan	酒泉
33	Jiuzhen	九真
34	Jiyin	濟陰
35	Julu	鉅鹿
36	Kuaiji	會稽
37	Lelang	樂浪
38	Liaodong	遼東
39	Liaoxi	遼西
40	Lingling	零陵
41	Longxi	隴西
42	Lujiang	廬江
43	Nanhai	南海
44	Nanjun	南郡
45	Nanyang	南陽
46	Pingyuan	平原
47	Rinan	日南
48	Runan	汝南
49	Shangdang	上黨
50	Shanggu	上谷
51	Shangjun	上郡
52	Shanyang	山陽
53	Shujun	蜀郡
54	Shuofang	朔方
55	Taishan	泰山

56	Taiyuan	太原
57	Weijun	魏郡
58	Wudu	武都
59	Wujun	吳郡
60	Wuling	武陵
61	Wuwei	武威
62	Wuyuan	五原
63	Xihe	西河
64	Xuantu	玄菟
65	Yanmen	鴈門
66	Yingchuan	穎川
67	Yizhou	益州
68	Yongchang	永昌
69	Youbeiping	右北平
71	Yuesui	越巂
72	Yulin	鬱林
73	Yunzhong	雲中
74	Yuyang	漁陽
75	Yuzhang	豫章
76	Zangke	牂柯
77	Zhangye	張掖
78	Zhuojun	涿郡

KINGDOMS

A	Anping	安平
B	Beihai	北海
C	Changshan	常山
D	Chen guo	陳
E	Dongping	東平
F	Hejian	河間
G	Jibei	濟北
H	Jinan	濟南
I	Langye	琅邪
J	Lean	樂安
K	Liang guo	梁
L	Lu guo	魯
M	Pei guo	沛
N	Pengcheng	彭城
O	Qi guo	齊
P	Qinghe	清河
Q	Rencheng	任城
R	Xiapi	下邳
S	Zhaoguo	趙
T	Zhongshan	中山

OLD METROPOLITAN AREA

30	*Jingzhao yin*	京兆尹
70	*You Fufeng*	右扶風
79	*Zuo Pingyi*	左馮翊

DEPENDENT STATES

i	Guanghan	廣漢
ii	Jianwei	犍爲
iii	Liaodong	遼東
iv	Shujun	蜀郡
v	Zhangye	張掖
vi	Zhangye Juyan	張掖 居延

Qin, Han and Xin Emperors

Name	Title	Born	Acceded	Died
Qin				
Ying Zhao	Shi Huangdi	259 BCE	246 BCE	210 BCE
Ying Huhai	Qin Er shi Huanghi	231/222 BCE	210 BCE	207 BCE
Western Han				
Liu Bang	Gaozu (Gaodi)	248 BCE	206/202	195
Liu Ying	Huidi	207	195	188
Lü Zhi	[Lü Hou]		188	180
	Shaodi Gong		188	?
	Shaodi Hong		184	180
Liu Heng	Wendi		180	157
Liu Qi	Jingdi	188	157	141
Liu Che	Wudi	?157	141	87
Liu Fuling	Zhaodi	94	87	74
Liu He (4)	—		74	59
Liu Bingyi	Xuandi	?92	74	48
Liu Shi	Yuandi	74	48	33
Liu Ao	Chengdi	51	33	7
Liu Xin	Aidi	?25	7	1
Liu Kan (Jizi)	Pingdi	?8	1	6 CE
Liu Ying	—	4 CE	6	25
Xin				
Wang Mang		46 BCE	9 CE	23
Eastern Han				
Liu Xiu	Guangwudi	5 BCE	25	57
Liu Yang	Mingdi	28 CE	57 CE	75 CE
Liu Da	Zhangdi	57	75	88
Liu Zhao	Hedi	79	88	106
Liu Long	Shangdi	105	106	106
Liu You	Andi	94	106	125
Liu Yi	Shaodi	?	125	125
Liu Bao	Shundi	115	125	144
Liu Bing	Chongdi	143	144	145
Liu Zuan	Zhidi	138	145	146
Liu Zhi	Huandi	132	146	168
Liu Hong	Lingdi	156	168	189
Liu Bian	Shaodi	173/176	189	190
Liu Xie	Xiandi	181	189	234★

★ Abdicated 220 CE.

Works Cited

Abbreviations

BMFEA	*Bulletin of the Museum of Far Eastern Antiquities*
CHOAC	*Cambridge History of Ancient China*
CHOC	*Cambridge History of China Volume I*
Crisis and Conflict	Loewe, *Crisis and Conflict in Han China*
DMM	Loewe, *Divination, Mythology and Monarchy in Han China*
HHS	*Hou Han shu* and *Xu Han zhi*
HHSJJ	Wang Xianqian, *Hou Han shu jijie*
HS	*Han shu*
Men Who Governed	Loewe, *The Men Who Governed Han China*
RCL	Hulsewé, *Remnants of Ch'in Law*
RHA	Loewe, *Records of Han Administration*
SJ	*Shiji*

Abbreviations used in the Notes for Further Reading sections after each chapter refer to authors and titles as given below.

Balazs, Etienne. *Chinese Civilization and Bureaucracy: Variations on a Theme*. New Haven and London: Yale University Press, 1964.

Ban Gu (32–92 CE) and others. *Han shu*. References are to the punctuated edition, Beijing: Zhonghua shuju, 1962. [*HS*]

Barbieri-Low, Anthony J. *Artisans in Early Imperial China*. Seattle: University of Washington Press (forthcoming, 2007).

Beasley, W. G. and E. G. Pulleyblank, eds. *Historians of China and Japan*. London: Oxford University Press, 1961.

Bielenstein, Hans. *The bureaucracy of Han times*. Cambridge: Cambridge University Press, 1980. [*Bureaucracy*]

——. 'The Census of China during the Period 2–742 A.D.'. *BMFEA* 19 (1947): 135–45.

——. '*The Restoration of the Han Dynasty*, vol. 1'. *BMFEA* 26 (1954).

Bodde, Derk. *China's First Unifier: A Study of the Ch'in Dynasty as Seen in the Life of Li Ssü 280?–208 B.C.* Leiden: E. J. Brill, 1938. Reprint, Hong Kong: Hong Kong University Press, 1967.

——. *Festivals in Classical China*. Princeton: Princeton University Press, and Hong Kong: The Chinese University of Hong Kong, 1975. [*Festivals*]

Cambridge History of Ancient China; see Loewe and Shaughnessy.

Cambridge History of China Volume I; see Twitchett and Loewe.

Chavannes, Édouard. *Les documents chinois découverts par Aurel Stein dans les sables du Turkestan Oriental.* Oxford: Oxford University Press, 1913.

———. *Les mémoires historiques de Se-ma Ts'ien.* Vols. I–V. Paris: Ernest Leroux, 1895–1905. Reprint, with vol. VI, Paris: Adrien Maisonneuve, 1969.

The Chinese Bronzes of Yunnan. Foreword by Jessica Rawson. London: Sidgwick and Jackson, and Beijing: Cultural Relics Publishing House, 1983.

Ch'ü T'ung-tsu. *Han Social Structure.* Ed. Jack L. Dull. Seattle and London: University of Washington Press, 1972.

de Bary, Wm. Theodore, *Sources of Chinese Tradition.* 2 vols. New York and London: Columbia University Press, 1960.

de Crespigny, Rafe. *A Biographical Dictionary of Later Han to the Three Kingdoms, 23–220 AD.* Leiden: Brill (forthcoming).

———. *Emperor Huan and Emperor Ling.* 2 vols. Canberra: Australian National University, 1989.

———. *The Last of the Han.* Canberra: Australian National University, 1969.

Diény, Jean-Pierre. *Les dix-neuf poèmes anciens.* Paris: Presses Universitaires de France, 1963.

Dubs, Homer H. *The History of the Former Han Dynasty.* 3 vols. Baltimore: Waverly Press, 1938–1955.

Fan Ye (398–446 CE) and others. *Hou Han shu and Xu Han zhi.* References are to the punctuated edition, Beijing: Zhonghua shuju, 1965. [*HHS*]

Gale, Esson M. *Discourses on Salt and Iron: A Debate on State Control of Commerce and Industry in Ancient China.* Leiden: E. J. Brill, 1931. Reprint, Taipei: Ch'eng-wen Publishing Company, 1967.

Giele, Enno. *Early Chinese Manuscripts.* http://www.lehigh.edu/

Han guan liu zhong. References are to the *Si bu beiyao* edition.

Han shu; see Ban Gu.

Hawkes, David. *The Songs of the South: An Anthology of Ancient Chinese Poems by Qu Yuan and Other Poets.* Harmondsworth, Eng.: Penguin Books, 1985.

Hervouet, Yves. *Un poéte de cour sous les Han: Sseu-ma Siang-jou.* Paris: Presses Universitaires de France, 1964.

Hou Han ji; see Yuan Hong.

Hou Han shu; see Fan Ye.

Hsu Cho-yun. *Han Agriculture.* Seattle and London: University of Washington Press, 1980.

Huan Kuan (*fl.* 50 BCE). *Yan tie lun.* References are to Wang Liqi. *Yan tie lun jiaozhu.* 2nd ed. 2 vols. Beijing: Zhonghua shuju, 1992.

Hulsewé, A.F.P. *China in Central Asia.* Leiden: E.J. Brill, 1979. [*CICA*]

———. 'A Lawsuit of A.D. 28'. In *Studia Sino-Mongolica: Festschrift für Herbert Franke,* ed. Wolfgang Bauer, 23–34. Wiesbaden: Franz Steiner Verlag GMBH, 1979.

———. *Remnants of Ch'in Law.* Leiden: E.J. Brill, 1985. [*RCL*]

———. *Remnants of Han Law.* Leiden: E.J. Brill, 1955. [*RHL*]

Kaogu 1958– (1955–58 entitled *Kaogu tongxun*). Beijing: Chinese Academy of Social Sciences.

Keightley, David N. *Sources of Shang History: The Oracle-Bone Inscriptions of Bronze Age China.* Berkeley: University of California Press, 1978. Reprint, 1985.

Knechtges, David R. *The Han Rhapsody: A Study of the* Fu *of Yang Hsiung (53 B.C.–A.D. 18).* Cambridge: Cambridge University Press, 1976.

———. Wen xuan *or* Selections of Refined Literature. 2 vols. Princeton: Princeton University Press, 1982–87.

Kroll, J.L. 'Toward a Study of the Economic Views of Sang Hongyang'. *Early China* 4 (1978–79): 11–18.

Lao Kan. 'Liang Han junguo mianji zhi guji ji koushu zengjian zhi tuice'. *Bulletin of the Institute of History and Philology* 5, part 2 (1935): 215–40.

Le Blanc, Charles and Rémi Mathieu. *Philosophes taoïstes II Huainan Zi.* Paris: Gallimard, 2003.

Lewis, Mark Edward. 'The City-State in Spring-and-Autumn China'. In *A Comparative Study of Thirty City-State Cultures,* ed. Mogens Herman Hansen, 359–73. Copenhagen: The Royal Danish Academy of Sciences and Letters, 2000.

Loewe, Michael. 'Attempts at Economic Co-operation during the Western Han Dynasty'. In *The Scope of State Power in China,* ed. Stuart R. Schram, 237–67. London: School of Oriental and African Studies; and Hong Kong: the Chinese University Press, 1985.

———. *A Biographical Dictionary of the Qin, Former Han and Xin Periods (221 BC–AD 24).* Leiden, Boston and Köln: Brill, 2000. [*Biographical Dictionary*]

———. 'The Campaigns of Han Wu-ti'. In *Chinese Ways in Warfare,* ed. Frank A. Kierman, Jr. and John K. Fairbank, 119–22. Cambridge, Mass.: Harvard University Press, 1974.

———. *Crisis and Conflict in Han China, 104 BC to AD 9.* London: George Allen and Unwin Ltd., 1974. Reprint, London: Routledge, 2004.

———. *Divination, Mythology and Monarchy in Han China.* Cambridge: Cambridge University Press, 1994.

——. 'Guangzhou: The Evidence of the Standard Histories from the *Shi ji* to the *Chen shu*, A Preliminary Survey'. In *Guangdong, Archaeology and Early Texts: Archäologie und frühe Texte (Zhou-Tang)*, ed. Shing Müller and others, 51–80. Wiesbaden: Harrassowitz, 2004.

——. 'The Han View of Comets'. *BMFEA* 52 (1980): 1–32.

——. 'He Bo Count of the River, Feng Yi and Li Bing'. In *A Birthday Book for Brother Stone: for David Hawkes, at Eighty*, ed. Rachel May and John Minford. Hong Kong: The Chinese University Press, 2003.

——. 'The Imperial Way of Death in Han China'. In *State and Court Ritual in China*, ed. Joseph P. McDermott. Cambridge: Cambridge University Press, 1999.

——. *The Men Who Governed Han China*. Leiden and Boston: Brill, 2004. [*Men Who Governed*]

——. 'The Orders of Aristocratic Rank of Han China'. *T'oung Pao* 48, nos. 1–3 (1960): 97–174.

——. *Records of Han Administration*. 2 vols. Cambridge: Cambridge University Press, 1967. Reprint London: Routledge, 2002.

——. 'State Funerals of the Han Empire'. *BMFEA* 71 (1999)[2002]: 5–72.

Loewe, Michael and Edward L. Shaughnessy, eds. *The Cambridge History of Ancient China: From the Origins of Civilization to 221 B.C.* Cambridge: Cambridge University Press, 1999. [*CHOAC*]

Mancheng Han mu fajue baogao. Beijing: Wenwu chubanshe, 1980.

Nienhauser, William H., Jr., ed. *The Grand Scribe's Records*. Vols. 1, 2 and 7. Bloomington and Indianapolis: Indiana University Press, 1994, 2002.

Nylan, Michael. 'The Legacies of the Chengdu Plain'. In *Ancient Sichuan*, ed. Robert Bagley. Seattle Art Museum, and Princeton: Princeton University Press, 2001.

Pearson, Margaret J. *Wang Fu and the* Comments of a Recluse. Tempe, Ariz.: Center for Asian Studies, 1989.

Pirazzoli-t'Serstevens, Michèle. *The Han Dynasty*. Trans. Janet Seligman. New York: Rizzoli International Publications Inc., 1982.

Rawson, Jessica. Foreword to *The Chinese Bronzes of Yunnan*. London: Sidgwick and Jackson, and Beijing: Cultural Relics Publishing House, 1983.

Shaughnessy, Edward L. *Sources of Western Zhou History: Inscribed Bronze Vessels*. Berkeley: University of California Press, 1991.

Shiji; see Sima Qian.

Shodō zenshū: Chūgoku 2 Kan. Tokyo: Heibonsha, 1958.

Shuihudi Qin mu zhujian. Beijing: Wenwu chubanshe, 1990. Reprint, 2001. [*Shuihudi*]

Sima Qian (ca. 145–ca. 86 BCE) and others. *Shiji*. References are to the punctuated edition, Beijing: Zhonghua shuju, 1959. [*SJ*]

Swann, Nancy Lee. *Food and Money in Ancient China: The Earliest Economic History of China to A.D. 25.* Princeton, N.J.: Princeton University Press, 1950.

Tsien Tsuen-hsuin. *Written on Bamboo and Silk: The Beginnings of Chinese Books and Inscriptions.* 1st ed., 1962. 2nd ed., with afterword by Edward L. Shaughnessy, Chicago and London: The University of Chicago Press, 2004.

Twitchett, Denis and Michael Loewe, eds. *The Cambridge History of China Volume I: The Ch'in and Han Empires, 221 B.C.–A.D. 220.* Cambridge: Cambridge University Press, 1986. [CHOC]

Vankeerberghen, Griet. *The Huainanzi and Liu An's Claim to Moral Authority.* Albany: State University of New York Press, 2001.

Vervoorn, Aat. *Men of the Cliffs and Caves.* Hong Kong: The Chinese University Press, 1990.

Wagner, Donald B. *The State and the Iron Industry in Han China.* Copenhagen: Nordic Institute of Asian Studies, 2001.

Wang Xianqian. *Hou Han shu jijie.* Changsha, 1924.

Watson, Burton. *Records of the Grand Historian of China: Translated from the Shih-chi of Ssu-ma Ch'ien.* 2 vols. New York and London: Columbia University Press, 1961.

Wilbur, Clarence Martin. *Slavery in China during the Former Han Dynasty, 206 B.C.–A.D. 25.* Chicago: Field Museum of Natural History, 1943.

Xu Han zhi; see Fan Ye.

Yinwan Han mu jiandu. Beijing: Zhonghua shuju, 1997.

Yü Ying-shih. *Trade and Expansion in Han China.* Berkeley and Los Angeles: University of California Press, 1967.

Yuan Hong (328–376 CE). *Hou Han ji.* References are to Zhou Tianyou. *Hou Han ji jiaozhu.* Tianjin: Tianjin guji chubanshe, 1987.

Yunnan Jinning Shizhai shan gu mu qun fajue baogao. Beijing: Wenwu chubanshe, 1959.

Zhangjia shan Han mu zhu jian ersiqi hao mu. Beijing: Wenwu chubanshe, 2001. [*Zhangjia shan*]

Index

abdication: of last Han emperor, xviii, 170, 179; suggested by Aidi, 184; of Yao, Shun, 179

academy, academicians, 25; pupils at, 74

accession of emperors, 178

accountancy, 117

administrative units of empire, list of, 117

administrators of nobilities, 47, 50

age distinctions, 141

agencies, of government, 156

agricultural colonies, 137

agriculture, new techniques, 153; promotion of, 151; regulations for, 152; statutes for, 152

Aidi, suggested abdication, 184

algebra, textbook of, 142

amnesty, 137

ancestors, respect for, 98

Andi, criticism of, 15, 194

animal products, 154

anonymous accusations, 124

Ao granary, 30, 53

appeal, by criminals, 129

appeasement of enemies, 189

archery tests, 116

archives of the central government, 117

arguments, presentation of, 187

Aristotle, 119

arms, search for, 26

arsenals, 34; at Chang'an, 65; report on contents, 114

artisans, 29, 154; directed by

shaofu, 31

astrology, 24

astronomy, instruments, 155; specialists in, 71

Athens, force of oratory at, 171

authority, for military action, 60

balance, in economic ventures, 191

Ban Biao, 14; on kings' destiny, 174

Ban Chao, xvii, 56, 61, 181; tactics of, 68

Ban Gu, ix

Ban Yong, xvii, 59, 181

bans: on certain types of work, 152; on office holding, 76; on unseemly rites, 164

banishment, 128

Bao Yu: additions to laws, 122; as commandery governor, 42

Beizhuang, 44

bounties, imperial, 13, 137

brand marks, on horses, 131

bribery, 196

brick making, 63, 117

bride, for non-Han chieftain, 156

bronze mirrors, 156

Buddhism, xvii

building supplies, 33

bureaus (*cao*), 47; of Merit, 40, 113; of Music, 32

Cai Lun, and proto-paper, 155

calendar, luni-solar, vi, xvi, 24, 25; copies of, 107;